# Lecture Notes in Computer Science 10620

Commenced Publication in 1973
Founding and Former Series Editors:
Gerhard Goos, Juris Hartmanis, and Jan van Leeuwen

## Editorial Board

More information about this series at http://www.springer.com/series/8637

Abdelkader Hameurlain · Josef Küng
Roland Wagner · Hendrik Decker (Eds.)

# Transactions on Large-Scale Data- and Knowledge- Centered Systems XXXIV

## Special Issue on Consistency and Inconsistency in Data-Centric Applications

Springer

*Editors-in-Chief*
Abdelkader Hameurlain
IRIT
Paul Sabatier University
Toulouse
France

Roland Wagner
FAW
University of Linz
Linz
Austria

Josef Küng
FAW
University of Linz
Linz
Austria

*Guest Editor*
Hendrik Decker
Polytechnic University of Valencia
Valencia
Spain

and

Ludwig Maximilian University of Munich
Munich
Germany

ISSN 0302-9743          ISSN 1611-3349   (electronic)
Lecture Notes in Computer Science
ISSN 1869-1994          ISSN 2510-4942   (electronic)
Transactions on Large-Scale Data- and Knowledge-Centered Systems
ISBN 978-3-662-55946-8      ISBN 978-3-662-55947-5   (eBook)
https://doi.org/10.1007/978-3-662-55947-5

Library of Congress Control Number: 2017956080

Printed on acid-free paper

This Springer imprint is published by Springer Nature
The registered company is Springer-Verlag GmbH Germany
The registered company address is: Heidelberger Platz 3, 14197 Berlin, Germany

# Preface

At long last, we have finished completing a TLDKS collection of articles about consistency and inconsistency in data-centric applications. The road toward that aim was rough and rugged. At the outset, there was the workshop COIN at DEXA 2016, where eight papers about that same subject were presented. Those papers have been published in the 2016 volume of the DEXA workshop proceedings series. Both scientifically and socially speaking, the workshop was a big success.

At one of its social dinners, some of the participants came up with the proposal to invite contributions of more elaborate versions of COIN workshop papers, as well as to call for papers from colleagues in related research communities that had not taken part in the workshop, for publication in a journal.

At first, the idea was encouraged enthusiastically by all participants. So, together with a colleague, the writer of these lines put himself behind the task of finding a journal, issuing the invitations, broadcasting a call for papers, organizing a two-round reviewing process, and editing the final outcome.

All of that was more easily agreed upon than actually done. In the end, only three papers from the COIN workshop made it into the present TLDKS volume. The other COIN participants had opted out, for various reasons (large overlap with papers already published or planned to be published elsewhere, priority to get done with a PhD thesis, change of career plans, personal preferences).

Fortunately, there was some response to the call for papers. Six additional submissions were considered for publication by the reviewers, and three of them received green light to work on an improved version for inclusion this TLDKS edition. However, each of them, and also the papers drawn from the workshop, had received controversial reviews. It took several more rounds of thorough reviews, considerate reconciliation, and further modifications for the final versions included this volume.

In addition to the accepted papers, we were fortunate to be able to include an invited article, written by Philippe Besnard, entitled "Basic Postulates for Inconsistency Measures". It advances a discussion that has been going on for several years about certain properties that inconsistency measures should have, or shouldn't, depending on the demands of applications or one's point of view.

Krishnamurthy Vidyasankar has contributed a paper entitled "Batch Composite Transactions in Stream Processing". The author has successfully applied his recognized expertise on transaction serializability to the concurrent execution of batches of streaming data.

In their paper entitled "Enhancing User Rating Database Consistency through Pruning", Dionisis Margaris and Costas Vassilakis describe a sophisticated technique for improving the quality of stored data in recommender systems, by reducing user profile inconsistencies that are bound to accumulate over time.

In his paper entitled "A Second Generation of Peer-to-Peer Semantic Wikis", Charbel Rahhal presents a mechanism for detecting inconsistencies in annotations of collaborative semantic wikis. Also the causes of the inconsistencies are spotted and visualized, in order to support their removal.

The article by Jørgen Villadsen and Anders Schlichtkrull, entitled "Formalizing a Paraconsistent Logic in the Isabelle Proof Assistant", features the capabilities of the automated proof assistant Isabelle. They are shown to not only support proofs in classical logic, but also the specification, modification, and execution of a paraconsistent logic.

Ricardo Queiroz de Araujo Fernandes, Edward Hermann Haeusler, and Luiz Carlos Pinheiro Dias Pereira have contributed an article on "A Proximity-Based Understanding of Conditionals". The authors propose a logic account of David Kellog Lewis' counterfactual conditionals, an interesting application of which is hypothetical reasoning in databases.

The paper by Hendrik Decker is entitled "Inconsistency-Tolerant Database Repairs and Simplified Repair Checking by Measure-Based Integrity Checking". It uses inconsistency measures for monitoring the dynamics of databases, as opposed to inconsistency measures such as those addressed in Besnard's paper, which are meant to be applied in static propositional logic theories.

Finally, I'd like to acknowledge the indefatigable support of Gabriela Wagner at the TLDKS office, and say "thank you" to all authors and reviewers involved in this project, for their tireless commitment and perseverance. The reviews, and not least the most critical ones, were highly appreciated by the authors, enabling them to come up with satisfactory camera-ready versions. What follows is a list of the reviewers' names, except those who prefer to remain anonymous: Ofer Arieli, Jesper Bengtson, Christoph Benzmüller, Walter Carnielli, Karen Davis, Valeria de Paiva, Hendrik Decker, Carlos F. Enguix, Hermann Haeusler, Leandro B. Marinho, Pedro Muñoz, Jyrki Nummenmaa, Denis Parra Santander, Lawrence Paulson, Andrei Popescu, Nuno Preguica, Norbert Ritter, Alexander Steen, Diego Torres, Christoph Trattner, Jørgen Villadsen, Gottfried Vossen, Makarius Wenzel, Yorick Wilks, Wolfram Wingerath, and Max Wisniewski. Many thanks to all of you!

August 2017                                                                 Hendrik Decker

# Editorial Board

# Contents

# Basic Postulates for Inconsistency Measures

Philippe Besnard[✉]

IRIT, CNRS, University of Toulouse, Toulouse, France
**besnard@irit.fr**

**Abstract.** Postulates for inconsistency measures are examined, the set of postulates proposed by Hunter and Konieczny being the starting point. The focus is on two postulates that were questioned by various authors. Studying the first suggests a systematic transformation to guard postulates against a certain kind of counter-examples. The second postulate under investigation here is devoted to independence, for which a general version is proposed that avoids the pitfalls mentioned in the literature. Combining these two additions with some postulates previously introduced by the same author, a set of basic postulates alternative to the core set given by Hunter and Konieczny arises.

## 1 Inconsistency Measures

There are plenty of reasons for belief bases to be inconsistent. Unfortunately, inconsistency is a nuisance on a number of counts (it makes deductive reasoning to collapse, it allows decision-making to simultaneaously enforce two mutually exclusive options, . . . ). In short, inconsistency in belief bases is bad. How bad? This is the question that inconsistency measures have been taking seriously. Informally speaking, an inconsistency measure tells *to what extent* a belief base is inconsistent. Indeed, there seems to be degrees. Consider e.g. the statement *"This item is robust and affordable"*. One way to contradict it is by means of the statement *"If it's robust then it is not affordable"*. Another way is by means of the statement *"It is neither robust nor affordable"*. The latter expresses that both claims (i.e., *"the item is robust"* and *"the item is affordable"*) in the initial statement are false but the former only objects that either *"the item is robust"* is false or *"the item is affordable"* is false. Accordingly, the belief base

$$K_1 = \left\{ \begin{array}{c} \textit{This item is robust and affordable} \\ \textit{If it's robust then it is not affordable} \end{array} \right\}$$

can be viewed as *less inconsistent than* the belief base

$$K_2 = \left\{ \begin{array}{c} \textit{This item is robust and affordable} \\ \textit{It is neither robust nor affordable} \end{array} \right\}.$$

Formally, for $I$ denoting an inconsistency measure,

$$I(K_1) < I(K_2).$$

© Springer-Verlag GmbH Germany 2017
A. Hameurlain et al. (Eds.): TLDKS XXXIV, LNCS 10620, pp. 1–12, 2017.
https://doi.org/10.1007/978-3-662-55947-5_1

A host of inconsistency measures exist, e.g., $[1,8,9,12,14,15,20,22,23]$. An example of a well-known inconsistency measure is $[10]$, an approach based on counting contradicted atoms (a belief base consists of propositional formulas). Using $\mathcal{A}|_K$ to denote the set of atoms occurring in $K$, it is defined as

$$I_{3Mod}(K) \stackrel{\text{def}}{=} \frac{\min_{M \in 3Mod(K)} |\{a \in \mathcal{A}|_K \colon M(a) = B\}|}{|\mathcal{A}|_K|}$$

where $3Mod$ is a system of $\{T, F, B\}$-valuations (with $T$ and $B$ being the designated truth-values) in which $T$ stands for $True$ and $F$ stands for $False$ while $Both$ stands for $True$ and $False$. The truth tables are:

| $\neg$ | |
|---|---|
| $F$ | $T$ |
| $T$ | $F$ |
| $B$ | $B$ |

| $\wedge$ | $F$ | $T$ | $B$ |
|---|---|---|---|
| $F$ | $F$ | $F$ | $F$ |
| $T$ | $F$ | $T$ | $B$ |
| $B$ | $F$ | $B$ | $B$ |

| $\rightarrow$ | $F$ | $T$ | $B$ |
|---|---|---|---|
| $F$ | $T$ | $T$ | $T$ |
| $T$ | $F$ | $T$ | $B$ |
| $B$ | $F$ | $T$ | $T$ |

Let the atom $a$ represent the statement *"the item is affordable"* and the atom $r$ represent the statement *"the item is robust"*. Then, the belief bases $K_1$ and $K_2$ above can be written formally as

$$K_1 = \{r \wedge a, r \rightarrow \neg a\}$$
$$K_2 = \{r \wedge a, \neg r \wedge \neg a\}$$

The $\{T, F, B\}$-models of $K_1$ are

$$3Mod(K_1) = \left\{ \begin{matrix} a \mapsto B \\ r \mapsto T \end{matrix}, \begin{matrix} a \mapsto B \\ r \mapsto B \end{matrix}, \begin{matrix} a \mapsto T \\ r \mapsto B \end{matrix} \right\}$$

of which the first and the third are such that only one atom is assigned the truth-value $B$ (whereas in the second model, $a$ and $r$ are assigned the truth-value $B$). Then, the minimum number of atoms that are assigned $B$ in models of $K_1$ is 1 (in symbols, $\min_{M \in 3Mod(K_1)} |\{a \in \mathcal{A}|_{K_1} \colon M(a) = B\}| = 1$). There are exactly two atoms occurring in $K_1$ hence $|\mathcal{A}|_K| = 2$. Therefore,

$$I_{3Mod}(K_1) = \frac{1}{2}.$$

There is a single $\{T, F, B\}$-model of $K_2$, namely

$$3Mod(K_2) = \left\{ \begin{matrix} a \mapsto B \\ r \mapsto B \end{matrix} \right\}$$

hence the minimum number of atoms assigned $B$ in models of $K_2$ is 2. Thus,

$$I_{3Mod}(K_2) = \frac{2}{2} = 1.$$

Summing up, $I_{3Mod}(K_1) < I_{3Mod}(K_2)$ which means that, according to the $I_{3Mod}$ inconsistency measure, $K_1$ is less inconsistent than $K_2$.

An approach based on counting formulas underlying contradictions is in [5]. Let $MI(K)$ denote the set of Minimal Unsatisfiable Subsets of $K$ (in symbols, $MI(K) = \{K' \subseteq K : K' \vdash \bot \text{ and } K' \setminus \{\varphi\} \nvdash \bot \text{ for all } \varphi \in K'\})$. Next, define

$$I_P(K) \stackrel{\text{def}}{=} \left| \bigcup MI(K) \right|.$$

Back to the above illustration, the only MUS of $\{r \wedge a, r \to \neg a\}$ is itself and the only MUS of $\{r \wedge a, \neg r \wedge \neg a\}$ is also itself. That is, $MI(K_1) = \{K_1\}$ and $MI(K_2) = \{K_2\}$. Despite contrary intuition (in fact, MUSes are not fine-grained enough to discriminate between contents of formulas), it follows that

$$I_P(K_1) = 2 = I_P(K_2).$$

Intuitively, an inconsistency measure $I$ is supposed to indicate how much inconsistency a knowledge base $K$ carries (where a more inconsistent belief base is ascribed a larger value). Of course, not every function $I$ can do! A list of requirements over $I$ is needed. To this end, postulates can ensure $I$ *to make sense* for the purpose of inconsistency measuring.

This note is an investigation into such requirements as postulates for inconsistency measures have indeed been proposed on the following grounds:

– The context is classical logic $\vdash$ over a language $\mathcal{L}$.
– Belief bases are finite sets of formulas of $\mathcal{L}$.
– $I$ maps all finite sets of formulas of $\mathcal{L}$ to values in $\mathbb{R}^+ \cup \{\infty\}$.

## 2  Postulates

Hunter and Konieczny [7] proposed a few postulates for inconsistency measures. The core set (of the Hunter-Konieczny postulates) is:

– $I(K) = 0$ iff $K \nvdash \bot$                                                    (*Consistency Null*)
– $I(K \cup K') \geq I(K)$                                                              (*Monotony*)
– If $\alpha \vdash \beta$ and $\alpha \nvdash \bot$ then $I(K \cup \{\alpha\}) \geq I(K \cup \{\beta\})$          (*Dominance*)
– If $\alpha$ is free for $K$ then $I(K \cup \{\alpha\}) = I(K)$     (*Free Formula Independence*)
   *where a formula $\varphi$ is free for $X$ iff $Y \cup \{\varphi\} \vdash \bot$ for no consistent subset $Y$ of $X$*

The last two postulates have been questioned on various grounds (see e.g., [13]). This note first gives a general principle that, among others, backs (Dominance) in a slightly amended form, and, second, proposes an independence postulate more sound than (Free Formula Independence) and also stronger than another well-known substitute [18] called (Safe Formula Independence).

In the course of this study, we emphasize the importance of the postulate for the elimination of tautologies (in a sense, the weakest independence postulate) and the role of the postulate expressing that the amount of inconsistency does not increase when a conjunction is replaced by one of its conjuncts.

In other words, we suggest a starting point for a body of postulates alternative to the core set provided by Hunter and Konieczny in their pioneering article.

## 2.1   Formalities

All the postulates to be discussed refer to propositional logic $\vdash$ with a language $\mathcal{L}$ based on a set of propositional variables denoted $Atoms(\mathcal{L})$ as well as the propositional constants $\bot$ and $\top$. The symbols we use for the connectives are $\neg$ (negation), $\wedge$ (conjunction), $\vee$ (disjunction). Turning to meta-level notation, $\equiv$ denotes logical equivalence, i.e., $p \equiv q$ means $p \vdash q$ and $q \vdash p$. In addition, $\alpha, \beta, \gamma, \ldots$ denote formulas of $\mathcal{L}$ while $K, K', \ldots$ are called belief bases and denote finite sets of formulas of $\mathcal{L}$. Lastly, $\mathcal{K}_{\mathcal{L}}$ is comprised of all belief bases over $\mathcal{L}$.

Formally, inconsistency measures are maps $I : \mathcal{K}_{\mathcal{L}} \to \mathbb{R}^+ \cup \{\infty\}$. Intuitively, $I(K)$ indicates how inconsistent a belief base $K \in \mathcal{K}_{\mathcal{L}}$ is: A more inconsistent $K$ is ascribed a larger value by $I$ (with 0 being the least).

A number of inconsistency measures actually have $[0, 1]$ as their codomain. Equivalently, they can be viewed as satisfying the following postulate from [7]

- $0 \leq I(K) \leq 1$                                     *(Normalization)*

In any case, postulates are meant to capture some aspects of rationality for inconsistency measures.

## 3   Restriction on Membership

As already mentioned, (Dominance) has been argued against on various grounds. Here is a specific illustration.

**Proposition 1.** *Assuming (Monotony), (Dominance) is equivalent with:*

- *For $\alpha \in K$, if $\alpha \not\vdash \bot$ and $\alpha \vdash \beta$ then $I(K \cup \{\beta\}) = I(K)$*        $(A_1)$

*Proof.* Let $\alpha$ and $\beta$ be such that $\alpha \not\vdash \bot$ and $\alpha \vdash \beta$. Assume $(A_1)$. Trivially, $\alpha \in K \cup \{\alpha\}$ so that $(A_1)$ applies to give $I(K \cup \{\alpha\} \cup \{\beta\}) = I(K \cup \{\alpha\})$. Due to (Monotony), $I(K \cup \{\alpha\} \cup \{\beta\}) \geq I(K \cup \{\beta\})$. By transitivity, it follows that $I(K \cup \{\alpha\}) \geq I(K \cup \{\beta\})$. Conversely, assume (Dominance). Consider $K$ such that $\alpha \in K$. As a consequence of (Dominance), $I(K \cup \{\alpha\}) \geq I(K \cup \{\beta\})$. Accordingly, $I(K) \geq I(K \cup \{\beta\})$ since $I(K \cup \{\alpha\}) = I(K)$ in view of $\alpha \in K$. The converse, i.e., $I(K \cup \{\beta\}) \geq I(K)$ holds by (Monotony).

Proposition 1 really pinpoints the fact that (Dominance) may get $I$ to go astray when $\alpha$ is in $K$, should $\beta$ be involved in a MUS of $K \cup \{\beta\}$. Indeed, $(A_1)$ then expresses that $I(K \cup \{\beta\}) = I(K)$ which may happen to be counterintuitive as the set of MUSes of $K$ and $K \cup \{\beta\}$ need not be the same.

*Example 1* (Adapted from [13]). Consider $K = \{p, \neg q, p \wedge q\}$. Take $\alpha = p \wedge q$ and $\beta = \neg p \vee q$. So, $\alpha \not\vdash \bot$ and $\alpha \vdash \beta$. By Proposition 1, (Dominance) would require $I(K \cup \{\beta\}) = I(K)$, i.e.,

$$ I\left(\left\{\begin{array}{l} p, \\ \neg q, \\ p \wedge q, \\ \neg p \vee q \end{array}\right\}\right) = I\left(\left\{\begin{array}{l} p, \\ \neg q, \\ p \wedge q \end{array}\right\}\right) $$

although the MUSes of $K$ consist of $\{\{\neg q, p \wedge q\}\}$ and the MUSes of $K \cup \{\beta\}$ consist of $\{\{\neg q, p \wedge q\}, \{p, \neg q, \neg p \vee q\}\}$.

This suggests a general principle, denoted *-*principle* in the sequel, as follows. Would-be postulates of the form

- if ... then $I(K \cup \{\alpha\}) \geq I(K \cup \{\beta\})$             (Postulate)

should be turned into the form

- for $\alpha \notin K$, if ... then $I(K \cup \{\alpha\}) \geq I(K \cup \{\beta\})$      (Postulate*)

The expected proviso $\beta \notin K$ is omitted because $I(K \cup \{\alpha\}) \geq I(K \cup \{\beta\})$ is ensured by (Monotony) for $\beta \in K$.

**Fact 1** *For all inconsistency measure $I$, if $I$ satisfies (Postulate) then $I$ also satisfies (Postulate*).*

The *-principle gives rise to a slightly restricted version of (Dominance), i.e.,

- For $\alpha \notin K$, if $\alpha \vdash \beta$ and $\alpha \nvdash \bot$ then $I(K \cup \{\alpha\}) \geq I(K \cup \{\beta\})$ (Dominance*)

Proposition 1 no longer holds if (Dominance) is replaced by (Dominance*). Moreover, (Dominance*) does not impose $I(K \cup \{\beta\}) = I(K)$ in Example 1. However, Example 2 introduced by Mu, Liu, Jin and Bell in [13] to show that the $I_{MI}$ inconsistency measure (it simply counts the number of MUSes, i.e., $I_{MI}(K) = |\{M \subseteq K : M \text{ is a MUS of } K\}|$) fails (Dominance) also shows that $I_{MI}$ fails (Dominance*).

*Example 2* [13]. Let $K = \{p, p \wedge r, \neg q\}$. Let $\alpha = p \wedge r \wedge (\neg p \vee q)$ and $\beta = \neg p \vee q$. $K \cup \{\alpha\}$ has a single MUS $\{\neg q, p \wedge r \wedge (\neg p \vee q)\}$ and $K \cup \{\beta\}$ has two MUSes, which are $\{p, \neg q, \neg p \vee q\}$ and $\{p \wedge r, \neg q, \neg p \vee q\}$, hence both (Dominance) and (Dominance*) fail here because $I_{MI}(K \cup \{\alpha\}) = 1 < 2 = I_{MI}(K \cup \{\beta\})$.

A most worthwhile application of the *-principle is with a postulate introduced in [3], to the effect that inconsistency does not increase when a conjunction is replaced by any one of its conjuncts. In symbols, $I(K \cup \{\alpha\}) \leq I(K \cup \{\alpha \wedge \beta\})$. This actually conveys the very same idea than (Monotony): Extra information (whether in the form of an extra formula or in the form of an extra conjunct) cannot make the amount of inconsistency to decrease. Keeping the non-starred name although applying the *-principle, the postulate writes

- If $\alpha \wedge \beta \notin K$ then $I(K \cup \{\alpha\}) \leq I(K \cup \{\alpha \wedge \beta\})$   (Conjunction Dominance)

The need for the proviso $\alpha \wedge \beta \notin K$ in (Conjunction Dominance) can be illustrated by means of Example 3.

*Example 3.* Let $K = \{p \wedge \neg p \wedge q\}$. Take $\alpha$ to be $p \wedge \neg p$ and take $\beta$ to be $q$. If it were not for the proviso $\alpha \wedge \beta \notin K$, (Conjunction Dominance) would give $I(\{p \wedge \neg p \wedge q, p \wedge \neg p\}) \leq I(\{p \wedge \neg p \wedge q\})$ —thereby precluding the intuitive possibility $I(\{p \wedge \neg p \wedge q, p \wedge \neg p\}) > I(\{p \wedge \neg p \wedge q\})$.

The *-principle extends in a natural way to would-be postulates of the form *if ... then $I(K \cup \{\alpha\}) = I(K \cup \{\beta\})$*, to be turned into *for $\alpha \notin K$ and $\beta \notin K$, if ... then $I(K \cup \{\alpha\}) = I(K \cup \{\beta\})$*.

## 4   Independence

A most welcome consequence of (Free Formula Independence) is

- If $\alpha \equiv \top$ then $I(K \cup \{\alpha\}) = I(K)$            *(Tautology Independence)*

Unless $\beta \not\vdash \bot$ (i.e., the case that would let (Dominance) to apply), there is unfortunately no guarantee that the following holds:

- for $\alpha \equiv \top$, if $\alpha \wedge \beta \notin K$ and $\beta \notin K$ then $I(K \cup \{\alpha \wedge \beta\}) = I(K \cup \{\beta\})$
                                            *($\top$-conjunct Independence)*

Addressing the concern that (Free Formula Independence) applies in some undesirable cases, Thimm [17] proposed a postulate called (Weak Independence) which was examined by Hunter and Konieczny [7] in the following form

- If $\alpha$ is safe for $K$ then $I(K \cup \{\alpha\}) = I(K)$     *(Safe Formula Independence)*
  where a formula $\varphi$ is safe for $X$ iff $\varphi \not\vdash \bot$ and $Atoms(\varphi) \cap Atoms(X) = \emptyset$

Unfortunately, (Safe Formula Independence) is weaker than expected. First, it may fail to apply to a formula $\alpha \wedge (p \vee \neg p)$ although applying to $\alpha$. Second, (Safe Formula Independence) does not entail (Tautology Independence).

Anyway, postulates about independence attempt to capture the idea that if a formula can be satisfied with no impact on the truth value of critical items then such a formula is not to count for measuring inconsistency. We now propose a general version. In order to express syntactically the fact that a subformula has a truth value determining the truth of the entire formula, we follow the $\mathcal{NP}$-form approach [16]. However, we focus on atoms and we can thus simplify Schütte's inductive definition, instead resorting to a special class of substitutions:

**Definition 1.** $\sigma : Atoms(\mathcal{L}) \rightarrow Atoms(\mathcal{L}) \cup \{\top, \bot\}$ *is a Boolean substitution iff for all $a \in Atoms(\mathcal{L})$, either $\sigma(a) = a$ or $\sigma(a) = \top$ or $\sigma(a) = \bot$.*

A generalization of the notion of a safe formula is now in order, according to the intuitions just expressed.

**Definition 2.** *A formula $\varphi$ is safely consistent for $X$ if there exists a Boolean substitution $\sigma$ such that $\sigma\varphi$ is a tautology and $\sigma(a) = a$ for all $a \in Atoms(X)$.*

A new independence postulate can then be formulated—with a due proviso from the *-principle—as follows.

- If $\alpha \wedge \beta \notin K$, $\beta \notin K$, and $\alpha$ is safely consistent for $K \cup \{\beta\}$
  then $I(K \cup \{\alpha \wedge \beta\}) = I(K \cup \{\beta\})$     *(Conjunct Independence)*

Clearly, if $\varphi$ is safely consistent for $K$ then $\varphi$ is free for $K$. This means that (Free Formula Independence) is at least as strong as (Conjunct Independence). Example 4 shows that the converse is untrue.

*Example 4.* Consider $K = \{p \wedge r, q \wedge \neg r\}$. Let $\alpha$ be $(\neg p \vee \neg q) \wedge \top$. Clearly, $\alpha$ is free for $K$ hence (Free Formula Independence) applies although $\neg p \vee \neg q$ causes a contradiction with two conjunctively consistent parts of formulas of $K$ (see [3]). In other words, $I(\{p \wedge r, q \wedge \neg r, (\neg p \vee \neg q) \wedge \top\}) = I(\{p \wedge r, q \wedge \neg r\})$ is required by (Free Formula Independence) but not by (Conjunct Independence).

The next results show that (Conjunct Independence) entails several other independence postulates, possibly with the help of (Tautology Independence).

**Proposition 2.** *(Conjunct Independence) entails ($\top$-conjunct Independence).*

*Proof.* For $\alpha$ tautologous, $\sigma$ can be taken to be identity. It is then possible to apply (Conjunct Independence) which gives $I(K \cup \{\alpha \wedge \beta)\}) = I(K \cup \{\beta\})$.

**Proposition 3.** *Assuming (Tautology Independence), (Conjunct Independence) entails*

– *if $\alpha$ is safely consistent for $K$ then $I(K \cup \{\alpha\}) = I(K)$*

*Proof.* If $\alpha \in K$ then $I(K \cup \{\alpha\}) = I(K)$. Therefore, assume $\alpha \notin K$. Since $K$ is finite, there exists $n$ such that $\alpha \wedge \bigwedge_{i=1}^{n} \top \notin K$ and $\bigwedge_{i=1}^{n} \top \notin K$. Clearly, (Tautology Independence) gives $I(K) = I(K \cup \{\bigwedge_{i=1}^{n} \top\})$. Since $\alpha$ is safely consistent for $K$, it is safely consistent for $K \cup \{\bigwedge_{i=1}^{n} \top\}$. Due to $\bigwedge_{i=1}^{n} \top \notin K$ and $\alpha \wedge \bigwedge_{i=1}^{n} \top \notin K$, (Conjunct Independence) can thus be applied so that $I(K \cup \{\bigwedge_{i=1}^{n} \top\}) = I(K \cup \{\alpha \wedge \bigwedge_{i=1}^{n} \top\})$ is obtained. In view of $\alpha \wedge \bigwedge_{i=1}^{n} \top \notin K$ and $\alpha \notin K$, it happens that $I(K \cup \{\alpha \wedge \{\bigwedge_{i=1}^{n} \top\}) = I(K \cup \{\alpha\})$ by means of ($\top$-conjunct Independence) which is available according to Proposition 2. Summing up, $I(K) = I(K \cup \{\alpha\})$.

**Proposition 4.** *Assuming (Tautology Independence), (Conjunct Independence) entails (Safe Formula Independence).*

*Proof.* Let $\alpha$ be safe for $K$, that is, $\alpha \not\vdash \bot$ and $Atoms(K) \cap Atoms(\alpha) = \emptyset$. From completeness of $\vdash$, there exists a valuation $v$ over $Atoms(\alpha)$ satisfying $v(\alpha) = true$. Thus, $\alpha$ has the truth value $true$ if each atom $a$ in $Atoms(\alpha)$ has the truth value $v(a)$. Define $\sigma$ as $\sigma(a) = a$ if $a \in \mathcal{L} \setminus Atoms(\alpha)$ whereas $\sigma(a) = \top$ for $a \in Atoms(\alpha)$ s. t. $v(a) = true$ and $\sigma(a) = \bot$ for $a \in Atoms(\alpha)$ s. t. $v(a) = false$. Accordingly, for all atomic formulas $a$ in $\alpha$, $v(a) = v(\sigma a)$. By induction, $v(\alpha) = v(\sigma \alpha)$. Thus, $\sigma \alpha$ is true under $v$. However, all atomic formulas in $\sigma \alpha$ are $\top$ and $\bot$ hence the truth value of $\sigma \alpha$ is independent of $v$. Since $\sigma \alpha$ is true under $v$, this means that $\sigma \alpha$ is a tautology. In view of $\sigma(a) = a$ for all $a \in \mathcal{L} \setminus Atoms(\alpha)$, it is clear that $\sigma(a) = a$ for all $a \in Atoms(K)$ because $Atoms(K) \cap Atoms(\alpha) = \emptyset$. Therefore, $\alpha$ is safely consistent for $K$. Finally, $I(K \cup \{\alpha\}) = I(K)$ by Proposition 3.

Example 5 shows that the converse of Proposition 4 is untrue.

*Example 5.* Consider $K = \{p \wedge q \wedge \neg q\}$ and let $\alpha$ be $\neg q \vee [r \leftrightarrow (s \wedge (q \vee \neg q))]$ (for readability, $\alpha$ is abbreviated using the symbol $\leftrightarrow$ with its usual meaning). Since $\alpha$ is not safe for $K$, (Safe Formula Independence) fails to apply. However, replacing $r$ and $s$ by $\bot$ in $\alpha$ results in a tautology, i.e., (Conjunct Independence) and (Tautology Independence) give $I(K \cup \{\alpha\}) = I(K)$ (see Proposition 3).

## 5   Paradigm

*Example 6.* A paradigmatic case is

$$K_0 = \left\{ \begin{array}{c} p \wedge \neg p \\ q \wedge \neg r \wedge s \end{array} \right\} \qquad K_1 = \left\{ \begin{array}{c} p \wedge \neg p \\ p \wedge \neg p \wedge s \end{array} \right\} \qquad K_2 = \left\{ \begin{array}{c} p \wedge \neg p \\ q \wedge \neg q \wedge s \end{array} \right\}$$

where it is expected that $I(K_0) \leq I(K_1)$ and $I(K_0) \leq I(K_2)$ *and* $I(K_2) \not\leq I(K_1)$.

The codomain of $I$ is totally ordered hence $I(K_2) \not\leq I(K_1)$ is in fact equivalent with $I(K_1) \leq I(K_2)$, and what is expected in Example 6 is in fact

$$I(K_0) \leq I(K_1) \leq I(K_2).$$

Intuition also suggests

$$I(K_0) < I(K_2).$$

Hence, either $I(K_0) < I(K_1)$ or $I(K_1) < I(K_2)$ (or both) must hold. That is,

- the number of occurrences of the *same* atomic contradiction makes a difference,
- or the number of *distinct* atomic contradictions makes a difference.

Now, $I(K_0) \leq I(K_1)$ (and $I(K_0) \leq I(K_2)$ in a similar way) can be shown using (Monotony) and (Safe Formula Independence) as follows. Since $q \wedge \neg r \wedge s$ is safe for $\{p \wedge \neg p\}$, (Safe Formula Independence) can be applied to give

$$I\left( \left\{ \begin{array}{c} p \wedge \neg p \\ q \wedge \neg r \wedge s \end{array} \right\} \right) = I\left( \{ p \wedge \neg p \} \right)$$

while (Monotony) of course gives

$$I\left( \{ p \wedge \neg p \} \right) \leq I\left( \left\{ \begin{array}{c} p \wedge \neg p \\ p \wedge \neg p \wedge s \end{array} \right\} \right)$$

and $I(K_0) \leq I(K_1)$ ensues by transitivity, i.e.,

$$I\left( \left\{ \begin{array}{c} p \wedge \neg p \\ q \wedge \neg r \wedge s \end{array} \right\} \right) \leq I\left( \left\{ \begin{array}{c} p \wedge \neg p \\ p \wedge \neg p \wedge s \end{array} \right\} \right)$$

However, (Safe Formula Independence) is not general enough to deal with a variant where an intuitively safe formula actually fails to be safe because it has a conjunct which is a tautology over an atom in $K$; e.g., for our running example:

$$K_0' = \left\{ \begin{array}{c} p \wedge \neg p \\ q \wedge \neg r \wedge s \wedge (p \vee \neg p) \end{array} \right\} \qquad K_1 = \left\{ \begin{array}{c} p \wedge \neg p \\ p \wedge \neg p \wedge s \end{array} \right\} \qquad K_2 = \left\{ \begin{array}{c} p \wedge \neg p \\ q \wedge \neg q \wedge s \end{array} \right\}$$

The combination "(Safe Formula Independence) + (Monotony)" can be generalized by substituting (Conjunct Independence) and (Tautology Independence) for (Safe Formula Independence). To generalize further, supplement (Monotony) with (Conjunction Dominance).

In the example, $I(K_0') = I(\{p \wedge \neg p\})$ is given by (Conjunct Independence) together with (Tautology Independence) whereas $I(\{p \wedge \neg p\}) \leq I(K_1)$ comes from (Monotony). That is, $I(K_0') \leq I(K_1)$ can be shown using these postulates.

## 6   Exhibiting Conjunctions

The reader might be concerned that some important postulates above explicitly mention a distinctive connective, namely conjunction. Such a concern is well-taken because there are a host of forms, $\neg(\neg\alpha \vee \neg\beta)$ for instance, under which conjunctions may hide. Display logic [2] tells us what to do: if a subformula $\alpha$ is in essence a conjunct of the whole formula then it is possible to rewrite the formula in such a way that $\alpha$ *actually* occurs as a conjunct. Fortunately, there is no need here to resort to the full-fledged system (display logic is meant to cover a large family of logics) because we are only interested in classical logic.

Thus, define $\alpha'$ to be a *prenormal form* of $\alpha$ if $\alpha'$ results from $\alpha$ by applying (possibly repeatedly) one or more of the principles: commutativity, associativity and distribution for $\wedge$ and $\vee$, De Morgan laws, double negation equivalence.

– If $\beta$ is a prenormal form of $\alpha$ then $I(K \cup \{\alpha\}) = I(K \cup \{\beta\})$     *(Rewriting)*

There is another way the form of a belief base should be irrelevant with respect to inconsistency measuring, and that is, the propositional symbols chosen to express formulas in a belief base must be interchangeable as follows.

– If $\sigma$ and $\sigma'$ are substitutions s.t. $\sigma K = K'$ and $\sigma' K' = K$ then $I(K) = I(K')$
     *(Variant Equality)*

It seems indeed rational to hold that $\{p, q \wedge \neg p\}$ for example conveys exactly the same amount of inconsistency than $\{r, s \wedge \neg r\}$ and the like.

## 7   Towards an Alternative Set of Basic Postulates

Summing up, an alternative set of basic postulates would be:

– $I(K) = 0$ iff $K \not\vdash \bot$                                             *(Consistency Null)*

– $I(K \cup K') \geq I(K)$                                                      *(Monotony)*

– For $\alpha \notin K$, if $\alpha \vdash \beta$ and $\alpha \not\vdash \bot$ then $I(K \cup \{\alpha\}) \geq I(K \cup \{\beta\})$ *(Dominance\*)*

– If $\alpha \equiv \top$ then $I(K \cup \{\alpha\}) = I(K)$                    *(Tautology Independence)*

– If $\alpha \wedge \beta \notin K$, $\beta \notin K$, and $\alpha$ is safely consistent for $K \cup \{\beta\}$
  then $I(K \cup \{\alpha \wedge \beta\}) = I(K \cup \{\beta\})$               *(Conjunct Independence)*

– If $\beta$ is a prenormal form of $\alpha$ then $I(K \cup \{\alpha\}) = I(K \cup \{\beta\})$     *(Rewriting)*

– If $\sigma$ and $\sigma'$ are substitutions s.t. $\sigma K = K'$ and $\sigma' K' = K$ then $I(K) = I(K')$
     *(Variant Equality)*

In a very insightful comparison, Thimm [21] checks many inconsistency measures against various postulates. An interesting conclusion is that no postulate except (Inconsistency Null) is satisfied by all those inconsistency measures. How well do our basic postulates would fare? In fact, all those inconsistency measures satisfy (Variant Equality) and (Rewriting). The other way around, an inconsistency measure such as $I_{MI^C}$ (defined in [6] by $I_{MI^C}(K) = \Sigma_{M \in MI(K)} 1/|M|$ with $MI(K)$ denoting the set of MUSes of $K$) satisfies all our basic postulates.

Despite the argument that (Monotony) is only one way to express that extra information cannot make the amount of inconsistency to decrease while another way is by means of the postulate

  – If $\alpha \wedge \beta \notin K$ then $I(K \cup \{\alpha\}) \leq I(K \cup \{\alpha \wedge \beta\})$   *(Conjunction Dominance)*

the latter is not in the set. The reason is that (Conjunction Dominance) rules out inconsistency measures based on Minimal Unsatisfiable Subsets. As an example, considering $K = \{p, \neg q, \neg r\}$ when taking $\alpha$ to be $s \wedge (\neg p \vee (q \wedge r))$ and taking $\beta$ to be $\neg p$ gives $I_{MI^C}(K \cup \{\alpha\}) = 1/3 + 1/3 > 1/2 = I_{MI^C}(K \cup \{\alpha \wedge \beta\})$. That is, (Conjunction Dominance) is failed by $I_{MI^C}$.

With the advent of a number of new inconsistency measures (see e.g. [9] as well as the special issue [11] in the Journal of Approximate Reasoning) or related approaches [4, 19], further investigations are afoot.

## 8    Conclusion

We have examined basic postulates for inconsistency measures, unearthing a simple transformation to secure would-be postulates against a family of counter-examples and investigating independence postulates. We have also considered a case study in the form of three belief bases close to each other, illustrating the impact of the linearity of the codomain of an inconsistency measure (so that an intuition about $I(K) \not< I(K')$ actually means $I(K) \geq I(K')$) leading to the fact that on some occasions it *must* either be that (1) the number of occurrences of the same atomic contradiction makes a difference, or be that (2) the number of distinct atomic contradictions makes a difference.

In the end, we propose a set of basic postulates that can be viewed as an alternative to the core set introduced by Hunter and Konieczny. Among these are two postulates expressing that changing the form of a belief base through e.g. exchanging the order of disjuncts in a disjunction or using fresh propositional symbols should be of no consequence when it comes to inconsistency measuring. We have also discussed a postulate along the lines of the rather uncontroversial (Monotony) postulate, to the effect that extending a belief base cannot make the amount of inconsistency to decrease, regardless of whether extra information comes in the form of an extra formula or of an extra conjunct. A major avenue for future work is exhaustiveness, both through providing further postulates and through offering criteria to fix bounds to the introduction of basic postulates for inconsistency measures.

# References

1. Ammoura, M., Raddaoui, B., Salhi, Y., Oukacha, B.: On an MCS-based inconsistency measure. J. Approximate Reasoning **80**, 443–459 (2017)
2. Belnap, N.D.: Display logic. Philos. Logic **11**, 375–417 (1982)
3. Besnard, P.: Revisiting Postulates for Inconsistency Measures. In: Fermé, E., Leite, J. (eds.) JELIA 2014. LNCS (LNAI), vol. 8761, pp. 383–396. Springer, Cham (2014). doi:10.1007/978-3-319-11558-0_27
4. De Bona, G., Hunter, A.: Localising iceberg inconsistencies. Artif. Intell. **246**, 118–151 (2017)
5. Grant, J., Hunter, A.: Measuring consistency gain and information loss in stepwise inconsistency resolution. In: Liu, W. (ed.) ECSQARU 2011. LNCS (LNAI), vol. 6717, pp. 362–373. Springer, Heidelberg (2011). doi:10.1007/978-3-642-22152-1_31
6. Hunter, A., Konieczny, S.: Measuring inconsistency through minimal inconsistent sets. In: Brewka, G., Lang, J. (eds.) 11th Conference on Principles of Knowledge Representation and Reasoning (KR 2008), pp. 358–366, Sydney, Australia, September 16–19, 2008. AAAI Press (2008)
7. Hunter, A., Konieczny, S.: On the measure of conflicts: shapley inconsistency values. Artif. Intell. **174**(14), 1007–1026 (2010)
8. Hunter, A., Parsons, S., Wooldridge, M.: Measuring inconsistency in multi-agent systems. Künstliche Intelligenz **28**, 169–178 (2014)
9. Jabbour, S., Ma, Y., Raddaoui, B., Saïs, L., Salhi, Y.: A MIS partition based framework for measuring inconsistency. In: Baral, C., Delgrande, J.P., Wolter, F. (eds.) 15th International Conference on Principles of Knowledge Representation and Reasoning (KR 2016), pp. 84–93, Cape Town, South Africa, April 25–29, 2016. AAAI Press (2016)
10. Konieczny, S., Lang, J., Marquis, P.: Quantifying information and contradiction in propositional logic through epistemic tests. In: Gottlob, G., Walsh, T. (eds.) 18th International Joint Conference on Artificial Intelligence (IJCAI 2003), pp. 106–111, Acapulco, Mexico, August 9–15, 2003. Morgan Kaufmann (2003)
11. Liu, W., Mu, K. eds.: Special Issue on Theories of Inconsistency Measures and their Applications. Journal of Approximate Reasoning (to appear, 2017)
12. McAreavey, K., Liu, W., Miller, P.C.: Computational approaches to finding and measuring inconsistency in arbitrary knowledge bases. J. Approximate Reasoning **55**(8), 1659–1693 (2014)
13. Kedian, M., Liu, W., Jin, Z., Bell, D.: A syntax-based approach to measuring the degree of inconsistency for belief bases. J. Approximate Reasoning **52**(7), 978–999 (2011)
14. Kedian, M., Wang, K., Wen, L.: Approaches to measuring inconsistency for stratified knowledge bases. J. Approximate Reasoning **55**(2), 529–556 (2014)
15. Potyka, N., Thimm, M.: Probabilistic reasoning with inconsistent beliefs using inconsistency measures. In: Yang, Q., Wooldridge, M., (eds.) 24th International Joint Conference on Artificial Intelligence (IJCAI 2015), pp. 3156–3163, Buenos Aires, Argentina, July 25–31, 2015. AAAI Press (2015)
16. Schütte, K.: Proof Theory. Springer, Heidelberg (1977)
17. Thimm, M.: Measuring inconsistency in probabilistic knowledge bases. In: Bilmes, J.A., Ng, A.Y. (eds.) 25th Conference on Uncertainty in Artificial Intelligence (UAI 2009), pp. 530–537, Montreal, QC, Canada, June 18–21, 2009. AUAI Press (2009)
18. Thimm, M.: Inconsistency measures for probabilistic logics. Artif. Intell. **197**, 1–24 (2013)

19. Thimm, M.: On the expressivity of inconsistency measures. Artif. Intell. **234**, 120–151 (2016)
20. Thimm, M.: Measuring inconsistency with many-valued logics. J. Approximate Reasoning **86**, 1–23 (2017)
21. Thimm, M.: On the compliance of rationality postulates for inconsistency measures: a more or less complete picture. Künstliche Intelligenz **31**(1), 31–39 (2017)
22. Thimm, M.: Stream-based inconsistency measurement. J. Approximate Reasoning **68**, 68–87 (2017)
23. Ulbricht, M., Thimm, M., Brewka, G.: Measuring inconsistency in answer set programs. In: Michael, L., Kakas, A. (eds.) JELIA 2016. LNCS (LNAI), vol. 10021, pp. 577–583. Springer, Cham (2016). doi:10.1007/978-3-319-48758-8_42

# Batch Composite Transactions
# in Stream Processing

K. Vidyasankar[✉]

Department of Computer Science, Memorial University,
St. John's, Newfoundland A1B 3X5, Canada
vidya@mun.ca

**Abstract.** Stream processing is about processing continuous streams of data by programs in a workflow. Continuous execution is discretized by grouping input stream tuples into batches and using one batch at a time for the execution of programs. As source input batches arrive continuously, several batches may be processed in the workflow simultaneously. Ensuring correctness of these concurrent executions is important. As in databases and several advanced applications, the transaction concept can be applied to regulate concurrent executions and ensure their correctness in stream processing. The first step is defining transactions corresponding to the executions in a meaningful way. A general requirement in stream processing is that each batch be processed completely in the workflow. That is, all the programs triggered by the batch, directly and transitively, in the workflow must be executed successfully. Then, considering each program execution as a transaction, all the transactions involved in processing a batch can be grouped into a single *batch composite transaction*, abbreviated as BCT, and transactional properties applied to these BCTs. This works well when a batch is processed individually and completely in isolation. However, when the batches are split, merged or overlapped along the workflow computation, the resulting BCTs will have some transactions in common and applying transactional properties for them becomes complicated. We overcome the problems by defining *nonblocking* BCTs that have disjoint collections of transactions. They satisfy some properties analogous to those of the database transactions and facilitate (i) defining correctness of concurrent executions in terms of equivalent serial executions of composite transactions and (ii) processing each batch either completely or not at all, and rolling back partially processed batches without affecting the processing of other batches. We also suggest an appropriate roll back mechanism.

## 1 Introduction

Stream processing is about processing continuous streams of data arriving from external sources by programs in a workflow. Continuous execution is discretized

---

This research is supported in part by the Natural Sciences and Engineering Research Council of Canada Discovery Grant 3182.

© Springer-Verlag GmbH Germany 2017
A. Hameurlain et al. (Eds.): TLDKS XXXIV, LNCS 10620, pp. 13–32, 2017.
https://doi.org/10.1007/978-3-662-55947-5_2

by grouping (input) stream tuples into batches and using one batch at a time for the execution of programs. As source input batches arrive continuously, several batches may be processed in the workflow simultaneously. Ensuring correctness of these concurrent executions is important.

As in databases and several advanced applications, the transaction concept can be applied to regulate concurrent executions and ensure their correctness in stream processing. To do this, the first step is defining transactions correspond-ing to the executions in a meaningful way. A general requirement in stream processing is that each batch be processed completely in the workflow. Each batch will trigger a set of programs in the workflow. Considering each execution of a program as a transaction, all the transactions involved in processing a batch can be grouped into a composite transaction, called *batch composite transac-tion*, abbreviated as BCT, for that batch. Then, transactional properties can be applied to the BCTs.

In the database context, a transaction is a partially ordered set of operations, but any such set does not qualify as a transaction. Certain properties and con-ventions are followed in the definition and execution of database transactions. We look at applying these properties to BCTs. In this paper, we focus on the following four properties, denoted *Transaction Properties*, abbreviated as TPs.

**TP1.** A transaction is a partially ordered set of operations such that *any two conflicting operations are ordered.*

**TP2.** The operations of each transaction are distinct. That is, no two transac-tions have any operations in common.

**TP3.** Each transaction can be executed independently of other transactions.

**TP4.** Partial execution of a transaction can be rolled back without affecting other transactions.

Denoting the operations of a transaction $T$ as $op(T)$ and partial order as $\prec_t$, TP1 states that conflicting operations in $T$ are ordered by $\prec_t$. Two operations are non-conflicting if their effects are the same in whichever order they are executed; they are conflicting otherwise. For example, a read and a write of a data item are conflicting. TP2 states that $op(T) \cap op(T')$ is empty for any two transactions $T$ and $T'$. Note that both $T$ and $T'$ may have similar operations like $read(x)$, for the same data item $x$, but the operations are different, not shared by both the transactions.

We now look at applying these properties to BCTs. They can be stated as follows, replacing 'transaction' by 'BCT' and 'operation' by 'transaction' in the above.

**BP1.** A BCT is a partially ordered set of transactions such that *any two con-flicting transactions are ordered.*

**BP2.** The transactions of each BCT are distinct. That is, no two BCTs have any transactions in common.

**BP3.** Each BCT can be executed independently of other BCTs.

**BP4.** Partial execution of a BCT can be rolled back without affecting other BCTs.

We note that conflicts among the transactions of a BCT are to be determined by the semantics of the operations in the transactions and the data items accessed by them in the application.

In many applications, all processing pertaining to an input batch is done *in isolation*. That is, if a transaction $T$ (which is an execution of a program $P$) takes as input a batch $a$ and produces as output a batch $a'$, and the output is fed to another transaction $T'$ (an execution of program $P'$), then $a'$ constitutes the input batch $b$ for $T'$. In such cases, BCTs defined as consisting of all transactions triggered by the individual batches satisfy the above properties. However, when the batches are merged or overlapped along the workflow computation, the resulting BCTs may not satisfy the above properties. For example, in the case of a merge, when $b$ contains tuples from the outputs of two executions of $P$, on two source input batches, the BCTs of both batches will contain $T'$ and so will not satisfy BP2-BP4. In this paper, to overcome this problem, we propose a new notion called *nonblocking* BCTs (NBCTs) which satisfy the properties BP1-BP4 and, in addition, the following requirements for processing batches.

**B1.** *Completion*: Each batch must be processed completely. If it is not possible, then partial processing, if any, must be rolled back *non-intrusively*, that is, without affecting the processing of other batches.

**B2.** *Monotonic execution*: At any time, for each batch, the amount of processing done on that batch should be a prefix of the workflow.

We describe a procedure for composing NBCTs, that is, figuring out the transactions of each NBCT, in a simple manner. We also describe a non-intrusive roll back mechanism.

With the new notion, the correctness of concurrent executions of the batches can be described in terms of equivalent serial executions of their NBCTs. Rolling back the executions pertaining to a batch can be accomplished by rolling back the NBCTs that process the batch.

The transaction concept was introduced first in the context of (centralized) database systems, characterized by ACID (Atomicity, Consistency, Isolation and Durability) properties, and then adopted in various advanced database and other applications, for example, in transactional processes [12], Web services [17], and electronic contracts [16]. In all these applications, the composite/nested transactions defined corresponding to the executions satisfy the properties BP1-BP4. There have been several studies on the application of the transaction concept in stream processing, including [2,3,6,9,18]. We elaborate the approaches in the Related Works section. Some of them define composite transactions for batches consisting of single tuples or batches executed in isolation. To our knowledge, none of them define composite transactions when the batches are split, merged or overlapped along the workflow computation.

We start with core definitions of compositions and transactions in stream processing environments in Sect. 2. We study the executions involving splits, merges and overlapping of batches and arrive at the definition of the NBCTs in Sect. 3. A recovery mechanism that supports BP4 and B1 for the NBCTs is given in Sect. 4. We initially consider only one source input stream. Inputs from multiple source streams are considered in Sect. 5. Concurrent execution of BCTs is dealt with in Sect. 6. We discuss related work in Sect. 7 and conclude in Sect. 8.

## 2     Executions in Stream Processing

A stream processing workflow is a composition of programs. Formally, a *composition* $\mathcal{C}$ is $(\mathcal{P}, \prec_p)$, where $\mathcal{P}$ is a set of *transaction programs* $\{P_1, P_2, \ldots, P_n\}$, simply called *programs*, and $\prec_p$ is a partial order, called *program order*, among them. The partial order consists of dataflow order (of the streams) and control order. We also include *conflict order*. We discuss conflict order in Sect. 6. We call the (acyclic) graph representing the partial order the *composition graph* $\mathcal{GC}(\mathcal{C})$. Stream data are sequences of tuples. Streams coming from outside the composition are called *source streams*. The output streams (of any program) are called *derived streams*. Each execution of a program yields a *transaction*.

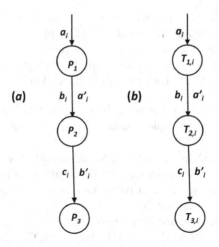

**Fig. 1.** A schema example

We use the simple composition, shown in Fig. 1, to illustrate the definitions. It is a workflow consisting of a sequence of three programs $P_1, P_2$ and $P_3$. Input batches will be denoted by unprimed variables $x_i$ and the corresponding outputs by primed variables $x'_i$. Stream inputs/outputs for $P_1, P_2$ and $P_3$ will be denoted by $a, b$ and $c$, respectively. The sequence of input batches for $P_1$ is $a_1, a_2, \ldots$, and the executions are transactions $T_{1,1}, T_{1,2}, \ldots$ (the first index is that of the program and the second index is that of the input batch), producing the output sequence $a'_1, a'_2 \ldots$.

The processing of a source input batch will involve executions of some of the programs in the workflow, resulting in a set of transactions with a partial order $\prec_t$, called *transaction order*. We call this a *batch composite transaction*, BCT, denoted as $T = (\{T_1, T_2, \ldots, T_m\}, \prec_t)$. We denote $\{T_1, T_2, \ldots, T_m\}$ as $set(T)$. The graph representing $\prec_t$ is called *transaction graph* $\mathcal{GT}(T)$. The transaction graphs are acyclic. We note that each $T_i$ is an execution of some program $P_j$. It is possible that $T$ has more than one execution of some $P_j$. The transaction partial order $\prec_t$ reflects the program partial order $\prec_p$, that is, if $T_i$ is an execution of $P_j$, $T_k$ is an execution of $P_l$ and $P_j \prec_p P_l$, then $T_i \prec_t T_k$. In addition, $\prec_t$ will contain triggering relationships, if any. (We note that, in this paper, we use the term 'transaction' exclusively to denote some $T_i$; a $T$ always denotes a 'batch composite transaction', that is, BCT.) We denote the BCT that is executed for source input batch $b$ as $T(b)$. In the execution shown in Fig. 1, the BCT for batch $a_i$, $T(a_i)$, is $\{T_{1,i}, T_{2,i}, T_{3,i}\}$ (omitting the transaction order for brevity).

Stream input batches arrive in sequence, for example, as $b_1, b_2, \ldots$. The batch order is denoted $\prec_b$. The batch $b_2$ and a few more batches may arrive before all the transactions in $T(b_1)$ are completely executed. Thus many BCTs may be executed concurrently.

General requirements for concurrent executions of BCTs can be stated as follows [14].

1. *Unit of atomicity.* Each BCT is executed either completely or not at all. That is, the entire $T$ is an *atomic unit* for each $T$.
2. *Serializability.* The execution is equivalent to a serial execution of the BCTs.
3. *Transaction order.* The effective execution order of the transactions of $T$ should obey the partial order $\prec_t$. That is, for any $i, j$, if $T_i \prec_t T_j$, then $T_i$ should precede $T_j$ in the serial execution.
4. *Batch order.* The serial execution should reflect the batch order $\prec_b$. That is, for $i < j$, (all the transactions in) $T(b_i)$ should precede (the transactions of) $T(b_j)$ in the equivalent serial execution.

We define nonblocking BCTs in the next section.

## 3    Batch Composite Transaction Model

Batch composite transactions are initiated by arrival of batches of tuples from source streams. Batch sizes vary. A batch may contain all the tuples with the same timestamp (time-based) or a certain number of tuples (count-based). A program may process one tuple at a time (as in selection and projection operations) or all the tuples in the batch together (as in join). We stipulate only that *each* execution of a program is a transaction. Therefore, with the all-or-nothing atomicity property, the result of the execution will be known only after the entire batch is processed. The intermediate results and states of the program will not be available. In general, smaller batches will reduce latency while larger ones, resulting in fewer executions of the program, may improve efficiency. Batch sizes may also be different for different programs, and even for different executions of the same program.

Batches may be split, merged or overlapped along the workflow computation [4,7]. For example, splitting may occur for processing the batches in parallel.

Subsequently, the resulting output batches may be merged. Merging and overlapping will also occur in aggregates computation. We assume arbitrary splitting, merging and overlapping in this paper. We consider several examples and come up with a definition of nonblocking BCTs and an execution model underlying the definition.

We first consider only one source input stream. (Note that in many applications where multiple input streams are involved, the tuples from the different streams are combined and input as one stream.) We consider multiple source streams in Sect. 5.

Details of the model are itemized with label M. Though we are dealing with concurrent processing of the batches and hence concurrent executions of their BCTs, we assume in this paper that:

**M1.** Each program in the workflow is executed serially.

It follows that each transaction in a BCT is executed atomically, akin to each operation in a database transaction being executed atomically.

We have identified the composite transaction *to be executed* for batch $b$ as the BCT $T(b)$. Suppose $b$ is input to transaction $T$. Then we define $T(b)$ as the union of $\{T\}$ and all the transactions triggered directly or indirectly by $T$ in the composition, with the corresponding partial order. Suppose $T_i$ precedes $T_j$. If the precedence is due to dataflow order, the execution of $T_j$ will start only after the execution of $T_i$ finishes. The same can be assumed for control order. We also assume an implementation such that if $T_i$ triggers $T_j$, the triggering is done only after $T_i$ commits. Then, in all cases, for $T_i$ preceding $T_j$, the execution of $T_j$ starts only after the execution of $T_i$ finishes. This is true whether $T_i$ and $T_j$ are conflicting or not. If $T_i$ and $T_j$ are executions of the same program, then the assumed serial execution of programs (M1) induces an ordering between the two transactions. Thus, BP1 will be satisfied for $T(b)$. In the following, we look at the properties BP2-BP4 for various cases. We use the composition shown in Fig. 1 to illustrate the cases.

**M2.** We model the dataflow, from an output stream of one program $P_i$ to an input stream of another program $P_j$, with a FIFO (first-in-first-out) queue $Q_{i,j}$; $P_i$ enqueues its output into $Q_{i,j}$ and $P_j$ dequeues its input from that queue. Both enqueueing and dequeueing a batch are assumed to be done atomically.

In the execution shown in Fig. 1, the dataflow between $P_1$ and $P_2$ is such that $b_i = a'_i$, that is, $P_2$ empties the queue $Q_{1,2}$ (in a serial execution of the batches), and similarly $P_3$ empties the queue $Q_{2,3}$ resulting in $c_i = b'_i$. Here, the BCT for batch $a_i$, $T(a_i)$, is $\{T_{1,i}, T_{2,i}, T_{3,i}\}$. Rolling back partially executed $T(a_i)$ involves rolling back the corresponding transactions in this set. Clearly, the BCT $T(a_i)$, for each $i$, satisfies all the properties BP1-BP4.

We note that, in a serial execution of the batches, all the queues are empty before the processing of $a_i$ starts, and all of them are empty after the processing is completed. This property captures the notion of *the batch being processed in isolation*.

In the following, we consider splits, merges, and overlapping of batches.

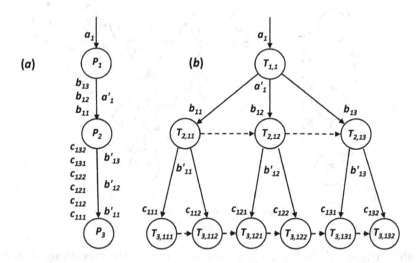

**Fig. 2.** Splitting of the batches

(a) *Splits*: Consider the following with respect to our composition example, depicted in Fig. 2. (In all the figures, horizontal edges denote batch order.)

- Input batch $a_1$ for $P_1$ results in execution of $T_{1,1}$, producing output batch $a'_1$.
- The batch $a'_1$ is split into three batches $b_{11}, b_{12}, b_{13}$, and each $b'_{1j}$ is split into two batches $c_{1j1}$ and $c_{1j2}$.
- Then the corresponding executions of $P_2$ are $T_{2,11}, T_{2,12}, T_{2,13}$. The batch order among the three batches translates to $T_{2,11} \prec_b T_{2,12} \prec_b T_{2,13}$.
- The executions of $P_3$ are $T_{3,111}, T_{3,112}, T_{3,121}, T_{3,122}, T_{3,131}, T_{3,132}$.

Here, $T(a_1)$ consists of all the transactions listed above. Again, to satisfy BP1, all conflicting transactions must be ordered. Imposing batch order on the split batches will guarantee this property. (We assume that any two executions of the same program are conflicting.) The other three properties, BP2–BP4, are clearly satisfied. We note that, here also, (again in a serial execution of the batches) all the queues are empty before the processing of $a_1$ starts and are empty after the processing is complete. That is, the batch $a_1$ is processed in isolation.

(b) *Merges*: Merging of the batches is depicted in Fig. 3:

- Input batches $a_1, a_2, \ldots, a_6$, for $P_1$, result in executions of $T_{1,1}, T_{1,2}, \ldots, T_{1,6}$, producing output batches $a'_1, a'_2, \ldots, a'_6$, respectively.

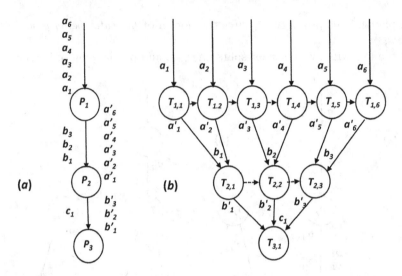

**Fig. 3.** Merging of batches

- Batch $b_1$ is $a'_2 \cdot a'_1$, $b_2$ is $a'_4 \cdot a'_3$, and $b_3$ is $a'_6 \cdot a'_5$ and the executions of $P_2$ are $T_{2,1}, T_{2,2}, T_{2,3}$. Here "." indicates concatenation, of the batches in the order of their arrival, that is, from right to left.
- Batch $c_1$ is $b'_3 \cdot b'_2 \cdot b'_1$, and the execution of $P_3$ yield $T_{3,1}$.

Here, $\mathcal{T}(a_1)$ is $\{T_{1,1}, T_{2,1}, T_{3,1}\}$ and $\mathcal{T}(a_2)$ is $\{T_{1,2}, T_{2,1}, T_{3,1}\}$. We note that these two sets have $\{T_{2,1}, T_{3,1}\}$ in common. Thus BP2 is not satisfied.

To satisfy BP2, keeping in mind the completion and monotonic execution requirements, B1 and B2, of the batches, we choose an appropriate prefix[1] of $\mathcal{T}(b)$ as a composite transaction for batch $b$. We can interpret that in the executions of a program where merges occur, on arrival of an earlier batch, the program *waits* (*blocks*) for further batches. For instance, in Fig. 3, after $a'_1$ arrives, $P_2$ waits for $a'_2$ for execution of $T_{1,2}$. We take this as the execution of the BCT for $a_1$ is complete when it cannot proceed any farther by itself, that is, once $a'_1$ is sent to $P_2$. Therefore, eliminating waiting for batches from other transactions, we can close the composition of the BCT with $\{T_{1,1}\}$. We call this *nonblocking* BCT, abbreviated as NBCT and denoted $\widetilde{\mathcal{T}}(a_1)$. Arguing along the same lines, the nonblocking batch composite transactions for other batches will be as follows.

- $\widetilde{\mathcal{T}}(a_2)$ is $\{T_{1,2}, T_{2,1}\}$.
- $\widetilde{\mathcal{T}}(a_3)$ is $\{T_{1,3}\}$.
- $\widetilde{\mathcal{T}}(a_4)$ is $\{T_{1,4}, T_{2,2}\}$.
- $\widetilde{\mathcal{T}}(a_5)$ is $\{T_{1,5}\}$.
- $\widetilde{\mathcal{T}}(a_6)$ is $\{T_{1,6}, T_{2,3}, T_{3,1}\}$.

---

[1] A subgraph $H$ of an acyclic graph $G$ is a prefix of $G$ if all the edges from $H$ to the rest of the graph are outdirected.

This approach is captured in the following definition.

**Definition 1.** For a batch $a$, the *nonblocking batch composite transaction* $\widetilde{T}(a)$ is the maximal prefix of $T(a)$ that is executed without inputs from subsequent batch composite transactions.

We note that with this definition, referring to the above example, the properties BP1-BP3 will be satisfied. Now, BP4 requires that roll back of any partial execution can be done without affecting other NBCTs. We describe a nonintrusive roll back mechanism that will accomplish this in the next section. As an example, in Fig. 3, suppose $T_{1,1}$, $T_{1,2}$ and $T_{1,3}$ have been executed by $P_1$, and $P_2$ has not yet executed $T_{2,1}$. Now, to roll back $\widetilde{T}(a_2)$, the state of $P_1$ is rolled back to the one before $T_{1,2}$ and $a_3$ is processed again. That is, we roll back the processing of subsequent batches also and then reprocess them. We note that the completion requirement for each batch is fulfilled jointly by the NBCTs of all batches.

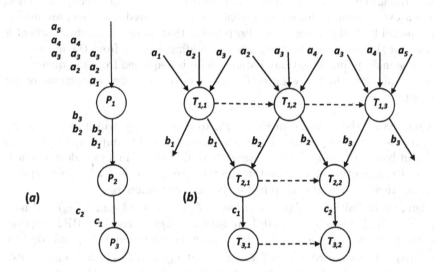

**Fig. 4.** Overlapping batches

(c) *Overlapping batches*: In the previous examples, the batches input to the executions of a program are disjoint. In some applications, the batches may overlap. For example, in the problem of computing an aggregate function every 5 min where the batch consists of the tuples received in the preceding 10 min, every two consecutive batches will overlap. Figure 4 depicts overlapping batches in our composition example. The transactions and batches used for them are:

– Input batches of $T_{1,1}, T_{1,2}$ and $T_{1,3}$ are $a_3 \cdot a_2 \cdot a_1$, $a_4 \cdot a_3 \cdot a_2$, and $a_5 \cdot a_4 \cdot a_3$; the respective output batches are $b_1, b_2$ and $b_3$.

- Input batches of $T_{2,1}$ and $T_{2,2}$ are $b_2 \cdot b_1$, and $b_3 \cdot b_2$; the respective output batches are $c_1$ and $c_2$;
- Input batches of $T_{3,1}$ and $T_{3,2}$ are $c_1$ and $c_2$, respectively.

Here, we can interpret as (i) an input batch is made up of several smaller batches and (ii) each such batch is input multiple times in the executions of a program. We can then consider BCTs of the smaller batches.

We extend our execution model to accommodate overlapping input batches as follows.

**M3.** With each program, for each stream input, we associate a *local* FIFO window. At the beginning of an execution, the input batches used for the computation are dequeued from the queues and placed (enqueued, let us say on top) in the respective windows. In the next execution of the program, either all or a part of the content (always from the bottom) is used. At the end of that execution, a part of the content, again from the bottom, is dequeued and discarded if and only if it is not used in any further executions. Then, in an overlapping window, some contents are removed and some are added, dequeued from the queue. It is also possible that an entire window content is used for the next computation, without adding a batch from the queue.

**M4.** The main point is that any batch (tuple) is dequeued from the queue (just once), but kept in the window for using in one or more executions of the program.

Considering the example in Fig. 4, $P_1$, to execute $T_{1,2}$, will have $a_2$ and $a_3$, concatenated as $a_3 \cdot a_2$ in its window, dequeue $a_4$ from its input queue to form the input batch $a_4 \cdot a_3 \cdot a_2$. The program $P_2$ would have $b_1$ in its window, dequeue $b_2$ after the execution of $T_{1,2}$, and merge them to get $b_2 \cdot b_1$ for the execution of $T_{2,1}$, and then clear $b_1$ but keep $b_2$ for the next execution $T_{2,2}$.

Here, by Definition 1, $\widetilde{T}(a_4)$ will have $\{T_{1,2}, T_{2,1}, T_{3,1}\}$ and $\widetilde{T}(a_5)$ will have $\{T_{1,3}, T_{2,2}, T_{3,2}\}$. Clearly, BP1-BP3 are satisfied. Let us consider BP4. Suppose after the execution of $T_{1,2}$ and $T_{2,1}$, but before the execution of $T_{3,1}$, it is decided that $\widetilde{T}(a_4)$ needs to be rolled back. Assume that $T_{1,3}$ and $T_{2,2}$ have been executed with $a_5$, and also, $T_{1,4}$ has been executed with $a_6$ (not shown in the figure). With the roll back of $\widetilde{T}(a_4)$, $P_1$ has to be reset to its state before $T_{1,2}$, and $P_2$ to its state before $T_{2,1}$.

**M5.** We define the states of the programs to include the states (that is, contents) of their windows also.

Thus, when $P_1$ is reset, its window will contain $a_3 \cdot a_2$ and when $P_2$ is reset, its window will have $b_1$. Then, we want $P_1$ to process $a_5$ again, and then $a_6$ again. With the resulting outputs, $P_2$ should execute (new) $T_{2,1}$, and then (new) $T_{2,2}$. This way, we achieve non-intrusive roll back. Here also, the completion requirement of each batch is satisfied jointly by several NBCTs.

# 4    A Roll Back Mechanism

In general, we assume that splits, merges and overlapping of batches could occur arbitrarily in an execution. The source input batches that transactions process can be kept track of as follows.

**M6.**   1. Index the source input batches serially.
2. For a batch $b$, we denote the source input batch set from which $b$ is derived as *sb-set*, denoted $\psi(b)$. If $b$ itself is a source input batch, then $\psi(b)$ contains just $b$.
3. We define sb-sets for transactions also. For a transaction $T$, let $\psi(T)$ denote the source input batch set that $T$ processes. It will be the union of $\psi(b)$ of all batches $b$ input to $T$.
4. Each of the output batches of $T$ will have sb-set equal to that of $\psi(T)$.

We observe that, for a batch $b_i$, $set(\mathcal{T}(b_i))$ is the set of all the transactions $T$ whose sb-set contains $b_i$. An alternate definition of $\widetilde{\mathcal{T}}(b_i)$ is the following.

**Definition 2.**   For a batch $b_i$, $\widetilde{\mathcal{T}}(b_i)$ is the subgraph of $\mathcal{T}(b_i)$ with all the transactions $T$ such that $i$ is the largest index of the batches in $\psi(T)$.

We note that if $b_i$ is in $\psi(T)$ of a transaction $T$, then $b_i$ is in $\psi(T')$ of all descendents $T'$ of $T$ also. Therefore, it follows that $\widetilde{\mathcal{T}}(b_i)$ is a prefix of $\mathcal{T}(b_i)$.
The roll back mechanism is as follows.

*Preliminaries*:

**M7.**   1. (a) We denote the completion of a BCT by *committing* it once all its transactions are successfully executed.
   (b) A source input batch $b$ can be *committed* when all the BCTs processing $b$ have been committed, that is, all the transactions in $\mathcal{T}(b)$ (*not* $\widetilde{\mathcal{T}}(b)$) have been executed successfully.
   (c) The batches are committed serially, in the order of their indices.
2. For each transaction $T$ of program $P$, we denote the state of $P$ before the execution of $T$ as $prev(P, T)$. Rolling back $T$ amounts to resetting $P$ to this state. Resetting will also roll back changes, if any, made by $T$ to objects in persistent storage.
3. We require each program $P$ to remember $prev(P, T)$ for $T$s corresponding to all the BCTs that are currently executed and not yet committed in the workflow. These are for transactions $T$ whose $\psi(T)$ contains an uncommitted batch; if all the batches in $\psi(T)$ are committed, then the $prev(P, T)$ can be discarded. Since we consider serial execution of the programs, a sequence of previous states can be kept corresponding to the executions.
4. In addition, we require $P_1$, the first program that processes source input batches, remembering (temporarily) all the uncommitted batches themselves. A batch is kept until it commits.

*Mechanism:*

1. Rolling back an NBCT $\widetilde{T}(b_i)$, of batch $b_i$ is done by resetting the programs of each of the transactions in that NBCT to the previous states corresponding to the *first* execution of that batch. This amounts to rolling back all the subsequent transactions of that program too, that is, a cascade roll back.
2. A subsequent batch might have been processed by a program that does not process $b_i$. Therefore, all the programs that have executed a transaction whose sb-set contains a batch with index greater than or equal to $i$ are rolled back.
3. The program $P_1$, after rolling back its state to the one prior to the first execution of the batch $b_i$, resumes executions of the successor batches, one by one. All other programs simply roll back their states to the ones prior to the first execution of that batch. Then they wait for normal execution.
4. Some derived batches of the ones that are rolled back may arrive to the other programs in the mean time. They should be ignored. To facilitate this, the reprocessed batches could be given new indices (that are greater than any previous index).
5. Each transaction could have modified different variables and thus state of the program differently. All these changes have to be rolled back, in reverse order.

A Stream Processing Engine (SPE) can regulate the executions.

**M8.** 1. The SPE will index the source input batches.
2. It will keep track of the transactions executed by programs, and their sb-sets.
3. Therefore, the SPE can figure out the composition of the NBCTs, that is the set of transactions in each NBCT. Note that this set can be completed only after the sb-sets of all transactions have been received.
4. It will determine commitment of the batches.
5. When a decision to roll back an NBCT is made, the SPE will figure out the programs that need to be rolled back and inform them. The actual roll back will be done by the programs themselves. Likewise, the previous states will also be maintained by the programs themselves.
6. The SPE, instead of $P_1$, could keep the uncommitted source batch sets.

We note that since $\widetilde{T}(b_i)$ is a prefix of $T(b_i)$, rolling back $\widetilde{T}(b_i)$ amounts to rolling back $T(b_i)$ itself, and thus rolling back the batch $b_i$, and it is done non-intrusively.

Stream tuples are usually not stored persistently. They are used in the computation and then discarded. Typically, as we have assumed, the tuples arriving from a source or derived by some transaction are written into a queue and read by the next program (transaction) in the workflow. Once the tuples are used, they are not available anymore. However, many recovery considerations require that the tuples are *available for a while* [8]. The duration of their availablity may vary from (i) only until they are used by the successor program(s), (ii) until a certain amount of downstream computations have been carried out, (iii) until the corresponding BCT commits, or (iv) until some time later or when a certain number of subsequent batches have been processed. Some of the (source or derived) batches may even be stored persistently as part of a checkpoint or for archival purposes. The recovery mechanism described above assumes the availability of source input batches until they are committed, and the availability of the previous states of transactions executed by programs. The previous states can be stored in terms of before-images of the changes each transaction makes. Then, resetting to a previous state of a transaction would amount to installing before-images of all the transactions up to that transaction in reverse order.

In some applications, source input streams, also called *raw* streams, should only be processed (by edge devices) and not stored anywhere, for example, for privacy reasons. In such cases, the derived batches at some downstream level can be stored for reprocessing. For example, in our composition schema, instead of remembering $a_i$'s at $P_1$, $b_i$'s can be remembered at $P_2$. Then, when $a_j$, for some $j$, needs to be rolled back, $b_j$ can be rolled back instead (and subsequent $b_i$'s reprocessed from $P_2$). This would amount to dropping $a_j$, literally after $P_1$ but semantically at $P_1$ itself.

We discuss another semantic adjustment in the following. In many applications, a source input batch is processed for several functionalities. We may find that a batch should be rolled back with respect to some functionality, but used for others. This will redefine the NBCT of that batch. We illustrate with an example.

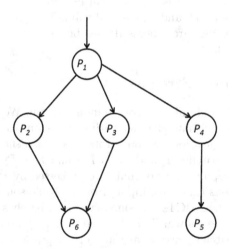

**Fig. 5.** A composition example

A simple composition is shown in Fig. 5, and its execution on input batch $a_1$, that is, the NBCT $\widetilde{T}(a_1)$, is shown in Fig. 6. In this example, $T_{1,1}$, the execution of $P_1$ on input $a_1$, produces two stream outputs $b_1$ and $c_1$. The batch $c_1$ is input to $P_3$. It is also input to $P_4$ split into two batches $c_{11}$ and $c_{12}$. The outputs

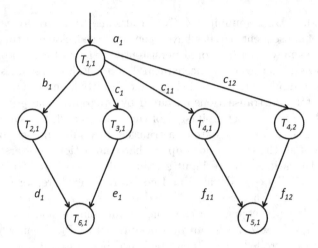

**Fig. 6.** A batch composite transaction

from the two executions of $P_4$, namely, $T_{4,1}$ and $T_{4,2}$, are merged and fed to one execution $T_{5,1}$ of $P_5$. The programs $P_2$ and $P_3$ process $b_1$ and $c_1$ respectively, and produce $d_1$ and $e_1$ which are processed together by $P_6$. Suppose that after $T_{4,1}$ and $T_{4,2}$ are executed but before $T_{5,1}$ is executed, it is decided to drop $c_{11}$. Then, $P_4$ has to be reset to $prev(P_4, T_{4,1})$ and it has to reprocess $c_{12}$. Then $P_5$ could execute just with (new) $f_{12}$. It is possible that $c_{11}$, and hence $c_1$, is processed for different functionality by $P_3$ and $T_{3,1}$ is still valid. Thus, wherever reprocessing is allowed, the batches that are processed must be stored until their source input batches are committed.

## 5   Multiple Source Streams

So far, we have considered only one source input stream. We now consider multiple streams. We start with an example with two streams to illustrate the problem. Consider the composition and one of its executions shown in Fig. 7. Here, program $P_1$ processes batches $a_1$ and $a_2$, in $T_{1,1}$ and $T_{1,2}$, $P_2$ processes batch $b_1$ from a different source, and their outputs are processed by $P_3$ as shown.

In some applications that have inputs from multiple source streams, it may be appropriate to define NBCTs for combinations of batches of different source inputs. For the example shown, $\widetilde{T}(a_1, b_1)$ and $\widetilde{T}(a_2, b_1)$ would be appropriate. However, when the batch $a_2$ arrives at the source input level, we may not know whether it will be processed downstream with $b_1$ or some other batch $b$. This problem arises even when batches from both sources are input to the same (first) program. Irrespective of how the NBCTs are identified, we would like to compose them as per Definitions 1 and 2. We resolve the issue as follows.

**M9.** We introduce a hypothetical program $P_0$ and let batches from all source streams be input to this program. This will be a *filter* program sorting out batches to be fed to the original source programs.

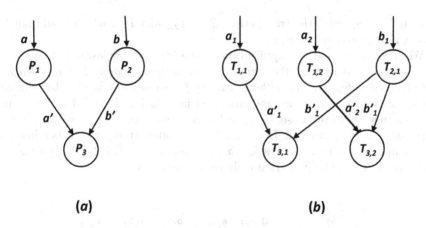

**Fig. 7.** Inputs from multiple source streams

The construction for the composition in Fig. 7 is shown in Fig. 8 with the hypothetical program in grey box. We identify the executions of $P_0$ first with $a_1$ and $b_1$, and then with $a_2$. In Fig. 8, we extend the execution in Fig. 7 with input $b_2$ next and then with $a_3$ and $b_3$. Now we can identify the NBCTs with the sets of *new* batches used in the executions of $P_0$; as per our notion, they will contain all the transactions triggered directly or transitively, but executed *without waiting for* subsequent batches. The NBCTs and their transactions are shown in the figure in part (i), omitting the transactions (hypothetically) executed by $P_0$. (The first and the third NBCTs are in one line, and the second and the fourth in the next line.) We apply this idea for any number of source streams. We stipulate only that each execution of $P_0$ will have a new batch that is dequeued from the appropriate queue, from at least one source. It may have new batches from any number of sources. Also, once dequeued into its window, a batch could be used for any number of executions.

Again, for each $a_i$ and $b_j$, $\widetilde{T}(a_i, b_j)$ would contain all transactions $T$ such that its sb-set contains $a_i$ but not $a_k$, for $k > i$, and similarly for $b_j$. Note that in $\widetilde{T}(a_i, b_j)$, $P_0$ is executed with $a_i$ and $b_j$, and hence all the transactions in the NBCT will have both $a_i$ and $b_j$. Hence, $\widetilde{T}(a_i, b_j)$ could as well be identified as $\widetilde{T}(a_i)$, and similarly as $\widetilde{T}(b_j)$. The execution of the hypothetical program $P_0$ can be managed by the SPE.

We note that each of the source input batches can be rolled back; the NBCT of that batch as per Definition 2 will be rolled back, with the result that the batch is not used for any NBCT at all. The roll back mechanism described in the last section is applicable here also. When the NBCT has several (new) batches in the execution of $P_0$, any number of those batches can be rolled back, and subsequent batches of the respective streams are reprocessed. We note that the reprocessing may produce different NBCTs, compared to the execution without roll back. For instance, in the example of Fig. 8, suppose $a_1$ is rolled back. Then we might end up with $\widetilde{T}(a_2, b_1)$ with the transactions $T_{1,2}$, $T_{2,1}$ and $T_{3,2}$, which would not be present if $a_1$ is not rolled back.

We have illustrated the application of the idea of *composing a batch composite transaction with all the transactions triggered by arrival of new batches and executed independently without waiting for subsequent batches* to different executions where batches are not processed in isolation. Part (ii) in Fig. 8 displays another interesting case. Here, each time, new pairs of batches from the two source streams are processed. However, $P_3$ accumulates the previous batches and uses them with the new batches for the next execution. This type of processing is described in [1]. The NBCTs are shown in the figure.

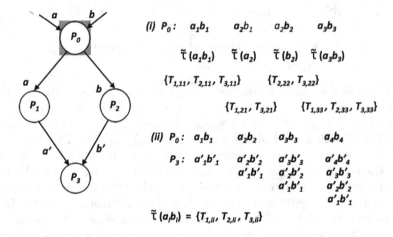

**Fig. 8.** Nonblocking batch composite transactions for multiple source streams

## 6    Concurrent Executions

In this section, we consider concurrent executions of NBCTs. Let **T** be a set of NBCTs. We define an *execution graph* $\mathcal{GE}(\mathbf{T})$ as the graph whose vertex set is the union of $set(\widetilde{T})$'s of all $\widetilde{T}$ in **T**, and edges for the following:

- the transaction partial order $\prec_t$ of each $\widetilde{T}$ in **T**;
- the serial order among the transactions of the same program, for each program in the workflow; and
- the conflict order among the transactions, as described below.

We associate conflicts between programs in a composition. Conflicts are to be determined based on the semantics of the operations executed by the programs and the data items that are operated on. In general, the execution order is important for conflicting operations and irrelevant for non-conflicting ones. We assume that the conflicts between programs carry over to their executions. For example, suppose programs $P_i$ and $P_j$, $i < j$, are conflicting. Then, we assume that every execution of $P_i$ conflicts with every execution of $P_j$. These executions may be for the same source input batch or different source input batches. We also assume that any two conflicting programs in a composition are related by the program order $\prec_p$. Then, since the program order will yield transaction partial order, conflicts between executions of the programs for the same input batch, that is, transactions of the same NBCT, are taken care of by the transaction order edges. For example, for executions $T_{i,m}$ and $T_{j,m}$ for the same source input batch $a_m$, a conflict edge from $T_{i,m}$ to $T_{j,m}$ need not be added since $T_{i,m} \prec_t T_{j,m}$ and hence the corresponding transaction order edge will be added. However, for different source input batches $a_m$ and $a_n$, $m < n$, the edges from $T_{i,m}$ to $T_{i,n}$, as well as from $T_{j,m}$ to $T_{i,n}$ need to be added. The former edges are already included in the serial order of the transactions of the same program; only the latter edges need to be added.

We note that the graph obtained as above is acyclic. There are no edges directed from a transaction of an NBCT of a batch $b_j$ to that of batch $b_i$, for $j > i$. (This is certainly true for conflict edges and those between the transactions of the same program. Consider a transaction order edge of $\widetilde{T}(b_j)$, say from an execution $T$ of $P_k$ to an execution $T'$ of $P_l$, for $k < l$. Now, $T'$ could be in $T(b_i)$, but it must be waiting for a batch derived from $b_j$. Then, by definition, $T'$ is not in $\widetilde{T}(b_i)$. Therefore, by contracting the subgraphs generated by the set of vertices of NBCTs $\widetilde{T}(b)$ into single vertices, we will indeed get a graph consisting of a single directed path whose vertices are the NBCTs and edges correspond to the batch order, that is, a serial execution of the NBCTs in $\mathbf{T}$, according to the batch order.

Again, note that the vertices of the execution graph $\mathcal{GE}(\mathbf{T})$ are the transactions, not the NBCTs, in $\mathbf{T}$. Therefore the graph can be constructed without waiting to know the composition of the NBCTs.

We note that, in the above discussions, we have insisted on the serial order of the NBCTs to be the same as the batch order among the batches. With multiple source input streams, the batch order will be the lexicographic order of the set (of indices) of the batches as they arrive for processing.

# 7   Related Work

Composite transactions have been defined in different ways in different heterogeneous distributed environments depending on the required/relaxed ACID properties appropriate to the applications. In most cases, they are defined as *sagas* and then the properties of the transactions constituting a *saga* are explored. With respect to atomicity (all-or-nothing property of composite transactions), an early proposal [10] was the schema $c^*[p]r^*$ denoting a partially ordered set of *compensatable* transactions followed by at most one *pivot* (which is non-compensatable) and then followed by a partially ordered set of *retriable* (*assured*) transactions. This schema has been extended, allowing multiple pivots, for Transactional processes [12], and then for Web services [17], Electronic contracts

[16] and recently for Internet of Things services [13]. In the latter applications, nested transactions were considered. The properties BP1-BP4, as applicable to sagas, were satisfied by the (high level) transactions. Our NBCTs are also nested transactions but treated as non-nested ones, capturing the top level of the nesting only.

The works in the context of stream processing include the following. A unified transaction model, called UTM, is proposed in [2]. It treats events also as transactions. It discusses splitting continuous executions into transactions. Isolation and atomicity properties are relaxed. Events and triggers in the context of Complex Event Processing over Event Streams are discussed in [18]. They also define *stream* ACID properties for transactions. The stream atomicity notion requires "all operations stimulated by a single input event should occur in their entirety". In S-Store [9], the unit of atomicity is the entire composite transaction. The batches are executed in isolation. In [6,11], entire read-only composite transactions reflecting "continuous queries reading updatable resources" are taken as units of atomicity. Such considerations are very useful especially in IoT environments, where monitoring and actuations are predominant and monitoring should be consistent. Reprocessing upstream batches is also considered in [11]. Other papers discussing stream transactions and compositions include [3,5]. None of these papers deal with executions arising with splitting, merging or overlapping of the batches and defining composite transactions satisfying properties considered in this paper. Splitting batches for parallel execution and merging them later have been considered in the literature, for example in [4,7].

This paper is closely related to [15]. There, the source input batches $b$ for which $\mathcal{T}(b)$ satisfies BP1-BP4 and B1-B2 are called *atomic* batches. (The properties BP1-BP4 are not brought out explicitly in that paper.) As observed in this paper, when splits, merges and overlapping of the batches occur in an execution, some source input batches may not be atomic. The contribution in [15] is showing that several source input batches can be grouped into a single atomic batch. In contrast, the goal in this paper is to define an NBCT for each source input batch individually to satisfy the properties BP1-BP4, at the expense of satisfying the completion requirement of batches jointly by several NBCTs and achieving non-intrusive roll back by rolling back some subsequent batches also and reprocessing them.

## 8    Conclusion

In stream processing, input stream tuples are processed in batches by programs in a workflow. Several batches are processed concurrently and the batches may be split, merged or overlapped along the workflow. In this paper, we have identified the executions corresponding to the batches in terms of nonblocking batch composite transactions (NBCTs) that satisfy some basic transactional properties BP1-BP4.

When BP1 is satisfied, the conflicting transactions in each NBCT are ordered. If the transactions that are ordered are executed strictly serially (as can be expected in stream processing), then all conflicts during the execution are between transactions of different NBCTs, and not between those of the same NBCT. Therefore, conflict-serializability of the NBCTs can be checked with a conflict graph consisting of nodes corresponding to NBCTs and directed edges representing conflicts among them. That is, there is no need to construct a graph with individual transactions of the NBCTs as vertices. Therefore, management of conflict graphs, and concurrency control, will be simpler.

In this paper, we have considered roll back of partially processed batches only. We have not considered compensation of the BCTs, after their commitment, at a later time. As in sagas, we can consider compensating BCTs. Further, these BCTs could be of *compensating* batches. Then, these BCTs could be executed like any other BCTs. The availability of compensating batches will be application-dependent.

# References

1. Akidau, T., Bradshaw, R., Chambers, C., Chernyak, S., Fernández-Moctezuma, R.J., Lax, R., McVeety, S., Mills, D., Perry, F., Schmidt, E., Whittle, S.: The dataflow model: a practical approach to balancing correctness, latency, and cost in massive-scale, unbounded, out-of-order data processing. Proc. VLDB Endow. **8**(12), 1792–1803 (2015). http://dx.doi.org/10.14778/2824032.2824076
2. Botan, I., Fischer, P.M., Kossmann, D., Tatbul, N.: Transactional stream processing. In: Proceedings of the 15th International Conference on Extending Database Technology EDBT 2012, pp. 204–215. ACM, New York (2012). http://doi.acm.org/10.1145/2247596.2247622
3. Conway, N.: Transactions and data stream processing. In: Online Publication, pp. 1–28 (2008). http://neilconway.org/docs/stream_txn.pdf
4. De Matteis, T., Mencagli, G.: Parallel patterns for window-based stateful operators on data streams: an algorithmic skeleton approach. Int. J. Parallel Prog., pp. 1–20 (2016)
5. Golab, L., Özsu, M.: Issues in data stream management. ACM SIGMOD Rec. **32**(2), 5–14 (2003)
6. Gürgen, L., Roncancio, C., Labbé, S., Olive, V.: Transactional issues in sensor data management. In: Proceedings of the 3rd International Workshop on Data Management for Sensor Networks (DMSN 2006), Seoul, South Korea, pp. 27–32 (2006)
7. Hirzel, M., Soulé, R., Schneider, S., Gedik, B., Grimm, R.: A catalog of stream processing optimizations. ACM Comput. Surv. **46**(4), 46: 1–46: 34 (2014). http://doi.acm.org/10.1145/2528412
8. Hummer, W., Satzger, B., Dustdar, S.: Elastic stream processing in the cloud. Wiley Interdisc. Rev. Data Min. Knowl. Disc. **3**, 333–345 (2013)
9. Meehan, J., Tatbul, N., Zdonik, S., Aslantas, C., Cetintemel, U., Du, J., Kraska, T., Madden, S., Maier, D., Pavlo, A., Stonebraker, M., Tufte, K., Wang, H.: S-store: streaming meets transaction processing. Proc. VLDB Endow. **8**(13), 2134–2145 (2015)
10. Mehrotra, S., Rastogi, R., Silberschatz, A., Korth, H.F.: A transaction model for multidatabase systems. In: Proceedings of the 12th International Conference on Distributed Computing Systems 1992, pp. 56–63. IEEE (1992)

11. Oyamada, M., Kawashima, H., Kitagawa, H.: Continuous query processing with concurrency control: reading updatable resources consistently. In: Proceedings of the 28th Annual ACM Symposium on Applied Computing SAC 2013, pp. 788–794. ACM, New York (2013). http://doi.acm.org/10.1145/2480362.2480514

12. Schuldt, H., Alonso, G., Beeri, C., Schek, H.: Atomicity and isolation for transactional processes. ACM Trans. Database Syst. **27**, 63–116 (2002)

13. Vidyasankar, K.: Transactional properties of compositions of internet of things services. In: 2015 IEEE First International Smart Cities Conference (ISC2), pp. 1–6, October 2015

14. Vidyasankar, K.: A transaction model for executions of compositions on internet of things services. In: Procedia Computer Science, pp. 195–202. Elsevier (2016)

15. Vidyasankar, K.: Atomicity of batches in stream processing. J. Ambient Intell. Humanized Comput. (2017)

16. Vidyasankar, K., Krishna, P.R., Karlapalem, K.: A multi-level model for activity commitments in e-contracts. In: Meersman, R., Tari, Z. (eds.) OTM 2007. LNCS, vol. 4803, pp. 300–317. Springer, Heidelberg (2007). doi:10.1007/978-3-540-76848-7_20

17. Vidyasankar, K., Vossen, G.: Multi-level modeling of web service compositions with transactional properties. Database Manag. **22**(2), 1–31 (2011)

18. Wang, D., Rundensteiner, E.A., , Ellison III, R.T.: Active complex event processing over event streams. In: Proceedings of the VLDB Endowment, pp. 634–645. ACM Press (2011)

# Enhancing User Rating Database Consistency Through Pruning

Dionisis Margaris[1] and Costas Vassilakis[2(✉)]

[1] Department of Informatics and Telecommunications,
University of Athens, Athens, Greece
margaris@di.uoa.gr
[2] Department of Informatics and Telecommunications,
University of the Peloponnese, Tripoli, Greece
costas@uop.gr

**Abstract.** Recommender systems are based on information about users' past behavior to formulate recommendations about their future actions. However, as time goes by the interests and likings of people may change: people listen to different singers or even different types of music, watch different types of movies, read different types of books and so on. Due to this type of changes, an amount of inconsistency is introduced in the database since a portion of it does not reflect the current preferences of the user, which is its intended purpose.

In this paper, we present a pruning technique that removes old aged user behavior data from the ratings database, which are bound to correspond to invalidated preferences of the user. Through pruning (1) inconsistencies are removed and data quality is upgraded, (2) better rating prediction generation times are achieved and (3) the ratings database size is reduced. We also propose an algorithm for determining the amount of pruning that should be performed, allowing the tuning and operation of the pruning algorithm in an unsupervised fashion.

The proposed technique is evaluated and compared against seven aging algorithms, which reduce the importance of aged ratings, and a state-of-the-art pruning algorithm, using datasets with varying characteristics. It is also validated using two distinct rating prediction computation strategies, namely collaborative filtering and matrix factorization. The proposed technique needs no extra information concerning the items' characteristics (e.g. categories that they belong to or attributes' values), can be used in all rating databases that include a timestamp and has been proved to be effective in any size of users-items database and under two rating prediction computation strategies.

**Keywords:** DB consistency · Recommender systems · Collaborative filtering · Matrix factorization · Pruning · Data quality · Evaluation

## 1  Introduction

An increasing number of applications and data sources continuously produce a massive amount of data. Examples of such applications and sources range from websites [7, 32] to smartphones and wearable computing [30, 31]. The collection of these data can be

A. Hameurlain et al. (Eds.): TLDKS XXXIV, LNCS 10620, pp. 33–64, 2017.
https://doi.org/10.1007/978-3-662-55947-5_3

used to promote the formulation of successful personalized suggestions over a wide range of domains, from movies and restaurants [32, 33] to smartphone apps [30] and from consumer products to travel and leisure [10, 12].

As far as recommender systems are concerned, collaborative filtering (CF) formulates personalized recommendations on the basis of ratings expressed by people having similar tastes to the user for whom the recommendation is generated; taste similarity is computed by examining the resemblance of already entered ratings [1]. CF works on the assumption that if users have similar tastes regarding choosing an item in the past then they are likely to have similar interests in the future too. Typically, for each user a set of "nearest neighbor" users is found, i.e. those users that display the strongest correlation to the target user. Scores for unseen items are predicted based on a combination of the scores given from the nearest neighbors [14]. Research has proven that the CF-based recommendation approach is the most successful and widely used approach for implementing recommender systems [2]. More recently, recommender systems have employed methods based on *matrix factorization* [35]. In its basic form, matrix factorization characterizes both items and users by vectors of factors inferred from item rating patterns. High correspondence between item and user factors leads to a recommendation. These methods have become popular in recent years by combining good scalability with prediction accuracy.

Within the recommendation process, typical recommender systems assume that the rating time is not relevant and ignore how old each user-item rating is. However, rating age can be exploited to substantially enhance recommendation quality, due to phenomena such as shift of interest [3, 4]. For instance, in domains such as music, users continuously listen to and rate songs. In this setting, user neighborhoods based on song ratings rapidly lose their validity; indeed the time span in which a user-based neighborhood remains valid is too short because new users –who are potential neighbor candidates- continuously join the system, and new user preferences are constantly added to the user rating database [11]. This necessitates the re-computation of the user neighborhood, which may be an excessively costly action if all rating data are retained and matched in the neighborhood re-computation process.

Another major issue that CF systems front is the storing and management of rating data (user ratings). On one hand, maintaining all ratings in an extensive primary database offers the advantage of reducing the "gray sheep" probability [15], i.e. the probability that some user's recorded preferences are unusual, as compared to the rest of the community, which leads to low quality recommendations. However, maintaining and processing the whole data bulk increases storage demands, as well as the time needed to generate recommendations (since computing the neighborhoods for all data and all users is costly); hence most of the times we either resort to techniques such as clustering [16–18] or we opt for small nearest neighbors' (NNs) number, and actually trade off recommendation quality for better online recommendation time.

In this paper, we contribute to the state of the art of recommender systems dataset quality enhancement by:

1. presenting a novel pruning algorithm to eliminate elements that have a high probability of being inconsistent with the current user preferences and likings, from the user rating database.

2. introducing an algorithm for determining the amount of pruning that should be performed, allowing thus the configuration and execution of the pruning algorithm in an unsupervised fashion.
3. validating the performance of the pruning algorithm by comparing the results produced by the two aging and one pruning algorithms presented in [34], as well as with the five aging algorithms described in [47], in terms of (i) prediction quality, (ii) execution performance, (iii) storage size gains and (iv) recommendation quality in the context of recommender systems. The tested algorithms exploit user rating timestamps in the rating prediction formulation process; user rating timestamps exist in many datasets, such as Movielens [7, 23] and Amazon [42]. The aging-based algorithms decrease the significance of old-aged ratings, while the presented pruning based algorithm removes user rating histories from the primary online database, based on their timestamps. We also compare the performance of our work against works on temporal dynamics, in terms of rating prediction quality.
4. showing that the proposed pruning algorithm can be used by different rating prediction formulation strategies, by evaluating its performance in user-user collaborative filtering-based and matrix factorization-based approaches.

The results show that the pruning algorithm presented in this work achieves the best results in all the evaluation datasets, leading to increased prediction accuracy and reduced prediction formulation times and storage size, at the same time.

Increased prediction accuracy is achieved through the increased consistency of the rating database, since pruning removes from the database data about user behavior which are inconsistent with the user's current preferences. The removed portions of the data have been found to effectively be aged and noisy ratings, which contribute to the computation of predictions with high absolute errors. On the contrary, aging of ratings in some cases marginally improves prediction quality, and in some others degrades it, without introducing any savings in prediction formulation time or database size gains. Additionally, the suggested pruning technique can be applied as a preprocessing step to any rating prediction algorithm, including algorithms that consider social network data (e.g. [13, 19]).

The rest of the paper is structured as follows: Sect. 2 overviews related work. Section 3 briefly reviews the aging algorithms presented in [34, 47] (which are used in our performance benchmarks), while Sect. 4 presents the proposed pruning algorithm, together with the pruning algorithm presented in [34] (which is again used in our performance benchmarks). In Sect. 5, the results of the conducted benchmarks are presented and discussed. Finally, Sect. 6 concludes the paper and outlines future work.

## 2  Related Work

The accuracy of CF systems is a topic that has attracted considerable research efforts. [8] proposes a new neighborhood-based model, which is based on formally optimizing a global cost function and leads to improved prediction accuracy, while maintaining merits of the neighborhood approach such as explainability of predictions and ability to handle new ratings (or new users) without retraining the model. In addition, it suggests a factorized version of the neighborhood model, which improves its computational complexity while retaining prediction accuracy. [9] proposes a filtering technique that applies to both unfairly positive and unfairly negative ratings in Bayesian reputation system. It is based on a reputation system and integrates a reputation systems filtering method, under the assumption that ratings provided by different raters on a given agent will follow more or less the same probability distribution.

Previous work [5, 6, 43] has identified the possibility that users may have changed preferences and likings, a phenomenon that has been termed as *concept drift*. [43] presents a survey of related models and algorithms. In this survey, concept drift handling methods are classified according to two dimensions, *data management* and *forgetting mechanism*. Regarding the data management dimension, two approaches are identified: the first is the *single example* approach where only the most recent input for each subject is stored in memory, and the subject model is updated taking into account only the current state of the subject model and the last input. The second approach is the *multiple examples* approach, where a set of recent inputs is maintained per subject, typically implemented as a sliding window. The subject model is then updated taking into account the current state of the subject model and the inputs within the subject's sliding window. Concerning the *forgetting mechanism*, it is again distinguished into two approaches. The first approach is *abrupt forgetting*, where a window is defined per subject and all data about the subject not included in the window is discarded, while the second approach is *gradual forgetting*, in which no data about subjects is discarded, but a fading factor is used to reduce the importance of old-aged data. Works such as [5, 6] address concept drift in an attempt to identify how user interests change, however without using the identified interests to generate recommendations.

[20] proposes an adaptation of the item-based CF algorithm to incorporate rating age influence in predictions, in order to analyze time influence in final prediction quality, following the *gradual forgetting* approach. The proposed approach is applied on a small-sized books-related dataset, exploring different values for the two fading factors used in their algorithm, also examining the temporal granularity at which ratings age should be measured. Results show that (a) prediction quality can be improved when using coarser temporal granularities (year instead of semesters), (b) it is beneficial to use only the ratings of the recent years and (c) active user preferences are closer to the most recent rated books than to older ones.

[34] presents two algorithms for aging (which follow the *gradual forgetting* approach) and one algorithm for pruning user histories (which follows the *abrupt forgetting* approach) in collaborative filtering systems. The algorithms presented in [34] exploit rating timestamps in the rating prediction formulation process, with the aging-based algorithm assigning weights to ratings based on their age (ratings with older ages are given smaller weights), and the pruning algorithm retaining only the N newest ratings of each user (same N for all dataset users).

[47] explores when the consideration of the temporal dimension is beneficial for traditional CF and also investigates the effect that the application of different time-decay functions have on the quality of rating prediction in the context of social tagging. Time decay can be applied either in the K-NN step, in which case it is termed *pre-filtering* or at the moment of picking the relevant items, in which case it is termed *post-filtering*. Post-filtering has been shown to outperform pre-filtering: pre-filtering

achieves better rating prediction quality only in one case (user-based CF with linear decay), but this is achieved at the cost of reducing coverage by 20%, approximately. Considering the decay functions, the *pow* function [41] was found to exhibit the best performance.

[44] creates a model tracking the time changing behavior throughout the life span of the data, aiming to make better distinctions between transient effects and long term patterns. This model is incorporated into a user-user based recommender and a matrix factorization-based recommender and evaluated against the Netflix dataset.

[45] explores a sliding window-based mechanism (which follows the abrupt change paradigm) and a fading factor-based mechanism (which follows the gradual forgetting paradigm). The results suggest that CF algorithms that use sliding windows, when compared to their versions using a growing window, reduce computational requirements, while not negatively affecting—and in some situations improving—predictive ability. Results also suggest that incremental algorithms (user-based algorithms that incrementally update user similarities every time new data is available) benefit from the use of fading factors, although the fading factor approach has more subtle improvements in time requirements. It is also confirmed that incremental algorithms are more scalable than non-incremental algorithms. However, the datasets tested are either artificial datasets (ART1 and ART2) or very small datasets, not typically employed in recommender system research (ELEARN and MUSIC). Finally, the experimental results were limited to abrupt change detection, either due to the data sets used in the experimental procedure or due to limitations of the presented approach.

Regarding the performance of CF-based systems, these have been proved to exhibit degraded performance in the presence of large volumes of data: clustering schemes have been proposed as a method to alleviate this problem [16–18]. Clustering schemes organize users and/or items into clusters based on appropriate characteristics, and in the rating prediction process firstly the similarity between the target user/item and the formulated clusters is computed, allowing for rapidly locating similar elements and limiting processing to elements within the identified clusters only.

[11] proposes a strategy to arbitrarily split the computation of user-to-user distances and neighbors into an off-line and on-line task which can temporarily satisfy the on-line time requirements, until a significant number of new users and ratings join the system. Additionally, in order to alleviate the scalability problem and to obtain a performance similar to that observed in ranking tasks, inverted indexes to evaluate queries efficiently were used. [46] proposes a multi-core CPU and a GPU implementation for the alternating least-squares algorithm, to compute recommendations based on implicit feedback datasets. One central feature of the reported implementation is an algorithm-specific kernel achieving compute-bound performance for the multiplication of two dense matrices scaled by a sparse diagonal matrix. Furthermore, it proposes to reorder the sequential system generation and system solve into a batched system generation and a batched solve, to compute many systems simultaneously.

None of the above mentioned works provides the following features: (a) improvement in prediction quality by cutting off rating predictions with high error, (b) reduction of the rating database size, as well as rating prediction formulation time, by pruning old and unhelpful user ratings and (c) the ability to be combined with other online time-reducing methods, e.g. clustering, as a preprocessing step.

This paper extends the work presented in [34] by (1) introducing a more successful pruning algorithm, (2) proposing an algorithm for determining the amount of pruning that should be performed, allowing thus the configuration and execution of the pruning algorithm in an unsupervised fashion, (3) validating the performance against widely used datasets with diverse characteristics and (4) showing that pruning can be used by different rating prediction computation strategies, by evaluating its performance in user-user collaborative filtering-based and matrix factorization-based approaches.

The newly introduced algorithm has been found to provide more accurate rating predictions and reduce storage requirement due to elimination of a portion of the ratings database (a portion contributing to the formulation of rating predictions with high errors). Moreover, the proposed algorithm achieves significant gains regarding the rating prediction formulation time, especially as compared to "full database" variants (i.e. executing a rating prediction algorithm without applying any pruning or aging) and to aging-based algorithms.

## 3  The Aging Algorithms

As presented in [34, 47], aging algorithms follow the general flow of standard CF algorithms [22], except for the fact that in some phase of the prediction computation, each rating is assigned a weight based on its age: recent ratings are assigned higher weights, while older ratings are assigned lower ones. This is based on the rationale that aged ratings may not accurately reflect the current state of users regarding their preferences, while recent ratings form a better basis for deriving user preferences.

The algorithms presented in [34] exploit rating timestamps by incorporating a weight for ratings in the user similarity computation process, adapting the standard user-user similarity computation as shown in Eq. 1:

$$sim(u, v) = \frac{\sum_{i \in I_u \cap I_v} (r_{u,i} - \overline{r_u}) * (r_{v,i} - \overline{r_v}) * w(r_{u,i}) * w(r_{v,i})}{\sqrt{\sum_{i \in I_{uv}} (r_{u,i} - \overline{r_u})^2} * \sqrt{\sum_{i \in I_{uv}} (r_{v,i} - \overline{r_v})^2}} \tag{1}$$

In the formula above, $I_u \cap I_v$ denotes the set of items that have been rated by both $u$ and $v$, $r_{u,i}$ represents the rating assigned by user $u$ to item $i$ and $\overline{r_u}$ denotes the mean value of ratings given by user $u$. Finally, $w(r_{u,i})$ represents the weight assigned to rating $r_{u,i}$. Two weight calculation functions are used in [34], the standard normalization function [27], which results to a variant termed *aging-N* and a sigmoid function [21], which results to a variant termed *aging-S*. This approach is based on the rationale that the users are "more similar" if the most recent ratings they have entered are alike. For more details on these functions and the setting of their parameters, the interested reader is referred to [34].

In [47], two ways for considering rating timestamps in the prediction computation process are explored. The first one is *pre-filtering*, which takes into account rating timestamps in the user similarity computation process, similarly to the case of [34]. The second option is *post-filtering*, user similarity computation is performed as in standard

CF algorithms [22], but when computing a prediction $p_{u,x}$ for the rating of user $u$ on item $x$, the computation formula is modified as shown in Eq. 2:

$$p_{u,x} = \overline{r_u} + \frac{\sum_{u' \in U} sim(u, u') * \left(r_{u',i} - \overline{r_{u'}}\right) * f\left(\Delta t\left(r'_{u,i}\right)\right)}{\sum_{u' \in U} sim(u, u') * f\left(\Delta t\left(r'_{u,i}\right)\right)} \qquad (2)$$

In Eq. 2, $f(t)$ is a time decay function and $\Delta t\left(r'_{u,i}\right)$ is the time that has elapsed since the posting of rating $r'_{u,i}$. The options for the time-decay function $f(t)$ explored in [47] are: exponential (*exp*), power (*pow*), linear (*lin*), logistic (*log*) and base-level learning (*bll*). All these functions involve a parameter $\lambda$ which controls the time-decay rate of the value assigned to ratings. For more information on the time-decay functions and the settings of their parameters, the interested reader is referred to [47].

Since [47] asserts that for the algorithms discussed therein, the *post-filtering* approach yields always better results than *pre-filtering*, in the evaluation section of this paper only the *post-filtering* approach will be considered for those algorithms.

In all cases, a set of users constituting the nearest neighborhood of user $u$ is required; regarding the size of the nearest neighborhood, we have used the value 20, suggested in [28]. Some users however have no nearest neighbors, due to the grey sheep problem [15], i.e. the fact that their ratings do not match with those of any other user within the ratings database. Since we want to offer a recommendation for all users, for these users we compute the prediction of item $X$ as the average item rating for item $X$ over the whole dataset.

# 4   The Pruning Algorithms

The pruning algorithms operate similarly to a standard rating prediction algorithm (such as a user-user CF algorithm [22] or a matrix factorization-based algorithm [35]), however they apply an offline preprocessing step to the dataset: this step retains only the more recent ratings per user, dropping all older ones. Then, prediction computation and recommendation formulation proceed as specified in the respective recommendation approach (user-user CF or matrix factorization).

Each pruning technique uses a criterion to select the data to be pruned. Ideally, the criterion should provide for removing from the database only those ratings that are inconsistent with the current preferences of the user.

Note that the removal of ratings from the database will increase the sparsity of the user-item matrix. In user-user CF based systems, this will decrease the number of users for whom it will be possible to generate rating predictions due to the gray sheep problem [15]. For instance, let us assume that user X has rated 5 items, which have also been rated by users Y and Z, but these ratings belong in Y's and Z's early histories (as earliness is defined by the current pruning technique). After pruning has been applied, X has no ratings in common with other users, and therefore no rating can be produced for X, while prior to pruning, formulation of a rating prediction was possible, based on other ratings entered by Y and Z. Rating predictions that could not be formulated due to pruning will be termed as *abolished*. It is worth noting however that the formulation of abolished predictions would have been based on inconsistent data, hence their absolute error metric would be high (and their actual usefulness for users would be low).

Increase of data sparsity also affects matrix factorization-based techniques [36], although it is manifested differently. Matrix factorization-based techniques *always* produce a prediction for a user's $u$ rating on an item $i$, through the formula

$$\hat{r}_{ui} = q_i^T * p_u \tag{3}$$

[35], where $q_i^T$ captures the relationship between item $i$ and the vector of latent factors identified by the matrix decomposition process and $p_u$ reflects the relationship between user $u$ and the latent factors. However, users who rate only a small portion of items could not get proper recommendations, and items with few ratings may not be recommended well [37]. This is owing to the fact that when a user $u$ has rated few items, there is a high probability that when computing a recommendation $\hat{r}_{ui}$ the set of the latent factors related to the user $u$ and the set of latent factors related to item $i$ is empty; and similarly for items with few ratings. When implementing a matrix decomposition-based prediction system using the LIBMF library (Matrix Factorization Library for Recommender Systems) [38, 39], predictions involving users or items having very few ratings degenerate to a dataset-dependent constant value. These predictions effectively convey no information, and will be considered as equivalent to the "no prediction" cases of user-user CF. Under this view, pruning leads to *abolished* predictions for matrix factorization-based techniques as well.

In practice, any pruning method would suffer from the existence of both *false positives* (i.e. removing from the ratings database elements that are consistent with the current user preferences) and *false negatives* (i.e. failing to remove from the ratings database elements that are inconsistent with the current user preferences). If the selectivity of the criterion for choosing the ratings to be removed is too low, the amount of false negatives would be high and henceforth some of the inconsistent data will remain in the database and will contribute to the formulation of rating predictions with high absolute error. At this point, increasing the selectivity factor of the pruning technique criterion is expected to remove from the database mainly inconsistent elements. Removal of these elements will lead to increased database sparsity and hence in some cases the rating prediction algorithm will be unable to generate rating predictions, due to the lack of nearest neighbors. However, the majority of these recommendations will have high absolute errors, because they would have been based on inconsistent data; some predictions with low absolute errors may also be abolished, due to the existence of false positives, yet their number will be significantly smaller than the abolished predictions with high absolute errors.

If, on the other hand, the selectivity of the criterion of the pruning algorithm is too high, the amount of false positives will increase and, effectively, the amount of data which are consistent with the current preferences of the users and will be removed, will be high. This will lead to the abolishment of a high number of predictions whose absolute error would be low. At this point, it would be beneficial to reduce the selectivity of the criterion of the pruning algorithm, so as to decrease the number of false positives.

Taking into account the above observations, we can conclude that there exists a specific setting for the pruning algorithm's selectivity criterion where any lower value will allow in the database more inconsistent ratings than consistent ones, whereas any higher value will remove from the database more consistent ratings than inconsistent ones. We use this conclusion to formulate an algorithm for automatically determining the optimal value for each pruning method's selectivity criterion. The algorithm proceeds as follows:

1. We compute *Pred(FullDB)*, i.e. the initial set of predictions generated by the rating prediction algorithm (with a non-pruned ratings database), their absolute errors and the respective MAE, which we denote as *MAE(FullDB)*. All predictions are generated during the testing phase. We then initialize the criterion selectivity factor *cur_sel_fact* to zero.

2. we increase the criterion selectivity factor by a step $\delta(sel\_fact)$, computing *sel_fact'* = *cur_sel_fact* + $\delta(sel\_fact)$. $\delta(sel\_fact)$ is pruning method-dependent and will be discussed in the following subsections, where pruning strategies are described. We then formulate the predictions $Pred(sel\_fact')$ and examine the absolute errors of the predictions that are abolished in the new state of the algorithm, i.e. the set $Pred_{abolished}(sel\_fact') = Pred(FullDB) - Pred(sel\_fact')$. If the majority of these predictions has an absolute error higher than *MAE(FullDB)* –or more formally $|p \in Pred_{abolished}(sel\_fact') : abs\_error(p) > \mathrm{MAE(FullDB)}| > \frac{|Pred_{abolished}(sel\_fact')|}{2}$ –then the increment of the selectivity factor is considered beneficial; we then set *cur_sel_fact* = *sel_fact'* and step 2 is repeated.

    If, however, the majority of the abolished predictions has an absolute error lower than *MAE(FullDB)*, then the increment in the selectivity factor leads to an undesirable state; then the algorithm terminates, returning *cur_sel_fact* as its result.

It is also possible that a threshold $Th_{abolished}$ is set, to exclude settings for *sel_fact'* where the percentage of abolished predictions is deemed excessive. Then, the result of the algorithm will be selected among the values of $sel_{fact'}$ for which $\frac{|Pred_{abolished}\left(sel_{fact'}\right)|}{|Pred(FullDB)|} \leq Th_{abolished}$. The value for $Th_{abolished}$ will be chosen by the recommender system administrators, so as to guarantee that an adequate percentage of the recommender system's users will receive recommendations. In the experimental evaluation section, we will consider $Th_{abolished} = 15\%$; recommender system administrators may use different values to suit the needs of their installations. It has to be noted here that abolished predictions are compensated by providing "default" values for gray sheep users (as an average of all ratings regarding the particular item); therefore the $Th_{abolished}$ threshold does not affect the percentage of users for which predictions can be computed, but it does determine the amount of users for which *personalized* (non-default) predictions can be calculated. Clearly, it is expected that in the context of a recommender system personalized predictions are indispensable, hence the $Th_{abolished}$ threshold is an important setting of the system.

In the following subsections, we provide details on the two pruning strategies considered in this paper.

## 4.1    Keeping the Last $K$ Ratings of Each User

As presented in [34], the first pruning algorithm retains in the primary database only the last $k$ ratings for each user. Effectively, this strategy applies the p-core pruning strategy [24, 25], exploiting however the age of ratings to select the ratings to be pruned. The number $k$ depends on the particular dataset that the algorithm is applied on: our experiments, reported in Sect. 5, have shown that different values may be suitable for different datasets. In general, lower values introduce more significant space and time savings and improve prediction quality, at the expense of reducing the percentage of users for whom a recommendation can be generated, due to the gray sheep problem [15]. In the following, we will denote this algorithm as *keep-k*.

In our experiments, reported in Sect. 5, we explored different values for the $k$ parameter, which determines the selectivity factor for this pruning method's criterion to select the data to be pruned. The goals of this exploration were (a) to gain insight regarding the effect that each value of $k$ has on the database size, the rating prediction formulation time and the quality of rating predictions and (b) to validate the algorithm presented in Sect. 4 regarding the identification of the optimal selectivity factor for the pruning method.

Regarding step $\delta(sel\_fact)$, this is set so as to lead to decrements of the ratings database size by 4% in each step, with a tolerance of 1%, i.e. the size reduction can range from 3% to 5%. Our experiments have shown that such a setting provides an adequately dense coverage of the search space, closely approximating the actual value of $k$ that is the optimal setting for the pruning criterion selectivity factor (if such a value exists, as will be shown in the experimental evaluation section). To identify the values of $k$ that provide the desired size reduction, we set $min_k = 5$ and $max_k = (meanRatingsPerUser * 10)$, where *meanRatingsPerUser* is the average number of ratings per user in the dataset, and then explore the interval $[min_k, max_k]$ using binary search, until all desired values of $\delta(sel\_fact)$ have been found (i.e. a first value $k_0$ leading to a reduction of the database size by 4%, a second value $k_1$ leading to a further reduction of the database size by 4% and so forth). The minimum value of $k$ considered is 10, since this is considered the minimum number of ratings for allowing users to participate in CF [51].

Similarly to the case of the aging algorithm, in order to offer recommendations for the "grey sheep" users, we compute for these users the prediction of item $X$ as the average item rating for item $X$ over the whole dataset.

## 4.2    Pruning Ratings in Users' Early Histories

The pruning algorithm proposed in this paper prunes each user's ratings that belong to her early history. More specifically, it prunes ratings having timestamp value less than

$$\min_{x \in Ratings(u)}(\mathrm{t}(r_{u,x})) \; + \; k_{early}\% \; * \; \left( \max_{x \in Ratings(u)}(\mathrm{t}(r_{u,x})) \; - \; \min_{x \in Ratings(u)}(\mathrm{t}(r_{u,x})) \right) \tag{4}$$

and then follows the rating prediction algorithm strategy, without assigning weights ($w(r_{u,i})$) to the users' ratings. Effectively, this pruning strategy splits each user's rating history in two time windows: the first window (*old ratings*) starts at the time point at which the user entered her first rating, and extends to the $k_{early}\%$ of the user's active rating period length. The second one (*recent ratings*) covers the remaining rating period. According to this pruning strategy, users that had been very active in entering ratings during their first time window but exhibited lower activity within the second will only have a small percentage of their ratings retained; on the contrary, users that had not been active in the first time window but have elevated their rating activity since, will have a high percentage of their ratings retained. For users that have a uniform level of rating activity, approximately $k_{early}\%$ of their ratings will be retained. In the following, we will denote this algorithm as $k_{early}$-N%.

In our experiments, reported in Sect. 5, we explored different values for the N parameter, which determines the selectivity factor for this pruning method's criterion to select the data to be pruned. Similarly to the previous algorithm variant, the goals of this exploration were (a) to gain insight regarding the effect that each value of N has on the database size, the rating prediction formulation time and the quality of rating predictions and (b) to validate the algorithm presented in Sect. 4 regarding the identification of the optimal data selection criterion selectivity factor.

Regarding step $\delta(sel\_fact)$, this is set so as to cover the following values of N: 1%, 5%, 10%, 20%, 30%, 40%, 50%, 60%, 70%, 80%, 90%, 99%. Our experiments have shown that this setting provides an adequately dense coverage of the search space, closely approximating the actual value of N that is the optimal setting for the pruning criterion selectivity factor. Naturally, subspaces of the above listed 10% intervals may be explored to locate values of N that are closer to the optimum value, if deemed necessary, by employing techniques such as hill climbing or simulated annealing [40].

Again, for "grey sheep" users, we compute the prediction of item X as the average item rating for item X over the whole dataset.

## 5   Performance Evaluation

In this section, we report on our experiments through which we compared (a) the two aging and the first pruning algorithms presented in [34] (Sects. 3 and 4.1), as well as the five aging algorithms described in [47], (b) the proposed pruning algorithm (Sect. 4.2) and (c) the plain CF algorithm which uses the full dataset, taking into account:

1. The quality of predictions; for this comparison, we used the mean absolute error (MAE) metric. We also provide a comparison regarding the recall@N metric [48], to gain insight on the performance of each algorithm in the context of recommender systems.

2. The database size.
3. The time needed to compute predictions.

To compute the MAE, we employed the standard "hide one" technique [26]: for each user in the database we hid her last rating, and then predicted its value based on the ratings on other non-hidden items. The MAE was therefore computed by considering all users in the database. The rationale behind hiding only the last rating of each user and then predicting it (as contrasted to hiding in turn each of the user's ratings) is owing to the fact that the value of each prediction should be computed based only on the user's ratings that existed in the database at the time the rating to be predicted was submitted. To further validate our results, we conducted an additional experiment, in each dataset, where the last rating of each user was dropped, and then the new last was hidden and predicted. The results of this test present negligible deviations from those obtained by hiding the last rating of each user, and are not presented in the following subsections due to space limitations.

For our experiments we used a laptop computer equipped with one dual core Intel CeleronN2840 @2.16 GHz CPU, with 4 GB of RAM and one 240 GB solid state drive with a transfer rate of 375 MBps, which hosted the datasets and ran the rating prediction formulation algorithms. Regarding the time measurements reported below, we note that the user-user CF implementation used in the experiments did not employ indexing or clustering techniques, therefore, the time gains reported may differ in settings where such techniques are employed. In all cases, the reported time gains provide a good insight about the speedup potential of the presented solutions. For the implementation of the matrix factorization-based predictions, we used the LIBMF library [38, 39].

In our experiments we use three datasets by Movielens [7, 23] as well as one dataset by Amazon [42], which are widely used in recommender systems research. These datasets contain "actual" timestamps, i.e. timestamps entered in real rating time and not in a batch mode. The used datasets vary with respect to the date of publication (published from 1998 until 2016) and size (from 2 MB to 486 MB). The properties of these datasets are summarized in Table 1.

In the following paragraphs, we report on our findings regarding the performance of the algorithm proposed in this work, versus the ones presented in [34, 47]; we also present our findings on the settings of parameters $k$ and $k_{early}$ in the pruning-based algorithms. Due to space limitations, we have not included the results of all pruning and aging variants that have been examined. In particular:

- For the pruning algorithms, variants with a drop in coverage higher than 15% were omitted, such an option would lead to the inability to formulate rating predictions for an excessive number of cases, and would therefore not be selected for any practical application of a recommender system, Additionally, variants that, due to low pruning levels, exhibit results almost identical to those of the unpruned variants are also omitted.
- For the temporal decay algorithms presented in [47], we have conducted experiments for the following values of the $\lambda$ parameter: 0.005, 0.01, 0.02, 0.05, 0.1, 0.2, 0.3, 0.4, 0.5, 0.6, 0.7, 0.8 and 0.9, and report only the results for the setting that has produced the predictions with the best quality (lowest MAE). Although the work in

**Table 1.** Datasets Summary

| Dataset name | #users | #ratings | #items | Avg. #ratings/user | DB Size (in text format) |
|---|---|---|---|---|---|
| MovieLens "Latest small" "recommended for education and development" http://grouplens.org/datasets/movielens/latest/ | 700 | 100,000 | 9,000 | 143 | 2.19 MB |
| MovieLens "Latest-20 M" "recommended for new research" http://grouplens.org/datasets/movielens/20m/ | 138,000 | 20,000,000 | 27,000 | 145 | 486 MB |
| MovieLens "100 K" dataset http://grouplens.org/datasets/movielens/100k/ | 1,000 | 100,000 | 1,700 | 100 | 2.04 MB |
| Amazon "Videogames" dataset http://jmcauley.ucsd.edu/data/amazon | 8,057 | 157,511 | 50,210 | 19.55 | 3.55 MB |

[47] has shown that the *Pow* decay function achieves the best results, our evaluation includes *all* decay functions surveyed in [47] (exponential, power, linear, logistic, BLL), since [47] reports findings on social bookmarking datasets, and it has not been verified that these results apply to other types of datasets.

## 5.1   The MovieLens "Latest-Small – Recommended for Education and Development" Dataset

Table 2 depicts the results obtained from the MovieLens "latest small – recommended for education and development" dataset, concerning the user-user CF strategy. For each algorithm, we report only on the variant that has achieved the best results:

- regarding the aging-based algorithms presented in [47] variants correspond to the value of the $\lambda$ parameter (discussed above), and the best-performing variant is the one that has produced the smaller value for the MAE metric;
- for the *keep-k* and $k_{early}$-$N\%$ algorithms, variants correspond to the amount of pruning that has been performed, and the method for selecting the best-performing variant is presented in Sect. 4.

Column "% DB size reduction" depicts the savings in space achieved by the pruning algorithm. Column "% coverage" corresponds to the percentage of cases for which the algorithm could compute *personalized* predictions (for some users, a personalized prediction could not be formulated due to the "gray sheep" phenomenon [15], e.g. in a user-user CF strategy, no prediction can be produced for users having no neighbor with a positive Pearson coefficient, i.e. no candidate recommenders [29]; recall that for each user, a "default" prediction was filled in for any item *X*, which was set as the average of all ratings for *X* in the database). When pruning was employed, the coverage dropped, due to the increased sparsity of the ratings database. The

**Table 2.** Results for the MovieLens "Latest small – recommended for education and development" dataset under the user-user CF strategy

| Method | % DB size reduction | % coverage | MAE (out of 9) | % no REC in MAE | % speedup |
|---|---|---|---|---|---|
| Full DB | – | 94.05 | 1.498 | – | – |
| aging-N | 0 | 94.05 | 1.504 | – | 0 |
| aging-S | 0 | 94.05 | 1.515 | – | 0 |
| exp@$\lambda = 0.8$ | 0 | 94.05 | 1.487 | – | 0 |
| pow@$\lambda = 0.1$ | 0 | 94.05 | 1.479 | – | 0 |
| lin@$\lambda = 0.8$ | 0 | 94.05 | 1.491 | – | 0 |
| log@$\lambda = 0.4$ | 0 | 94.05 | 1.488 | – | 0 |
| bll@$\lambda = 0.05$ | 0 | 94.05 | 1.489 | – | 0 |
| keep-300 | 25 | 91.07 | 1.527 | 67 | 48 |
| $k_{early}$-60% | 55 | 87.35 | 1.476 | 49 | 70 |

aging-based algorithms did not drop any portions of the dataset, hence the coverage remains the same with the case of the plain CF algorithm using the full dataset.

Column "MAE" corresponds to the mean absolute error of the predictions that each algorithm was able to formulate. For the computation of MAE, "default" predictions generated for the grey sheep users were taken into account.

Column "% no REC in MAE" considers the predictions that were abolished due to the increment in the pruning method's criterion selectivity factor, and corresponds to the ratio of the abolished predictions having absolute error lower than the full database MAE to the total number of abolished predictions. Clearly, these predictions are useful and it is desirable that the value in this column remains low.

Finally, column "%speedup" corresponds to the savings in time that were achieved, as a consequence of the database size reduction and mainly affects the user similarity computation phase.

The aging-based variants described in [34, 47] use the full dataset and perform minimally more computations (to calculate and use the rating weights), so their performance both space-wise and time-wise is identical to the full version. Contrary, the pruning-based variants introduce significant savings in both the DB-size and the time needed to compute the predictions.

In the two aging variants described in [34], the MAE is larger to the full database version; all the aging-based variants described in [47] achieve a reduction in the MAE, with the $pow@\lambda = 0.1$ (i.e. the variant based on the power decay function with parameter $\lambda$ set to 0.1) variant exhibiting the best results. For the keep-k algorithm, the best performing variant is keep-300, however the percentage of the predictions that are abolished and have an absolute error smaller than the respective full DB MAE is 67% (greater or equal to the 50% threshold), hence the keep-k pruning algorithm is proven inappropriate for this case. Finally, the best performing variant of the $k_{early}$-N% algorithm is $k_{early}$-60%, achieving an improvement in MAE by 1.46% against the full DB variant.

Figure 1 illustrates the performance of the different algorithms under the user-user CF strategy regarding (a) the MAE metric and (b) the coverage (i.e. the ability of the algorithm to formulate personalized predictions).

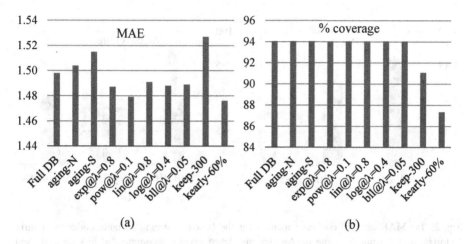

(a)                                                        (b)

**Fig. 1.** (a) MAE and (b) coverage metrics for the best performing variants under the user-user CF strategy, using the MovieLens "latest small – recommended for education and development" dataset

Table 3 depicts the results obtained from the MovieLens "latest small – recommended for education and development" dataset, concerning the matrix factorization CF strategy. Please note that the aging-based algorithms presented in [34, 47] are not directly applicable in the case of matrix factorization, hence they are not reported in this table. Again, for each algorithm, we report only on the variant that has achieved the best results (c.f. Sect. 4). Note also that under the matrix factorization strategy, column "%speedup" corresponds to the savings in time that were achieved during the matrix factorization process only, since the rating prediction formulation time is constant.

**Table 3.** Results for the MovieLens "Latest small – recommended for education and development" dataset, under the matrix factorization strategy

| Method | % DB size reduction | % coverage | MAE (out of 9) | % no REC in MAE | % speedup |
|---|---|---|---|---|---|
| Full DB | – | 97.47 | 1.482 | – | – |
| keep-300 | 25 | 88.54 | 1.479 | 29.2 | 39 |
| $k_{early}$-80% | 86 | 90.92 | 1.466 | 25.0 | 57 |

In Table 3 we notice that the MAE is minimally affected by the application of the *keep-k* pruning algorithm, however there is a considerable drop (approximately 9%) in the coverage, as compared to the coverage of the full database variant. The $k_{early}$-N%

improves MAE by approximately 1%, while it additionally reduces the database size by 86% and the matrix factorization time by 57%.

Figure 2 illustrates the performance of the different algorithms under the matrix factorization CF strategy regarding (a) the MAE metric and (b) the coverage.

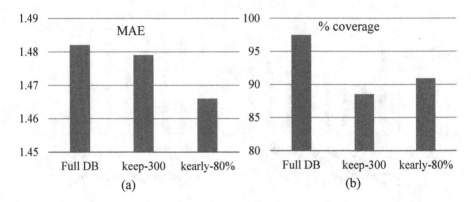

**Fig. 2.** (a) MAE and (b) coverage metrics for the best performing variants under the matrix factorization CF strategy, using the MovieLens "latest small – recommended for education and development" dataset

We performed a two-tailed paired t-test to test the following null hypothesis $H_0$: "the mean of the absolute errors of predictions produced by the winner pruning algorithm is equal to the mean of the absolute error of predictions produced by the full database case". In the case of user-user CF (winner: $k_{early}$-60%) the test yielded a p-value equal to 0.05092, hence the null hypothesis cannot be rejected (or, equivalently, the benefits observed are not statistically significant) at a confidence level of 95%. No statistical significance was established either when comparing $k_{early}$-60% and $pow@\lambda = 0.1$ (p-value = 0.0744).

In the case of matrix factorization-based predictions, the statistical significance test between the winner variant $k_{early}$-80% and the runner-up *keep-300*, yielded a p-value equal to 0.0497, hence the null hypothesis can be rejected (or, equivalently, the benefits observed are statistically significant) with a confidence level of 95%.

### 5.2 The MovieLens "Latest 20 M – Recommended for New Research" Dataset

Table 4 depicts the results obtained from the MovieLens "latest 20 M – recommended for new research" dataset, concerning the user-user CF strategy.

The two aging variants presented in [34] prove practically equivalent to the full database case. All the aging-based variants presented in [47] reduce the MAE, with the $log@\lambda = 0.2$ variant achieving the best results. All *keep-N* variants were found to deteriorate the MAE, through abolishing a high percentage of predictions having errors lower than the MAE, therefore the *keep-k* pruning algorithm is inappropriate for this

**Table 4.** Results for the MovieLens "Latest 20 M – recommended for education and development" dataset under the user-user CF strategy

| Method | % DB size reduction | % coverage | MAE (out of 9) | % no REC in MAE | % speedup |
|---|---|---|---|---|---|
| Full DB | – | 99.96 | 1.390 | – | – |
| aging-N | 0 | 99.96 | 1.390 | – | 0 |
| aging-S | 0 | 99.96 | 1.391 | – | 0 |
| exp@λ = 0.005 | 0 | 99.96 | 1.378 | – | 0 |
| pow@λ = 0.1 | 0 | 99.96 | 1.378 | – | 0 |
| lin@λ = 0.1 | 0 | 99.96 | 1.379 | – | 0 |
| log@λ = 0.2 | 0 | 99.96 | 1.371 | – | 0 |
| bll@λ = 0.7 | 0 | 99.96 | 1.398 | – | 0 |
| keep-1200 | 5 | 99.86 | 1.393 | 57 | 2 |
| $k_{early}$-50% | 32 | 99.95 | 1.364 | 33 | 60 |

case; the variant with the smaller MAE (which was also the one abolishing the smaller percentage of low-error ratings) was keep-1200. The variant of $k_{early}$-N% that is selected by the algorithm presented in Sect. 4 is $k_{early}$-50%, which is the one achieving the lowest MAE compared to other algorithms, while also delivering a database size reduction of 32% and a speedup equal to 60%.

Figure 3 illustrates the performance of the different algorithms under the user-user CF strategy regarding (a) the MAE metric and (b) the coverage (i.e. the ability of the algorithm to formulate personalized predictions).

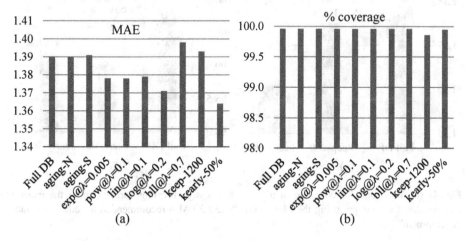

**Fig. 3.** (a) MAE and (b) coverage metrics for the best performing variants under the user-user CF strategy, using the MovieLens "latest 20 M – recommended for education and development" dataset

Table 5 depicts the results obtained from the MovieLens "latest 20 M – recommended for education and development" dataset, concerning the matrix factorization CF strategy. In Table 5 we notice that the MAE is minimally affected by the application of the *keep-k* pruning algorithm, which is achieved by the *keep-200* variant, at the expense of a drop in the coverage amounting for approximately 0.9%. The best-performing variant of $k_{early}$-$N\%$ is $k_{early}$-$90\%$, which improves the MAE by 1.16%, while the drop in coverage in this case is limited to 0.5%. While the gains in terms of MAE are not significant, benefits regarding the database size and speedup can be harvested.

Figure 4 illustrates the performance of the different algorithms under the matrix factorization CF strategy regarding (a) the MAE metric and (b) the coverage.

**Table 5.** Results for the MovieLens "Latest small – recommended for education and development" dataset, under the matrix factorization strategy

| Method | % DB size reduction | % coverage | MAE (out of 9) | % no REC in MAE | % speedup |
|---|---|---|---|---|---|
| Full DB | – | 99.96 | 1.377 | – | – |
| keep-200 | 30 | 99.07 | 1.375 | 45 | 32 |
| $k_{early}$-90% | 56 | 99.43 | 1.361 | 28.3 | 27 |

Figure 4 illustrates the performance of the different algorithms under the matrix factorization CF strategy regarding (a) the MAE metric and (b) the coverage.

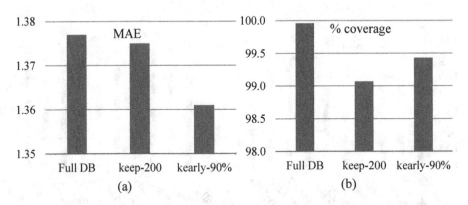

**Fig. 4.** (a) MAE and (b) coverage metrics for the best performing variants under the matrix factorization CF strategy, using the MovieLens "latest 20 M – recommended for education and development" dataset

We performed a two-tailed paired t-test to test the following null hypothesis $H_0$: "the mean of the absolute errors of predictions produced by the winner pruning algorithm is equal to the mean of the absolute error of predictions produced by the full database case". In the case of user-user CF (winner: $k_{early}$-50%) the test yielded a p-value equal to 0.04228, hence the null hypothesis can be rejected (or, equivalently, the benefits observed are statistically significant) at a confidence level of 95%. No statistical significance was however established when comparing $k_{early}$-50% and $log@\lambda = 0.2$ (p-value = 0.1037).

In the case of matrix factorization-based predictions, the statistical significance test between the winner variant $k_{early}$-90% and the runner-up *keep-200*, yielded a p-value equal to 0.0494, hence the null hypothesis can be rejected (or, equivalently, the benefits observed are statistically significant) with a confidence level of 95%.

## 5.3   The MovieLens "100 K" Dataset

Table 6 depicts the results obtained from the MovieLens "100 K" dataset, concerning the user-user CF strategy.

**Table 6.** Results for the MovieLens "100 K" dataset under the user-user CF strategy

| Method | % DB size reduction | % coverage | MAE (out of 4) | % no REC in MAE | % speedup |
|---|---|---|---|---|---|
| Full DB | – | 99.79 | 0.810 | – | – |
| aging-N | 0 | 99.79 | 0.828 | – | – |
| aging-S | 0 | 99.79 | 0.822 | – | – |
| exp@$\lambda$ = 0.8 | 0 | 99.79 | 0.833 | – | – |
| pow@$\lambda$ = 0.02 | 0 | 99.79 | 0.826 | – | – |
| lin@$\lambda$ = 0.9 | 0 | 99.79 | 0.822 | – | – |
| log@$\lambda$ = 0.5 | 0 | 99.79 | 0.818 | – | – |
| bll@$\lambda$ = 0.4 | 0 | 99.79 | 0.874 | – | – |
| keep-20 | 81 | 93.63 | 0.816 | 44 | 94 |
| $k_{early}$-50% | 62 | 98.73 | 0.802 | 33 | 74 |

The two aging variants presented in [34], as well as those presented in [47] have been found to deteriorate the MAE. The same applies to all *keep-N* variants; it is worth noting that the best performing variant is *keep-20*, however variants that maintain more ratings per user have been actually found to perform worse than *keep-20*, abolishing a large number of predictions with low error; the percentage of predictions with low error that are abolished is greater than 50% in all cases except *keep-20*, and because of this fact the algorithm presented in Sect. 4 would not consider *keep-20* at all (since pruning stops when the percentage of abolished predictions with low error exceeds 50%).

The variant of $k_{early}$-N% that is selected by the algorithm presented in Sect. 4 is $k_{early}$-50%, which is the one achieving the lowest MAE compared to other algorithms, while also delivering a database size reduction of 62% and a speedup equal to 74%.

Figure 5 illustrates the performance of the different algorithms under the user-user CF strategy regarding (a) the MAE metric and (b) the coverage (i.e. the ability of the algorithm to formulate personalized predictions).

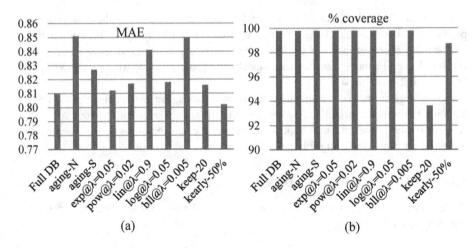

**Fig. 5.** (a) MAE and (b) coverage metrics for the best performing variants under the user-user CF strategy, using the MovieLens "100 K" dataset

Table 7 depicts the results obtained from the MovieLens "100 K" dataset, concerning the matrix factorization CF strategy. In Table 7 we notice that the *keep-50* variant achieves an improvement of 0.32% against the full database variant considering the MAE, however the winning variant of $k_{early}$-N%, which is $k_{early}$-*80%*, attains a considerably higher improvement, equal to 1.69%. Both pruning algorithms introduce significant speedups and savings in database size, with the coverage drop being limited to less than 1%.

**Table 7.** Results for the MovieLens "100 K" dataset, under the matrix factorization strategy

| Method | % DB size reduction | % coverage | MAE (out of 4) | % no REC in MAE | % speedup |
|---|---|---|---|---|---|
| Full DB | – | 99.96 | 0.7406 | – | – |
| keep-50 | 60 | 99.15 | 0.7382 | 37.5 | 33 |
| $k_{early}$-80% | 80 | 99.15 | 0.7281 | 35.0 | 36 |

Figure 6 illustrates the performance of the different algorithms under the matrix factorization CF strategy regarding (a) the MAE metric and (b) the coverage.

We performed a two-tailed paired t-test to test the following null hypothesis $H_0$: "the mean of the absolute errors of predictions produced by the winner pruning algorithm is equal to the mean of the absolute error of predictions produced by the full database case". In the case of user-user CF (winner: $k_{early}$-*50%*) the test yielded a p-value equal to 0.0543, hence the null hypothesis cannot be rejected (or, equivalently, the benefits observed are not statistically significant) at a confidence level of 95%. No statistical significance was established either when comparing $k_{early}$-*60%* and *exp@λ = 0.05* (p-value = 0.0531).

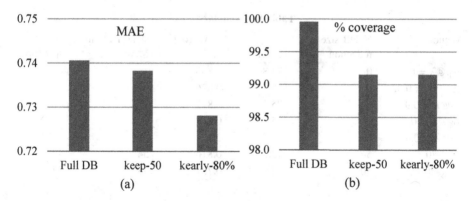

**Fig. 6.** (a) MAE and (b) coverage metrics for the best performing variants under the matrix factorization CF strategy, using the MovieLens "100 K" dataset

In the case of matrix factorization-based predictions, the statistical significance test between the winner variant $k_{early}$-80% and the runner-up keep-50, yielded a p-value equal to 0.0462, hence the null hypothesis can be rejected (or, equivalently, the benefits observed are statistically significant) with a confidence level of 95%.

## 5.4   The Amazon "Videogames" Dataset

The Amazon "Videogames" dataset differs from the three previous datasets in regards to the fact that the number of ratings per user is significantly smaller (19.55 ratings per user as compared to 100-145 ratings per user in the other three datasets), hence the probability of "gray sheep" increases. It is therefore important to gain insight into whether after such a sparse dataset is pruned, (a) the coverage of rating prediction formulation remains at acceptable levels and (b) benefits in MAE still apply.

Table 8 depicts the results obtained from the Amazon "Videogames" dataset, concerning the user-user CF strategy. The two aging variants described in [34] increase the MAE, and so do all five aging-based variants discussed in [47]. All keep-k variants also deteriorate the MAE, through abolishing a high percentage of predictions having errors lower than the MAE, therefore the keep-k pruning algorithm is inappropriate for this case too. The variant of $k_{early}$-N% that is selected by the algorithm presented in Sect. 4 is $k_{early}$-20%, which is the one achieving the lowest MAE compared to other algorithms (improved by 3.2% against the full database variant), while also delivering a database size reduction of 30% and a speedup equal to 37%.

**Table 8.** Results for the Amazon "Videogames" dataset under the user-user CF strategy

| Method | % DB size reduction | % coverage | MAE (out of 4) | % no REC in MAE | % speedup |
|---|---|---|---|---|---|
| Full DB | – | 75.8 | 0.813 | – | – |
| aging-N | 0 | 75.8 | 0.828 | – | – |
| aging-S | 0 | 75.8 | 0.822 | – | – |

(*continued*)

**Table 8.** (*continued*)

| Method | % DB size reduction | % coverage | MAE (out of 4) | % no REC in MAE | % speedup |
|---|---|---|---|---|---|
| exp@λ = 0.8 | 0 | 75.8 | 0.833 | – | – |
| pow@λ = 0.02 | 0 | 75.8 | 0.826 | – | – |
| lin@λ = 0.9 | 0 | 75.8 | 0.822 | – | – |
| log@λ = 0.5 | 0 | 75.8 | 0.818 | – | – |
| bll@λ = 0.4 | 0 | 75.8 | 0.874 | – | – |
| keep-80 | 5 | 73.2 | 0.816 | 54 | 4 |
| $k_{early}$-20% | 30 | 65.9 | 0.787 | 48 | 37 |

Figure 7 illustrates the performance of the different algorithms under the user-user CF strategy regarding (a) the MAE metric and (b) the coverage (i.e. the ability of the algorithm to formulate personalized predictions).

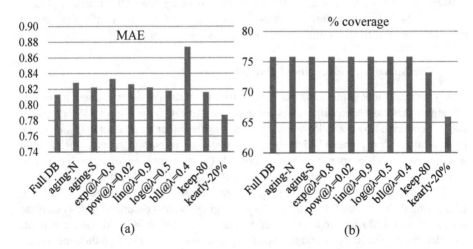

**Fig. 7.** (a) MAE and (b) coverage metrics for the best performing variants under the user-user CF strategy, using the Amazon "Videogames" dataset

Table 9 depicts the results obtained from the Amazon "Games" dataset, concerning the matrix factorization CF strategy. In Table 9 we notice that the *keep-30* variant achieves an improvement of 1.05% against the full database variant considering the MAE, however the winning variant of $k_{early}$-*N%*, which is $k_{early}$-*10%*, attains a higher improvement, equal to 1.40%. Both pruning algorithms introduce speedups and savings in database size, however the coverage drop in this case is higher, yet tolerable.

Figure 8 illustrates the performance of the different algorithms under the matrix factorization CF strategy regarding (a) the MAE metric and (b) the coverage.

**Table 9.** Results for the Amazon "Videogames" dataset, under the matrix factorization strategy

| Method | % DB size reduction | % coverage | MAE (out of 4) | % no REC in MAE | % speedup |
|---|---|---|---|---|---|
| Full DB | – | 68.92 | 0.571 | – | – |
| keep-30 | 16 | 59.77 | 0.565 | 22.7 | 6 |
| $k_{early}$-10% | 23 | 58.67 | 0.563 | 26.7 | 10 |

We performed a two-tailed paired t-test to test the following null hypothesis $H_0$: "the mean of the absolute errors of predictions produced by the winner pruning algorithm is equal to the mean of the absolute error of predictions produced by the full database case". In the case of user-user CF (winner: $k_{early}$-20%) the test yielded a p-value equal to 0.05131, hence the null hypothesis cannot be rejected (or, equivalently, the benefits observed are not statistically significant) at a confidence level of 95%.

In the case of matrix factorization-based predictions, the statistical significance test between the winner variant $k_{early}$-10% and the runner-up (keep-30), yielded a p-value equal to 0.0923, hence the null hypothesis cannot be rejected (or, equivalently, the benefits observed are not statistically significant) with a confidence level of 95%.

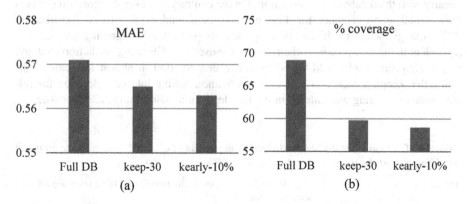

**Fig. 8.** (a) MAE and (b) coverage metrics for the best performing variants under the matrix factorization CF strategy, using the Amazon "Videogames" dataset

### 5.5 Discussion

In this section we summarize and discuss our findings of our experiments which concern (a) the newly introduced pruning algorithm $k_{early}$-N% and (b) the algorithm presented in this paper for determining an optimal amount of pruning.

Table 10 compares the performance of the $k_{early}$-N% variant chosen by the algorithm proposed in this paper, against the performance of the runner-up, under a user-user CF prediction formulation scheme; and Table 11 presents the same information under a matrix factorization prediction formulation scheme. We can see that the selected variant of the $k_{early}$-N% algorithm achieves better results than its contenders in all datasets, improvements range from 0.45% to 1.5%, with performance enhancements being statistically significant at a 95% confidence interval under all matrix factorization-based test cases and in one out of four cases where user-user CF is employed. In the remaining cases, no statistical significance of the improvements could be established. The ability of the proposed approach to improve the MAE in all datasets under the matrix factorization approach with statistical significance is considered to be very important, since matrix factorization clearly achieves better results than user-user CF, and is thus more prominent to be used in real-world applications.

Besides the improvement in the MAE, the $k_{early}$-N% pruning techniques introduces considerable improvements in the ratings database size and rating prediction formulation time, which are achieved at the expense of a reduction in the coverage, which ranges from negligible to tolerable.

Figure 9 illustrates how the MAE is affected by the reduction of the database size (only the pruning-based algorithms are considered, since aging-based algorithms do not affect the database size). The performance of the full database variant is used as a yardstick for measuring improvement/deterioration (point 0% on the y-axis). The value plotted on the figure corresponds to the average value of MAE change among the four datasets. On this diagram, we observe that the $k_{early}$-N% algorithm achieves MAE improvements (reductions) in all cases, and this improvement scales approximately linearly with the database size reduction. On the contrary, the keep-k algorithm delivers some small improvements for low pruning rates under the matrix factorization (MF) strategy, while for higher pruning rates its performance regarding the MAE is equivalent to the non-pruned variant. Under the user-user CF rating prediction strategy, keep-k algorithm leads to MAE performance deterioration in almost any case, indicating that keeping each user's last ratings, without taking into consideration the relative time each rating was entered in the DB, leads to a major rating DB inconsistency.

**Table 10.** Comparison of the MAE achieved by the variant of $k_{early}$-N% chosen by the proposed algorithm, against the runner-up, under user-user CF

| Dataset | $k_{early}$-N% variant selected by the proposed algorithm | | Best performing variant of all other algorithms | | |
|---|---|---|---|---|---|
| | Variant | MAE | Variant | MAE | Statistically significant@a = 0.95? |
| MovieLens "Latest small" "Recommended for education and development" | $k_{early}$-60% | 1.476 | pow@$\lambda$ = 0.1 | 1.477 | No |
| MovieLens "Latest-20 M" "recommended for new research" | $k_{early}$-50% | 1.364 | log@$\lambda$ = 0.2 | 1.371 | No |
| MovieLens "100 K" dataset | $k_{early}$-50% | 0.802 | Plain CF | 0.810 | No |
| Amazon "Videogames" dataset | $k_{early}$-20% | 0.787 | Plain CF | 0.813 | Yes |

**Table 11.** Comparison of the MAE achieved by the variant of $k_{early}$-$N$% chosen by the proposed algorithm, against the runner-up, under matrix factorization

| Dataset | $k_{early}$-$N$% variant selected by the proposed algorithm | | Best performing variant of all other algorithms | | |
|---|---|---|---|---|---|
| | Variant | MAE | Variant | MAE | Statistically significant@a = 0.95? |
| MovieLens "Latest Datasets" "Recommended for education and development" | $k_{early}$-80% | 1.466 | keep-300 | 1.479 | Yes |
| MovieLens "Latest-20 M" "recommended for new research" | $k_{early}$-90% | 1.361 | keep-200 | 1.375 | Yes |
| MovieLens "100 K" dataset | $k_{early}$-80% | 0.7281 | keep-50 | 0.7382 | Yes |
| Amazon "Videogames" dataset | $k_{early}$-10% | 0.563 | keep-30 | 0.565 | No |

Figure 10 depicts how the percentage of the predictions abolished due to pruning and having absolute error lower than the plain CF MAE varies with the database size reduction (the average among the four datasets is used). Again, only the pruning-based algorithms are considered, since in aging-based algorithms coverage remains constant. We notice that for the range that the "no REC in MAE%" metric remains below 50% (which is the range of interest, since beyond that threshold too many desired predictions are abolished), the $k_{early}$-$N$% algorithm proposed in this paper clearly outperforms the *keep-k* algorithm, dropping less useful predictions. This behavior is consistent across both rating prediction strategies, i.e. user-user CF and matrix factorization.

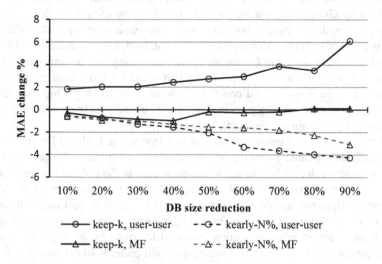

**Fig. 9.** Average MAE change comparison between the *keep-k* and $k_{early}$-$N$% algorithms, for both rating prediction strategies

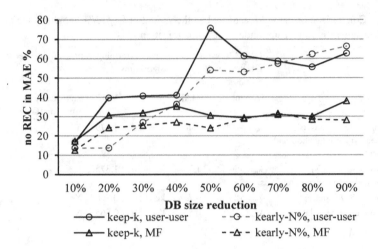

**Fig. 10.** Average "no REC in MAE%" metric for the *keep-k* and $k_{early}$-*N%* algorithms, with respect to the database size reduction

One of the major uses of rating prediction is within recommender systems, with the latter proposing to the user those items that she has not seen, and which are predicted to have the highest ratings for the user. Research has asserted that improved prediction algorithms indicate better recommendations [49]. However, to quantify the performance of the proposed algorithms in this context, we have measured the recall@N metric [48] for all the evaluated techniques. For the recall@N metric, we have set $N = 5$, taking into account the results of measurements, which show that the top-5 suggestions by Google account for more than 75% of the click-through rate [50]. To compute the recall@N metric, we performed cross-validation by first dividing the dataset in two parts: (i) the training part, which contained, for each user, the 80% of her earliest-submitted ratings and (ii) the test part, accounting for the remaining 20% of each user's ratings. Then, using the training part only, we formulated predictions for the elements in the test part, and computed how many of the top-5 highest-predicted items for each user are actually perceived as "good" by the user (within the top 20% of the user's ratings within the test part).

The results obtained from this evaluation are depicted in Table 12 for the user-user CF approach and in Table 13 for the matrix factorization approach. We can see that the $k_{early}$-*N%* variant selected by the algorithm presented in Sect. 4, consistently outperforms the runner-up algorithm, for all datasets and under both user-user CF and matrix factorization. The performance edge of the selected $k_{early}$-*N%* variant ranges from 26% to 87% under user-user CF and from 38% to 82% under matrix factorization. Table 14 depicts some example recommendation produced for users by the $k_{early}$-*N%* variants, for different datasets (one dense and one sparse) and under both the user-user CF and the matrix factorization approaches. In these examples we can observe that the $k_{early}$-*N%* variants include in their recommendations items that the corresponding users have rated in the top 50% of the rating scale ($\geq 3$ for 5-star rating scale and $\geq 6$ for a 9-star rating scale), and that the matrix factorization approach formulates better recommendations, i.e. includes in its recommendations items to which the user has assigned higher marks, as compared to the items included in the recommendations generated by the user-user CF approach.

**Table 12.** Comparison of the recall@5 metric achieved by the variant of $k_{early}$-$N\%$ chosen by the proposed algorithm, against the runner-up, under user-user CF

| Dataset | $k_{early}$-$N\%$ variant selected by the proposed algorithm | | Best performing variant of all other algorithms | |
|---|---|---|---|---|
| | Variant | recall@5 | Variant | recall@5 |
| MovieLens "Latest Datasets" "Recommended for education and development" | $k_{early}$-60% | 0.55 | pow@$\lambda$ = 0.1 | 0.41 |
| MovieLens "Latest-20 M" "recommended for new research" | $k_{early}$-50% | 0.54 | log@$\lambda$ = 0.2 | 0.43 |
| MovieLens "100 K" dataset | $k_{early}$-50% | 0.15 | pow@$\lambda$ = 0.02 | 0.08 |
| Amazon "Videogames" dataset | $k_{early}$-20% | 0.32 | pow@$\lambda$ = 0.02 | 0.24 |

**Table 13.** Comparison of the recall@5 metric achieved by the variant of $k_{early}$-$N\%$ chosen by the proposed algorithm, against the runner-up, under matrix factorization

| Dataset | $k_{early}$-$N\%$ variant selected by the proposed algorithm | | Best performing variant of all other algorithms | |
|---|---|---|---|---|
| | Variant | recall@5 | Variant | recall@5 |
| MovieLens "Latest Datasets" "Recommended for education and development" | $k_{early}$-80% | 0.62 | keep-300 | 0.45 |
| MovieLens "Latest-20 M" "recommended for new research" | $k_{early}$-90% | 0.61 | keep-200 | 0.41 |
| MovieLens "100 K" dataset | $k_{early}$-80% | 0.31 | keep-50 | 0.17 |
| Amazon "Videogames" dataset | $k_{early}$-10% | 0.39 | keep-30 | 0.26 |

**Table 14.** Example recommendations produced by the $k_{early}$-$N\%$ variants

| Dataset | Approach/variant | Recommendation (item ids with top-5 rating predictions, together with their original ratings) |
|---|---|---|
| MovieLens "Latest-20 M" "recommended for new research" (max rating = 9) | user-user/$k_{early}$-50% | User ML1: 104/6, 136/7, 165/7, 78/6, 109/7 |
| | | User ML2: 67/9, 3497/7, 251/7, 100/7, 576/9 |
| | | User ML3: 9990/8, 2334/8, 6292/6, 1602/7, 2488/8 |
| | | User ML4: 7174/8, 3864/8, 1747/6, 1434/7, 6454/7 |
| | | User ML5: 739/9, 2833/7, 28/8, 80/8, 314/7 |

(continued)

**Table 14.**  (*continued*)

| Dataset | Approach/variant | Recommendation (item ids with top-5 rating predictions, together with their original ratings) |
|---|---|---|
| | MF/$k_{early}$-90% | User ML1: 136/7, 165/7, 104/6, 162/7, 62/6 |
| | | User ML2: 67/9, 3497/7, 576/9, 558/9, 251/7 |
| | | User ML3: 2334/8, 1352/8, 2488/8, 6981/7, 456/8 |
| | | User ML4: 7174/8, 3864/8, 8203/7, 12570/8, 6454/7 |
| | | User ML5: 739/9, 80/8, 125/9, 654/9, 314/7 |
| Amazon "Videogames" dataset (max rating = 5) | User-user/$k_{early}$-20% | User AV1: 38132/5, 47425/4, 10095/4, 40574/5, 35096/4 |
| | | User AV2 28296/5, 38877/5, 38054/5, 42165/4, 33398/3 |
| | | User AV3: 6515/5, 6447/3, 5074/4, 4936/3, 1317/4 |
| | | User AV4: 40425/5, 44756/4, 28243/5, 40744/5, 49447/5 |
| | | User AV5: 46327/4, 46326/4, 34611/5, 42164/3, 49684/4 |
| | MF/$k_{early}$-10% | User AV1: 38132/5, 40574/5, 10095/4, 35096/4, 28934/4 |
| | | User AV2 6515/5, 5074/4, 4936/3, 1317/4, 6447/3 |
| | | User AV3: 6515/5, 6447/3, 5074/4, 4936/34013, 1317/4 |
| | | User AV4: 40744/5, 40425/5, 44756/4, 26204/5, 49409/5 |
| | | User AV5: 46327/4, 34611/5, 49684/4, 41783/4, 46206/4 |

Considering other works on recommender systems exploiting the ratings' timestamps, the approach presented in [20] achieves an improvement in MAE by 0.2%. In the work presented by Koren [44] –which to the best of our knowledge is the top-performing algorithm considering temporal dynamics and concept drift that has been presented insofar– under the user-user CF rating prediction strategy an improvement of MAE by 1.3% is achieved. Under the matrix factorization-based prediction scheme, the SVD++ method proposed in [44] achieves improvements in MAE from 0.1% to 1.1%, depending on factor dimensionality (higher dimensionalities perform better), while the timeSVD++ method also proposed in [44] performs better, achieving improvements in MAE between 1.8% and 2.5%, again depending on factor dimensionality.

The $k_{early}$-N% algorithm presented in this paper achieves improvements in the MAE ranging from 1% to 2.45% under the user-user CF rating prediction strategy and from 1.08% to 2.55% under the matrix factorization-based prediction scheme (for both rating prediction schemes, the reported percentages depict the difference between the full DB variant and the variant chosen by the algorithm proposed in Sect. 4). In this respect, the benefits of the proposed algorithm are comparable to those presented in [44] regarding the MAE; however the algorithm proposed in this paper additionally achieves considerable reductions in the database size and improvements in execution time, being at the same time simpler to implement.

Finally, the variant selection algorithm presented in Sect. 4, always achieves to select an optimal setting for the pruning level.

# 6 Conclusion and Future Work

In this paper we present a new algorithm ($k_{early}$-$N\%$) for pruning user histories in rating prediction systems. The algorithm operates on each individual user's history, dropping the oldest ratings, enhancing the rating DB consistency. We present an algorithm for tuning the parameter of the proposed pruning algorithm, allowing the configuration and execution of the pruning algorithm in an unsupervised fashion. The proposed pruning algorithm is evaluated against four datasets in terms of prediction accuracy, storage size gains and execution speedup, and is compared to the seven aging-based and one pruning-based algorithm presented in the literature, while it is also verified that the introduced parameter tuning algorithm correctly selects an optimal parameter setting. Finally, we show that the proposed algorithm can be used in different rating prediction strategies, by evaluating its performance in user-user CF-based and matrix factorization-based approaches. The proposed algorithm is also compared against works on temporal dynamics and concept drift.

The results show that among aging-based and pruning-based algorithms, only the pruning algorithm proposed in this work ($k_{early}$-$N\%$) increases the rating DB consistency –and consequently prediction quality–, since it achieves to prune old "noisy" ratings, and at the same time decreases prediction computation time, while achieving considerable database size gains. On the other hand, both of the aging algorithms presented in [34] exhibit performance similar to that of a typical CF algorithm, while the aging algorithms presented in [47] achieve MAE improvements in some cases, yet inferior to those achieved by the proposed algorithm. It is important to note that none of the aging-based algorithms can be directly applied in combination with matrix factorization. The pruning algorithm *keep-k* presented in [34] proved inappropriate, since by keeping the same number of ratings for each user, actually for some users we keep all of their history (users with initially less than $k$ ratings), no matter how old each rating is and for some others (users with many ratings) we may prune many of their recent ratings, which are consistent with their current interests and preferences. In relation to the works on temporal dynamics and concept drift that have been presented in the literature, the proposed approach achieves comparable results, being easier to implement and also introducing gains in rating database size and rating prediction formulation time.

Conclusively, the merits of the suggested pruning technique are that (1) it can be used in all rating databases that include a timestamp, (2) it has been proved to be effective in any size of user rating dataset, from a few hundreds of users and a few thousands of ratings to hundreds of thousands of users and millions of ratings and (3) it can be applied as a preprocessing step to any rating prediction algorithm (including different rating prediction strategies, clustering techniques, algorithms taking into account social network data and so forth).

Our future work will focus on further elaborating on the portions of the user histories that should be kept, employing different pruning settings for each user, depending on the timestamp distribution and contents of her history. Efficient and accurate sampling methods for avoiding computing predictions for all users to determine the MAE of each algorithm will be also examined. Finally, as new ratings are constantly added in the ratings database, the formulation of triggering conditions for executing the pruning algorithm will be studied.

# References

1. Bakshy, E., Eckles, D., Yan, R., Rosenn, I.: Social influence in social advertising: evidence from field experiments. In: Proceedings of the 13th ACM Conference on Electronic Commerce, pp. 146–161 (2012)
2. Schafer, J.B., Frankowski, D., Herlocker, J., Sen, S.: Collaborative filtering recommender systems. In: Brusilovsky, P., Kobsa, A., Nejdl, W. (eds.) The Adaptive Web. LNCS, vol. 4321, pp. 291–324. Springer, Heidelberg (2007). doi:10.1007/978-3-540-72079-9_9
3. Song, Y., Elkahky, A.M., He, X.: Multi-rate deep learning for temporal recommendation. In: Proceedings of the 39th International ACM SIGIR Conference on Research and Development in Information Retrieval, SIGIR 2016 (2016)
4. Li, L., Zheng, L., Yang, F., Li, T.: Modeling and broadening temporal user interest in personalized news recommendation. Expert Syst. Appl. **41**(7), 3168–3177 (2014)
5. Minku, L., Yao, X.: DDD: a new ensemble approach for dealing with concept drift. IEEE Trans. Knowl. Data Eng. **24**(4), 619–633 (2012)
6. Yin, D., Hong, L., Xue, Z., Davison, B.D.: Temporal dynamics of user interests in tagging systems. In: Proceedings of the 25th AAAI Conference on Artificial Intelligence (AAAI 2011), pp. 1279–1285 (2011)
7. MovieLens datasets. http://grouplens.org/datasets/movielens/
8. Koren, Y.: Factor in the neighbors: scalable and accurate collaborative filtering. ACM Trans. Knowl. Discov. Data (TKDD) **4**(1), 1 (2010)
9. Whitby, A., Jøsang, A., Indulska, J.: Filtering out unfair ratings in Bayesian reputation systems. In: Proceedings of the Workshop on Trust in Agent Societies, at the Autonomous Agents and Multi Agent Systems Conference (AAMAS 2004), New York, July 2004
10. Nilashi, M., Ibrahim, O.-B., Ithnin, N., Sarmin, N.H.: A multi-criteria collaborative filtering recommender system for the tourism domain using Expectation Maximization (EM) and PCA–ANFIS. Electron. Commer. Res. Appl. **14**(6), 542–562 (2015)
11. Anthony, V., Ayala, A., Alzoghbi, A., Przyjaciel-Zablocki, M., Schätzle, A., Lausen, G.: Speeding up collaborative filtering with parametrized preprocessing. In: Proceeding of the 6th International Workshop on Social Recommender Systems (SRS 2015), in Conjunction with the 2015 ACM SIGKDD Conference on Knowledge Discovery and Data Mining (KDD 2015), Sydney, Australia, August 2015
12. Margaris, D., Vassilakis, C., Georgiadis, P.: Knowledge-based leisure time recommendations in social networks. In: Current Trends on Knowledge-Based Systems. Intelligent Systems Reference Library, vol. 120, pp. 23–48 (2017)
13. Liu, F., Joo Lee, H.: Use of social network information to enhance collaborative filtering performance. Expert Syst. Appl. Int. J. Arch. **37**(7), 4772–4778 (2010)
14. Balabanovic, M., Shoham, Y.: Fab: content-based, collaborative recommendation. Commun. ACM **40**(3), 66–72 (1997)
15. Burke, R.: Hybrid recommender systems: Survey and experiments. User Model. User-Adap. Inter. **12**(4), 331–370 (2002)
16. Gong, S.: A collaborative filtering recommendation algorithm based on user clustering and item clustering. J. Softw. **5**(7), 745–752 (2010)

17. Das, A., Datar, M., Garg, A., Rajaram, S.: Google news personalization: scalable online collaborative filtering. In: Proceedings of the 16th international conference on World Wide Web, pp. 271–280 (2007)
18. Margaris, D., Georgiadis, P., Vassilakis, C.: A collaborative filtering algorithm with clustering for personalized web service selection in business processes. In: Proceedings of RCIS 2015, Athens, Greece, pp. 169–180 (2015)
19. Bakshy, E., Rosenn, I., Marlow, C., Adamic L.: The role of social networks in information diffusion. In: Proceeding of the 21st international conference on World Wide Web, pp. 519–528 (2012)
20. Vaz, P.C., Ribeiro, R., de Matos, D.M.: Understanding temporal dynamics of ratings in the book recommendation scenario. In: Proceeding of the 2013 International Conference on Information Systems and Design of Communication, pp. 11–15 (2013)
21. Han, J., Morag, C.: The influence of the sigmoid function parameters on the speed of backpropagation learning. In Mira, J., Sandoval, F. (eds.) From Natural to Artificial Neural Computation, pp. 195–201 (1995)
22. Ekstrand, M.D., Riedl, J.T., Konstan, J.A.: Collaborative filtering recommender systems. Found. Trends Hum.-Comput. Interact. 4(2), 81–173 (2011)
23. Maxwell Harper, F., Konstan, J.A.: The MovieLens datasets: history and context. ACM Trans. Interact. Intell. Syst. (TiiS) 5(4), 19 (2015)
24. Jaschke, R., Marinho, L., Hotho, A., Schmidt-Thieme, L., Stumme, G.: Tag recommendations in Folksonomies. In: Proceedings of the 11th European Conference on Principles and Practice of Knowledge Discovery in Databases (PKDD 2007), pp. 506–514 (2007)
25. Parra-Santander, D., Brusilovsky, P.: Improving collaborative filtering in social tagging systems for the recommendation of scientific articles. In: Proceedings of Web Intelligence 2010, pp. 136–142 (2010)
26. Yu, K., Schwaighofer, A., Tresp, V., Xu, X., Kriegel, H.P.: Probabilistic memory-based collaborative filtering. IEEE Trans. Knowl. Data Eng. 16(1), 56–69 (2004)
27. He, D., Wu, D.: Toward a robust data fusion for document retrieval. In: Proceedings of the IEEE 4th International Conference on Natural Language Processing and Knowledge Engineering – NLP-KE (2008)
28. Herlocker, J., Konstan, J.A., Riedl, J.: An empirical analysis of design choices in neighborhood-based collaborative filtering algorithms. Inf. Retrieval 5(4), 287–310 (2002)
29. Shardanand, U., Maes, P.: Social information filtering: algorithms for automating "Word of Mouth". In: Proceedings of the SIGCHI Conference on Human Factors in Computing Systems, pp. 210–217 (1995)
30. Frey, R.M., Xu, R., Ilic, A.: A novel recommender system in IoT. In: Proceedings of the 5th International Conference on the Internet of Things (IoT) (2015)
31. Munoz-Organero, M., Ramirez, G.A., Merino, P.M., Kloos, C.D.: A collaborative recommender system based on space-time similarities for an Internet of Things. IEEE Perv. Comput. 9(3), 81–87 (2010)
32. Suggest Movie recommendation system. http://www.suggestmemovie.com/
33. The Table recommendation system. http://thetable.me/
34. Margaris, D., Vassilakis, C.: Pruning and aging for user histories in collaborative filtering. In: Proceedings of the 2016 IEEE Symposium Series on Computational Intelligence (2016)
35. Koren, Y., Bell, R., Volinsky, C.: Matrix factorization techniques for recommender systems. In: IEEE Computer, pp. 42–49, August 2009
36. Zhang, Y., Zhang, M., Liu, Y., Ma, S., Feng, S.: Localized matrix factorization for recommendation based on matrix block diagonal forms. In: Proceedings of the 22nd international conference on World Wide Web (WWW 2013), pp. 1511–1520 (2013)

37. Wen, H., Ding, G., Liu, C., Wang, J.: Matrix factorization meets cosine similarity: addressing sparsity problem in collaborative filtering recommender system. In: Chen, L., Jia, Y., Sellis, T., Liu, G. (eds.) APWeb 2014. LNCS, vol. 8709, pp. 306–317. Springer, Cham (2014). doi:10.1007/978-3-319-11116-2_27

38. Chin, W.-S., Zhuang, Y., Juan, Y.-C., Lin, C.-J.: A fast parallel stochastic gradient method for matrix factorization in shared memory systems. ACM Trans. Intell. Syst. Technol. 6(1), 24 (2015). Article 2

39. Chin, W.-S., Zhuang, Y., Juan, Y.-C., Lin, C.-J.: A learning-rate schedule for stochastic gradient methods to matrix factorization. In: PAKDD, 2015 (2015)

40. Press, W.H., Teukolsky, S.A., Vetterling, W.T., Flannery, B.P.: Section 10.12. simulated annealing methods. In: Numerical Recipes: The Art of Scientific Computing, 3rd edn. Cambridge University Press, New York (2007). ISBN 978-0-521-88068-8

41. Wu, D., Yuan, Z., Yu, K., Pan, H.: Temporal social tagging based collaborative filtering recommender for digital library. In: Proceeding of ICADL 2012, pp. 199–208 (2012)

42. McAuley, J., Targett, C., Shi, J., van den Hengel, A.: Image-based recommendations on styles and substitutes. SIGIR (2015)

43. Gama, J., Zliobaite, I., Bifet, A., Pechenizkiy, M., Bouchachia, A.: A survey on concept drift adaptation. ACM Comput. Surv. 46(4), 37 (2014). Article 44

44. Koren, Y.: Collaborative filtering with temporal dynamics. In: Proceedings of the 15th ACM SIGKDD International Conference on Knowledge Discovery and Data Mining, pp. 447–456 (2009)

45. Vinagre, J., Jorge, A.M.: Forgetting mechanisms for scalable collaborative filtering. J. Braz. Comput. Soc. 18(4), 271–282 (2012)

46. Gates, M., Anzt, H., Kurzak, J., Dongarra, J.: Accelerating collaborative filtering using concepts from high performance computing. In: Proceedings of the 2015 IEEE International Conference on Big Data (2015)

47. Larrain, S., Trattner, C., Parra, D., Graells-Garrido, E., Nørvåg, K.: Good times bad times: a study on recency effects in collaborative filtering for social tagging. In: Proceedings of the 9th ACM Conference on Recommender Systems (RecSys 2015), pp. 269–272 (2015)

48. Baeza-Yates, R.A., Ribeiro-Neto, B.: Modern Information Retrieval: The Concepts and Technology behind Search. Addison-Wesley Professional, New York (2011)

49. Papagelis, M., Plexousakis, D.: Qualitative analysis of user-based and item-based prediction algorithms for recommendation agents. Eng. Appl. Artif. Intell. 18(7), 781–789 (2005)

50. Chitika: The Value of Google Result Positioning. https://chitika.com/google-positioning-value. Accessed 29 Apr 2017

51. Aggarwal, C.C., Wolf, J.L., Wu, K.-L., Yu, P.S.: Horting hatches an egg: a new graph-theoretic approach to collaborative filtering. In: Proceeding of the fifth ACM SIGKDD International Conference on Knowledge Discovery and Data Mining (KDD 1999), pp. 201–212. ACM (1999)

# A Second Generation of Peer-to-Peer Semantic Wikis

Charbel Rahhal[(✉)]

Faculty of Science, Lebanese University, Zahlé, Lebanon
charbelrahhal@gmail.com

**Abstract.** P2P Semantic Wikis (P2PSW) constitute a collaborative editing tool for knowledge and ontology creation, share and management. They ensure a massive collaboration in a distributed manner on replicated data composed of semantic wikis pages and semantic annotations. P2PSW are an instantiation of the optimistic replication model for semantic wikis. They ensure eventual syntactical consistency, i.e. that the wiki pages and semantic annotations store of the peers will eventually become identical. In spite of their advantages, these Wikis do not support a mechanism to maintain the quality of their semantic annotations. Thus, the content of the semantic wiki pages could be inconsistent for many reasons: the merge of the changes is made automatically by the wiki not by the users, missing information or inconsistent information added by the users of the peers. In this paper, I present a semantic inconsistency detection mechanism (SIDM) developed for P2PSW. SIDM detects the semantic inconsistency of the annotations in the semantic pages and improves the quality of the knowledge and the functionality of P2PSW. It indicates not only the existence of the semantic inconsistency in the wiki pages but also specifies the reason of the inconsistency. SIDM also facilitates the semantic inconsistency removal by determining exactly the position of the inconsistent annotations in the wiki pages and highlighting them via a semantic inconsistency visualization mechanism we developed.

**Keywords:** Semantic web · P2P semantic wikis · Semantic consistency

## 1 Introduction

P2P Semantic Wikis (P2PSW) [1] constitute a collaborative editing tool for knowledge and ontology creation, share and management. They ensure a massive collaboration in a distributed manner on a replicated data composed of semantic wikis pages and semantic annotations. In P2PSW, the number of peers can be very large, it can grow to thousands of thousands of peers. This happens without affecting the scalability and the functionality of the wiki. Research academics can work on common research projects and collaborate to produce their publications, people of same interests can produce and share same knowledge,

© Springer-Verlag GmbH Germany 2017
A. Hameurlain et al. (Eds.): TLDKS XXXIV, LNCS 10620, pp. 65–91, 2017.
https://doi.org/10.1007/978-3-662-55947-5_4

and domains' experts can build common taxonomies and ontologies in an easy way using P2PSW.

P2PSW combine the advantages of P2P wikis and the semantic wikis [2]. The replication of the semantic wiki pages in a distributed network enhances the performance, scalability, and fault-tolerance. The integration of the semantic aspect in P2PSW, improves the navigation, the search, and the knowledge extraction in the wikis. The semantic annotations in the wiki pages can be processed automatically by machines and they are exploited by semantic queries. P2PSW were first distributed on unstructured P2P networks, a recent work [3] proposed P2PSW distributed on structured P2P networks.

A P2P semantic wiki is a P2P network of autonomous semantic wiki servers (called also peers or nodes) that can dynamically join and leave the network. Every peer of a P2PSW hosts a copy of semantic wiki pages and a store for the semantic annotations extracted from these pages. As in any wiki system, the basic element is a semantic wiki page and every semantic wiki page is assigned a unique identifier PageID, which is the name of the page. A semantic wiki page is an ordinary wiki page that contains semantic annotations. It can be seen as an ordered sequence of lines. The semantic annotations can be written as typed links. For instance, a semantic wiki page about "Jaguar" could be written as shown in Fig. 1.

```
Jaguar is a Native American word means "he who kills with one blow".
It is the third biggest cat behind the [isBiggest::Tiger].
Jaguar has many colors such as [hasColor:=Brown] one.
[category::Animal]
```

Fig. 1. Semantic Wiki Page about Jaguar

It contains four lines and three semantic annotations [isBiggest::Tiger], [hasColor:= Brown], and [category::Animal] about "Jaguar". Text and semantic annotations are stored in separate persistent storages. Text can be stored in files or a database. The semantic annotations are mapped into RDF statements where the subject is the page name. For example, the [isBiggest::Tiger] annotation will be stored as <"Jaguar", "isBiggest", "Tiger">. These annotations are stored in the peer triple store separate from text since relational database is not an ideal type of storage for semantic data. An RDF triple store organizes information in graphs rather than in fixed database tables. It is designed to answer queries in the SPARQL query language and to provide reasoning features on the ontological elements they store.

P2PSW are based on an optimistic replication model [4]. When a peer updates its local replica of a semantic wiki page, the replicas of the peers diverge. An update of a replica generates the corresponding operations i.e. insert or delete a line. An operation is processed in four steps: it is executed immediately against the local replica of the peer, broadcasted through the P2P network to other peers, received by the other peers and integrated to their local replica. P2PSW use an optimistic synchronization algorithm to integrate the changes represented by operations and eventually ensure syntactic consistency. After integrating the same operations, wikis pages of the peers and their semantic annotations stores will become identical. The convergence of replicas is reached while preserving the execution order of the operations, and their intention independently of the concurrency. Each time the inserted or deleted line contains annotations, these annotations are extracted from the line, transformed into RDF statements and the local RDF triple store of the peer is updated. So, the merge of changes in P2PSW is made automatically by the synchronization algorithm and not by the users.

The first generation of P2PSW focused on ensuring syntactic convergence. They do not take in consideration the semantic consistency aspect of their content. While the syntactic consistency ensures that the semantic wiki pages of the peers and their stores will converge when integrating the same changes otherwise they diverge. The semantic consistency will be concerned with the consistency of the annotations in the semantic wiki pages of the peers. In other words, it will focus on ensuring that the common understanding of the users about the annotations is respected. The semantic consistency is not defined in the current P2PSWs. Current P2PSW do not support a mechanism to check the semantic consistency of the annotations in the semantic wiki pages. A user on a peer is not able to detect whether the annotations in a semantic wiki page are consistent or not. There is difference between the syntactic consistency and the semantic consistency, we explain it by running an example.

Consider two sites Site1 and Site2 replicating a semantic wiki page about "Jaguar", the page could be referring to a car for someone and an animal for another. Initially, the wiki page contains one line and is the same on both sites as shown in the Fig. 2. Suppose that a user on Site1 inserts the line "[category::Car]" at position2. Concurrently, a user on Site2 inserts the line "[category::Animal]" at the same position. The change on Site1 generates op1 = insert ("[category::Car]", 2) and the change on Site2 generates op2 = insert ("[category::Animal]", 2). The two operations are integrated locally, broadcasted through the network and eventually integrated on both sites. In P2PSW, the optimistic replication algorithm integrates op1 and op2 as follows. On Site1, first it inserts "[category::Car]" between line at position 1 and the end line of the page. When op2 is received on Site1, op2 specifies that "[category::Animal]" must be inserted between the same positions. The replication algorithm serializes op1 and op2 to make the operations commute and consequently to ensure convergence of the replicas on both sites. The Woot replication algorithm [5] uses the site identifiers in the synchronization which are unique and ordered. op2 is received from Site2 having an identifier greater than Site1, then "[category::Animal]" will be inserted after "[category::Car]". The same processing is made on Site2 and "[category::Car]" will be inserted before "[category::Animal]". The Logoot replication [6] generates a unique position between line 1 and the end line for line "[category::Car]" on Site1 and another unique position for "[category::Animal]" on Site2.

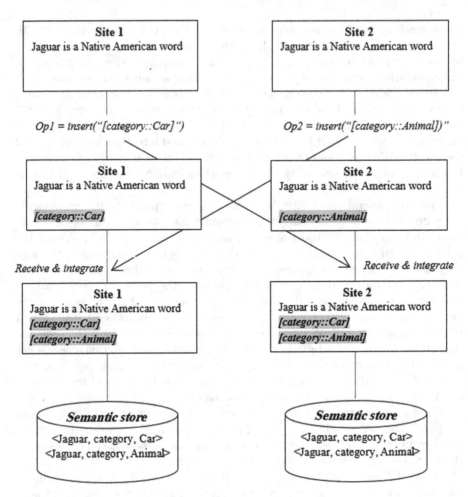

**Fig. 2.** Concurrent edition in P2PSW

Consequently, the lines "[category::Car]" and "[category::Animal]" will be inserted in the same order on both sites. The final result of an optimistic replication algorithm in P2PSW ensures that both sites ensure that the lines are inserted in the same order in the wiki pages and the triple stores contain the same semantic annotations as shown in Fig. 2. Both sites are syntactically convergent. However, a jaguar cannot have two disjoint categories Animal and Car at the same time. This statement cannot be made in the first generation of P2PSW. Thus, the obtained result is semantically inconsistent. Based on this result, running a semantic query to classify jaguars based on their category will return an erroneous result.

In the current P2PSWs, the result of the automatic merge could be anything and does not take in consideration the semantic consistency. There is no mechanism that helps the users to specify this constraint that the Animal and Car categories are distinct. The following annotations added by mistake [name:=3.2], [size:= −13], [birthdate:=2017-02-31], [brother::Apple Inc.] and the page is about a human and Apple is a company are examples about semantically inconsistent annotations that can be found in a semantic wiki page of a peer.

In spite the important role that play the semantic annotations in the P2PSW, working with semantically inconsistent annotations may lead to a loss of those benefits. Determining whether a semantic wiki page is semantically consistent requires checking the semantic consistency of its semantic annotations. This is not currently available in P2PSW. The annotations of a wiki page can be considered semantically consistent if they satisfy all the semantic rules on which they apply. For instance, a semantic rule will specify that a semantic wiki page should not belong to two or more disjoint categories.

The goal of this research work is to provide P2PSW with a generic semantic inconsistency detection mechanism (SIDM) that detects and proposes a solution for semantic inconsistency in P2PSW. SIDM will indicate not only the existence of the semantic inconsistency in the wiki pages but also the violated semantic rules. In addition, the inconsistency among the pages will also be detected. The semantic inconsistency is presented using a visualization mechanism we developed. **The outcome of this work is a second generation of P2PSW with an enhanced quality of content and knowledge.** Obviously, ensuring that the semantic annotations are semantically consistent has a major effect on the functionality of the P2PSW. It will improve the quality of the structured data in the different peers of the P2PSW.

The work focused on the design and the build of the semantic inconsistency detection mechanism. It includes defining semantic consistency in the context of P2PSW and the semantic rules (i.e. constraints) that determine the consistency of the annotations in the semantic wiki pages. The appropriate interfaces are created to write the semantic rules as special semantic wiki pages. The algorithm for the detection of the semantic inconsistency is developed. It detects the inconsistency existence and the inconsistent annotations. How the SIDM can be integrated in P2PSW and the semantic inconsistency is visualized follow.

The rest of the paper is organized as follows: Sect. 2 presents a state of art about the first generation of P2PSW. Section 3 discusses related work. Section 4 details the proposal that includes the algorithm, and the architecture. It describes the main steps followed in the development of the semantic inconsistency detection mechanism for P2PSW. Section 5 describes how to integrate SIDM in P2PSWs. Section 6 shows how the entire approach works. The last section concludes the paper and points to future work.

## 2   Peer-to-Peer Semantic Wikis

P2P Semantic Wikis constitute a collaborative editing tool for knowledge and ontology creation, share and management. They combine the advantages of semantic wikis and P2P wikis, also their technologies. They ensure a massive collaboration in a distributed manner by replicating their data composed of semantic wikis pages and semantic annotations. Their main focus was to ensure the syntactic consistency of their replicated data.

P2PSW as a wiki constitute an easy to use collaborative editor for any type of users who aim to collaborate and to produce data and knowledge in a simple manner. The number of peers in that wiki can be huge, it is variable and can grow to thousands of thousands. Since these wikis were designed for mass collaboration they can generate huge amount of data called nowadays big data by very large number of users on the peers. The users on the peers can create as many as they want of semantic wiki pages. These pages will be replicated and their annotations are stored in triple stores that can handle billion of RDF triples. The users of these wikis can be researchers and professors or experts in ontology and taxonomy building or people with no experience in Semantic Web such as business managers, students, etc. The data in P2PSW can be reused later on as a reference or as a part in other projects or systems. Data are locally stored at the users' side and not on some distant servers owned by private companies.

The semantic aspect in P2PSW improves the organization and the extraction of knowledge from these data. In addition it enables users to produce a common understanding and vocabulary. The linked data represented as semantic annotations in the wiki pages are actually manipulated in P2PSW using the Semantic Web technologies. The annotations are translated into RDF triples, extracted and stored in the triple stores via SPARQL query language [14].

What distinguishes P2PSW from any other collaborative ontologies/knowledge editors in the Semantic Web is the real nature of collaborative editing. Many users can edit the wiki at the same time. Concurrent editions are handled and changes are merged automatically. It is not only about sharing or indexing the knowledge as other tools are limited to. There are two ways to build a P2PSW either by integrating the Semantic Web technologies in a P2P wiki or by distributing the architecture of a Semantic Wiki. Two P2PSW were developed SWOOKI and DSMW. SWOOKI followed the first way while DSMW adopted the second one. Both are based on an instantiation of the optimistic replication model in the context of semantic wikis. They ensure the CCI consistency model (Causality, Convergence, Intention) [4] of the replicated data. Next, I will briefly present these two P2PSW.

## 2.1  SWOOKI

SWOOKI [9] is the first P2P semantic wiki. A SWOOKI network is a set of interconnected semantic wiki servers. Each server hosts a replica of semantically annotated wiki pages and a triple store. It addresses specifically the problems of scalability and fault tolerance. SWOOKI adopts a total replication of the data on every peer of the network. Each peer can join and leave the network at any time. The produced knowledge can be searched, queried and extracted locally on each peer. SWOOKI uses Woot [5] as an optimistic replication mechanism to maintain the syntactic consistency of the replicated wiki pages and the replicated RDF repositories i.e. their convergence. It ensures the CCI consistency model.

SWOOKI was implemented in Java under the GPL license. You can download and test it last release 0.9 at http://sourceforge.net/projects/wooki.

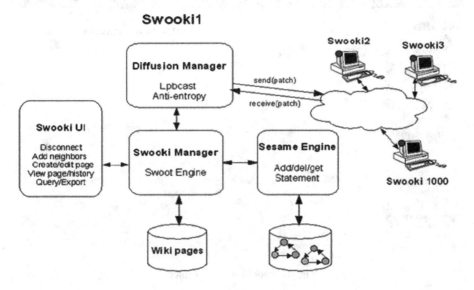

**Fig. 3.** Swooki architecture

**SWOOKI Architecture.** A SWOOKI server is composed of the following components (see Fig. 3):

- **User Interface:** The SWOOKI user interface (UI) component (see Fig. 4) is basically a regular wiki editor. It allows users to edit a view of a page by getting the page from the SWOOKI manager. Users can disconnect their peer to work in an off-line mode. They can add new neighbors in their list to work with. The UI allows users to see the history of a page, to search for pages having some annotation, to execute semantic queries, and to export the semantic annotations of the wiki pages in an RDF format.
- **SWOOKI Manager:** The SWOOKI manager is responsible for the generation and the integration of the editing patches which are sets of insert/delete operations. It implements the Woot algorithm. Its main method is to integrate all operations contained in the patch. Requesting and modifying a page or resolving a semantic query in the RDF repository pass through this manager.
- **Sesame Engine:** Sesame 2.0 is the RDF repository used in SWOOKI. Sesame is controlled by the SWOOKI manager for storing and retrieving RDF triples. This component allows also generating dynamic content for wiki pages using queries embedded in the wiki pages. It provides also a feature to export RDF graphs.
- **Diffusion Manager:** The diffusion manager is in charge to maintain the membership of the unstructured network and to implement a reliable broadcast.

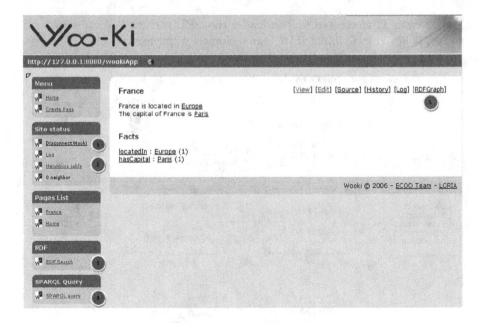

**Fig. 4.** Swooki user interface

## 2.2 Distributed Semantic Media Wiki (DSMW)

DSMW [10] is the second developed P2P Semantic Wiki. It allows to build a semantic Friend-to-Friend social network and to support multiple collaborative editing processes. In DSMW, a new model of collaboration called Push/Pull was developed. It is based on the notion of feeds. The idea was inspired from the work in Distributed Version Control Systems like Git. A generic ontology that covers the semantic wikis pages and their annotations, the changes and their history was proposed. Every DSMW element is an instantiation of this ontology and can be exploited semantically. DSMW is also based on an optimistic replication for the semantic wiki pages. It uses Logoot [6] for synchronization and to ensure the syntactic convergence of the replicated data.

DSWM allows users to build their own cooperation networks, every user declares explicitly with whom he would like to cooperate. Every user can have a DSMW server installed on his machine. He can create and edit his own semantic wiki pages as in a normal semantic wiki system. Later, he can decide to share or not these semantic wiki pages and decide with whom to share. The replication of data and the communication between servers is made through channels (push/pull feeds). These channels contain the changes made in the semantic wiki pages that can be shared and exchanged among peers. They are implemented as special semantic wiki pages.

When a semantic wiki page is updated on a multi-synchronous semantic wiki server, it generates a corresponding operation. This operation is processed in four steps: (1) it is executed immediately against the page, (2) published locally to the corresponding channels, (3) pulled remotely by authorized servers, and (4) integrated to their local replica of the page. If needed, the integration process merges this modification with concurrent ones, generated either locally or received from a remote server. DSMW was implemented as an extension of Semantic MediaWiki which is also an extension of Wikipedia's wiki engine. The latest version of DSMW 1.2 can be downloaded and tested at http://momo54. github.io/DSMW.

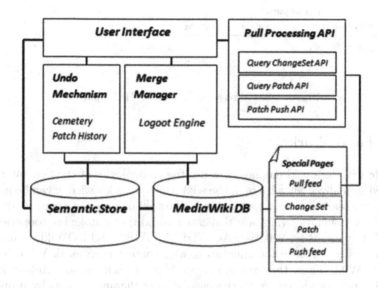

**Fig. 5.** DSMW architecture

**DSMW Architecture.** The DSMW architecture is illustrated in Fig. 5. Its components are given below:

- **User interface (UI):** Each semantic wiki page is associated with a special page (see Fig. 6) that shows the patches (i.e. the set of operations) integrated on that page, and the pushfeed to which it belongs.
- **Merge Manager:** is in charge of the integration of the operations. It synchronizes automatically the changes by implementing Logoot.
- **Diffusion manager:** This component is responsible for the generation and the propagation of the operations that represent the changes.
- **Data storage:** This component is constituted of a database that stores separately the semantic wiki pages and their annotations. It contains different namespaces (PullFeed, PushFeed, ChangeSet, Patch, and Operation) to separate the semantic wiki pages from the special ones.
- **Undo mechanism:** This component allows undoing changes at any time.

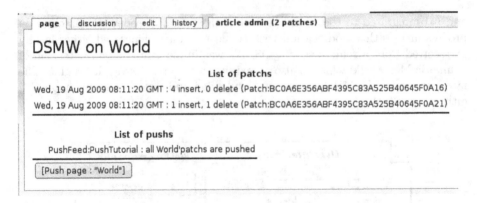

**Fig. 6.** DSMW page associated to 'Hello' page

## 3    Related Work

Semantic wikis are wiki engines that use the technologies of the Semantic Web to embed formalized knowledge in the wiki pages. This knowledge can be used to enhance the search and the navigation in the wiki or to update content dynamically. Some semantic wikis are dedicated to editing ontologies cooperatively such as Platypus, Rise, WikiSar, AceWiki, OntoWiki, and BOWiki. Others use ontologies as a reference for annotating wiki content such as IkeWiki, SWiM, and SweetWiki. Thus, they require to load/use a background ontology in the wiki. This provides guidance to the users during the annotations by proposing only valid completions. Semantic MediaWiki merged both approaches. First, it allowed users to add various types of ontological information to the wiki and to export these information later on. Then, it was extended by enabling importing ontologies in the wiki by authorized users. Based on the ontology, the system offers automatic classification of articles and supports the user in editing the wiki knowledge base. Many of the semantic wikis implement RDF and RDFs layer. Their vocabulary is not domain specific and thus does not allow to infer about domain specific relations.

Most of the semantic wikis do not check the consistency of the ontology they produce and do not support a reasoning feature [7]. Reasoning engine can perform consistency checks and derive additional implicit knowledge from the facts entered into the system. It uses predefined or user-defined rules in the knowledge base. Although reasoning is an important feature, it is only supported by a small number of wikis. The reasons for this might be that it is time-consuming, memory intensive, and can yield results that are not expected and/or traceable by the user. A reasoner may require significant resources (both in terms of processing and memory) which could slow down the wiki considerably. Consequently, it cannot be used to check the consistency of the P2PSW content which are designed for massive collaboration.

Some of the semantic wikis export the annotations or the ontologies defined in the wiki and check them by an external reasoning engine. Semantic MediaWiki uses external reasoner KAON2 to reason with the ontology it imports. This offers an automatic classification of its articles by adding a category to articles inferred from the ontology. It aims also supporting the users in editing the wiki knowledge base in a logically consistent manner. The users will be warned about inconsistencies in the wiki knowledge detected by the reasoner.

Semantic wikis are centralized based on servers. In case of concurrent changes in a semantic wiki, a conflict in the edition is presented to the user. It is up to him to solve the conflict and to make the merge manually or undoing its changes. The save of changes generates a new version of the wiki page. In semantic wikis, handling a semantic inconsistency is possible by either preventing the save of inconsistent semantic wiki pages or by checking the consistency of the saved wiki page modified by a user. An example of these wikis is BOWiki [8] that is destinated for collaborative editing of biomedical ontologies and gene data. It uses an OWL ontology with a description logic reasoner in order to perform consistency checks and queries. It evaluates newly entered data using an ontology in OWL-DL format. Only consistent semantic data will be stored in its semantic store. If an inconsistency is detected, the edited page is rejected with an explanation of the inconsistency. The use of these wikis could be hard for some users and the way they handle semantic inconsistency cannot be applied in the context of P2PSW. In P2PSW, the semantic consistency of remote changes can be only checked after they are received and integrated since the merge is automatically made by the wiki and not by the users.

## 4    Semantic Inconsistency Detection Mechanism

This section describes the proposal and is structured as follows. First the semantic consistency in the context of P2PSW and the semantic consistency rules are defined. Then the semantic inconsistency detection approach and the developed algorithm are presented.

### 4.1    Semantic Consistency in Peer-to-Peer Semantic Wikis

I define the semantic consistency in P2PSW as follows: A P2PSW is semantically consistent if all its semantic wiki pages are semantically consistent. A semantic wiki page is semantically consistent if its all semantic annotations are semantically consistent. The semantic annotations of a wiki page are semantically consistent when they are in a state in which all the semantic rules concerning these annotations are satisfied. Otherwise, the annotations are considered semantically inconsistent also their pages. So, what actually determines the consistency of the annotations are the semantic rules. In the absence of those rules, no information can be given about the consistency of the annotations.

First, we studied the existent constraints and restrictions that cán be expressed in RDF schemas (RDFS) and OWL and then we derived the consistency rules that cover these. The constraints can be extended easily if necessary.

They can be expressed as semantic annotations and their satisfaction can be checked using SPARQL queries. Many research works on semantic consistency checking such in [12, 13] focused on defining axioms and checking their consistency. In our approach, we followed the same principle.

In ontological terms, the annotations in a wiki page could represent a part of the ABox of an ontology i.e. the sets of assertions about the individuals which are instances of concepts. The semantic rules we define will represent the TBox of an ontology i.e. the set of concepts and their properties to formally describe a domain. In our consistency check of the P2PSW content, we are interested in only one major task of a reasoner which is checking the consistency of ABox with respect to TBox i.e. determining whether individuals in ABox do not violate axioms described by TBox.

Before detailing the semantic rules and their use, I will explain how the annotations in a semantic wiki page will be extracted, mapped into RDF triples and stored in the triple stores in the second generation of P2PSWs. I clarify three terms: instance, property, and concept in the context of P2PSW:

1. **Instance:** Every semantic wiki page that contains the annotation [category::Concept] is an instance of the Concept. Like in Object Oriented Programming, an instance can be seen as an object of the class Concept. A semantic wiki page can be an instance of many concepts, i.e. contains many annotations $[category::Concept_i]_{i=1,..,n}$.

2. **Property:** In semantic wiki pages, a property or predicate describes a relation between the semantic wiki page and another page or a characteristic of that page. It can be written as [property1::SemWikiPage2] or [property1:=Value].

3. **Concept:** Concepts are classes that provide an abstraction mechanism for grouping with similar characteristics. A concept can be seen as a category used to group a set of semantic wiki pages.

**Example.** We illustrate the three previous terms through the example given below:

```
Jaguar is the third biggest cat behind the [isBiggest::Tiger].
It has many colors but they are beautiful with [hasColor:=Darkest] one.
It has [hasLegs:=4] legs and runs very fast.
[category::Animal]
```

1. The semantic wiki page "Jaguar" is an instance of Animal. This annotation is mapped into an RDF triple and stored in the triple store as follows:
   <Jaguar> <rdf:type> <Concepts/Animal>
2. The properties of "Jaguar" page are isBiggest, hasColor, and hasLegs. They are stored in the triple store with the corresponding objects as follows:
   <Jaguar><Properties/isBiggest><Tiger>
   <Jaguar><Properties/hasColor>"Darkest"
   <Jaguar><Properties/hasLegs>"4"
3. There is the "Animal" concept to which belongs the "Jaguar" instance.

## 4.2 Semantic Consistency Rules

I define semantic consistency rules in P2PSW as the constraints that can applied on the semantic annotations. They are similar to integrity constraints applied to data in databases. These rules represent the constraints defined on the properties and the concepts. The rules on properties concern the domain and the range of the Properties, while the rules on concepts concern the cardinality of the properties in a Concept and the relations between Concepts. To be integrated in P2PSWs, first the properties and the concepts pages should be created. Then the annotations that represent the constraints are inserted in these pages.

**Semantic Consistency Rule on Properties.** I decided to use *domain* and *range* as semantic consistency rules on properties as shown in Table 1. I borrowed the idea from RDF Schema that uses them to associate constraints to properties. *rdfs:domain* and *rdfs:range* allow making statements about the contexts in which certain properties "make sense". The role of these constraints is:

- **rdfs:range** is used to constrain property values.
- **rdfs:domain** is used to specify a class on which a property may be used.

To define these constraints on a property, we create a special semantic wiki page for that property. The namespace *Properties* will be used for all the property pages.

**Table 1.** Property constraints

| Constraints on properties | |
|---|---|
| P2PSW annotations | RDF |
| [domain::URI] | rdfs:domain |
| [range::URI \|Literal] | rdfs:range |

We insert the annotations [domain::URI] ([range::URI \|Literal] respectively) in the semantic wiki page property1 to specify that property1 has a domain URI (has range a URI or a literal respectively). Each annotation has its equivalent in RDF as shown in Table 1. When saved, the annotations of the property1 are updated in the triple store. First, the triples of that property are removed from the store and then the annotations of the saved page are mapped into RDF triples and stored in the triple store.

We map these annotations into RDF triples as shown below:

<Properties/property1><rdfs:domain><Concepts/URI>
<Properties/property1><rdfs:range><Concepts/URI>                          Or
<Properties/property1><rdfs:range>
            <http://www.w3.org/2000/01/rdf-schema#Literal>.

In fact, the range of a property could be an URI i.e. some concept or a literal i.e. one of the datatypes: an integer, a float, a boolean, a string, a symbol, etc.

**Example of Constraints Definition on Properties.** To define the domain and range of isBiggest property, we create a semantic wiki page "isBiggest" in the *Properties* namespace and insert the appropriate annotations as illustrated in the following text:

```
[domain::Animal]
[range::Cat]
```

**Semantic Consistency Rule on Concepts.** I define two types of semantic consistency rules on a concept: (1) the cardinality of the concept properties and (2) the relations between this concept and other concepts. To define these constraints on a concept, a user on a peer must create a special semantic wiki page for that concept. The namespace *Concepts* will be used for all the concept pages. I defined the semantic annotations that can be added in the concepts. They express the constraints that can be applied on concepts. These annotations and their equivalence in OWL language [11] are given in Table 2. Actually, cardinality constraints can be used to make a property required (at least one), to allow only a specific number of values for that property, or to insist that a property must not occur. OWL provides three constructs for restricting the cardinality of properties locally within a class context. $owl : minCardinality$, $owl : maxCardinality$, and $owl : cardinality$ describe a class of all individuals that have at least $N$, at most $N$, and exactly $N$ semantically distinct values for the concerned property, where $N$ is the value of the cardinality constraint. On the other hand, C1 $rdfs : subClassOf$ C2, C1 $owl : equivalentClass$ C2, or C1 $owl : disjointWith$ C2 allow to say that the set of instances of C1 is a subset, the same, or has no instance in common with the set of instances of C2, where C1 and C2 are two concepts. I map the annotations inserted in concepts into RDF triples as shown below:

| | | |
|---|---|---|
| \<Concepts/concept1\> | \<owl:equivalentClass\> | \<Concepts/URI\> |
| \<Concepts/concept1\> | \<owl:disjointWith\> | \<Concepts/URI\> |
| \<Concepts/concept1\> | \<rdfs:subClassOf\> | \<Concepts/URI\> |
| \<Concepts/concept1\> | \<property\> | "value:max" |
| \<Concepts/concept1\> | \<property\> | "value:min" |
| \<Concepts/concept1\> | \<property\> | "value:exactly" |

When saved, the annotations i.e. the constraints of the concept1 page are inserted in the triple store.

**Example of constraints definition on concepts.** We can define an Animal concept as a class that has at least one color, at least two legs, and one isBiggest property. We can say also that an Animal is not a Car. To do so, we create a semantic wiki page "Animal" with the following annotations.

**Table 2.** Concept constraints

| Constraints on concepts | |
| --- | --- |
| P2PSW annotations | OWL |
| [equivalent::URI] | owl:equivalentClass |
| [disjoint::URI] | owl:disjointWith |
| [property:min=value] | owl:minCardinality |
| [property:max=value] | owl:maxCardinality |
| [property:exactly=value] | owl:cardinality |
| [subClass:URI] | rdfs:subClassOf |

```
[hasLegs:min=2]        [hasColor:min=1]
[disjoint::Car]        [isBiggest:exactly=1]
```

### 4.3  Semantic Inconsistency Detection Approach

The semantic inconsistency detection approach I developed is made of many components shown in the Fig. 7. The semantic inconsistency checker detects inconsistency on three levels: the semantic wiki page, the concept, and the property level. A user can check whether a page is consistent or select a property or concept to check in order to identify if there are semantic wiki pages that violate it. The checker works by running SPARQL queries [14] on the triple store of the P2PSW peer. The result of the query is displayed using a visualization mechanism that shows the inconsistency when it exists. In this section, I describe the possible inconsistencies that can take place, how they are detected on every level, and the developed algorithm.

**Check Consistency on Semantic Wiki Page Level.** To check the consistency of a semantic wiki page (SWP), we check the satisfaction of the semantic consistency rules on concepts and properties associated with the semantic annotations of that page. A semantic inconsistency occurs when one or many semantic consistency rules are violated. I consider that there is no contradiction in the semantic consistency rules definition. In addition, checking the inconsistency by a user on a peer can be made at any time. The inconsistency detection is made via SPARQL queries since both the semantic annotations and the semantic consistency rules are stored as RDF triples in the triple store of the peer. To detect the semantic inconsistency in a semantic wiki page SWP, we follow these steps:

1. Select all the semantic annotations in SWP. If there are no annotations in the result then there is nothing to check. We consider a semantic wiki page without annotations as a semantically consistent one. Otherwise, go to step2.
2. Check the satisfaction of the semantic consistency rules on the concepts of SWP. Select the concepts, let SC be the set of these concepts. Two cases exist:

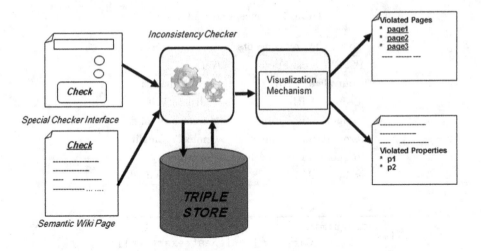

**Fig. 7.** The semantic consistency checker components

 2.1. There is no concept found, SC is empty, i.e. SWP does not belong to any concept. In this case, check the satisfaction of the semantic rules on the properties of SWP, go to step 5.

 2.2. SC is not empty, SC = $\{C_1, C_2, \ldots, C_n\}$. Check the disjoint constraints on these concepts go to step 3.

3. Compute SDC the set of disjoint concepts in SC. Two cases exist:

 3.1. There are disjoint concepts, i.e. SDC = $\{C_k\}_{1<=k<=n}$. Display SWP is semantically inconsistent and the properties of every concept in SDC. The semantic inconsistency checker stops.

 3.2. There is no disjoint concept, SDC is empty. Check the constraints on every concept C in SC, go to step 4.

4. For each concept C in SC, select the properties SP in C.

 For each property P in SP:

 4.1. Check the cardinality constraint of P. It consists of two steps:

  4.1.1. Compute the cardinality $cp$ of P in SWP i.e. the number of times P is present in SWP with different values.

  4.1.2. Compare $cp$ with the cardinality constraints on P in the concept C. If ($cp$ < minCardinality) or ($cp$ > maxCardinality) or ($cp$ <> cardinality) then Display semantic inconsistency on the cardinality of P in C.

 4.2. Check the range constraint of P. It consists of two steps:

  4.2.1. Compute the range R of P in SWP.

   – If the *value* of P i.e. the object in SWP is another semantic wiki page SWP' then check if SWP' exists. If SWP' does not exist then there is no information whether the range R of that property P is violated or not. If SWP' exists, we compute the set of concepts (i.e. ranges) SR to which belongs SWP'.

   – If the *value* of P in SWP is a literal, let us call it SR.

4.2.2 Compare SR with the range R" of P defined in the semantic wiki page of the property P only if SR is not empty. If R' <> SR then Display semantic inconsistency on the range of P.

5. Check the satisfaction of the semantic rules on the properties of SWP. Here we check the constraints on the properties that do not belong to any concept of SWP, i.e. only the unchecked properties. Let us call SUP the set of those properties.

For each property P in SUP:

5.1. Check the domain constraint on P. If the domain concept DC of P does not exist i.e. is not defined or the set of concepts SC in SWP is empty then there is no information else Display there is a possible semantic inconsistency of the domain of P in SWP.

5.2. Check the range constraint of P, go to step 4.2.

Some choices we made in the SIDM are presented below:

1. The check stops when two or more disjoint concepts are found in a semantic wiki page. To facilitate solving the inconsistency, we display the concepts and their properties. Another alternative could be letting the algorithm to continue checking the semantic inconsistency of the properties in SWP that belong to the non-disjoint concepts and that do not belong to any concept.

2. We consider the existence of a *possible* semantic inconsistency when the domain of a property defined in the property page is different than the categories of the SWP where the property is used. For instance, consider that the domain of a property is Bike, and the categories of SWP are Vehicle and Bicycle. If we compare Bike with the categories, they are different; however Bike and Bicycle are the same. In the context of Semantic Web, two concepts are equivalent if there is an explicit statement stating so. In the context of P2PSW, we can compare the equivalence and the disjoint of the categories with the domain of the property to possibly detect the inconsistency if it exists. We decided to leave that to the users.

3. To ensure scalability, we can use the construct SPARQL queries to extract at once all the required information for the SIDM algorithm from the store. The result is an RDF graph that will be used to detect the inconsistency and there is no need to interrogate the triple store again multiple times.

**Check Consistency on Concept Level.** Four types of constraints can be defined in concept pages which are subclass, disjoint, equivalent, and the cardinality of the properties that could be present in the concept. The constraints definitions and their violation detection are presented as follows:

1. **Subclass constraint:** a concept C is a subclass of a concept C' if every instance of C is an instance of C'. The constraint is violated when an instance of C doesn't belong to C'. An instance is a semantic wiki page. In other words, the constraint is violated when there exists a semantic wiki page that belongs to the category C and not to C'.

2. **Disjoint constraint:** a concept C is disjoint with a concept C' if every instance of C is not an instance of C'. The semantic wiki pages that belong to disjoint categories with C will be extracted and displayed. In the semantic consistency checker, we check only the satisfaction of the rules [disjoint::C'] defined in the Concept C page. We do not consider the case [disjoint::C] defined in C'.

3. **Equivalent constraint:** Two concepts C and C' are equivalent if they have the same instance set called a class extension. The constraint is violated when a semantic wiki page belongs to C and not to C'.

4. **Cardinality constraint:** Three types of constraints can be defined on the properties cardinality in a concept C. The constraints on the properties cardinality can be minimum cardinality, maximum cardinality, and exact cardinality. The checker detects the satisfaction or the violation of these constraints. We defined a function called checkCardinality() that takes as parameter a concept C and returns the set of pages that contain a property of C with a violated constraint. The function works as follows: first we extract the properties present in the concept C, then for each one of them we extract the pages that belong to C violating the properties cardinality constraints defined in C. A detailed description of the checkCardinality function is given in Algorithm 1.

**Function** *checkCardinality (Concept C)*
> $VPS \leftarrow \{\}$; //set of violated pages ;
> $PRS \leftarrow \{prop \in Properties/$ [prop:min=V] $\vee$ [prop:max=V'] $\vee$
> [prop:exactly=V"] $\in$ C $\}$;
> **if** $(PRS = \{\})$ **then**
> > | return VPS;
> 
> **else**
> > PGS $\leftarrow$ {page $\in$ Pages / [category::C] $\in$ page};
> > **if** $(PGS = \{\})$ **then**
> > > | return VPS;
> > 
> > **else**
> > > **for** *each page $\in$ PGS* **do**
> > > > **for** *each prop $\in$ PRS* **do**
> > > > > cp $\leftarrow$ Cardinality {prop, page};
> > > > > **if** $((cp < V) \vee (cp > V') \vee (cp \neq V''))$ **then**
> > > > > > | VPS = VPS $\cup$ {page};
> > > > > 
> > > > > **end**
> > > > 
> > > > **end**
> > > 
> > > **end**
> > > return VPS;
> > 
> > **end**
> 
> **end**

**Algorithm 1.** The checkCardinality function

**Check Consistency on Property Level.** In a property page, two types of constraints can be defined which are the domain and the range constraints of a property.

**Domain constraint:** This constraint specifies the concept that represents the domain of a property. This constraint is violated if the property belongs to a page that is an instance of one or many concepts disjoint with the domain of that property. We define the checkDomain( ) function that takes the property name as parameter and returns the pages that violate this constraint. A detailed description of the checkDomain function is given in Algorithm 2.

---

**Function** *checkDomain (Property P)*
   $VPS \leftarrow \{\}$; //set of violated pages ;
   $D \leftarrow$ Domain(P);
   **if** *($\nexists$ D)* **then**
     | return VPS;
   **else**
     PGS $\leftarrow$ {page $\in$ Pages / [P::V] $\vee$ [P:=V'] $\in$ page};
     **if** $(PGS = \{\})$ **then**
       | return VPS;
     **else**
       **for** *each page* $\in$ *PGS* **do**
         CS $\leftarrow$ {C $\in$ Concepts/ [category::C] $\in$ page};
         **if** $(CS = \{\})$ **then**
           | continue;
         **else**
           **if** *(D $\notin$ CS)* **then**
             | VPS = VPS $\cup$ {page};
           **end**
         **end**
       **end**
       return VPS;
     **end**
   **end**

**Algorithm 2.** The checkDomain function

---

**Range constraint:** This constraint gives the range concept of a property P. It is violated when [P::v] or [P:=v] is found in the checked semantic wiki page and v is different than the defined range in P. If v is a literal, we compare directly the data type of v with the range. However, when v is a URI (a semantic wiki page), we compute the concepts of that page and compare them with the range. If they are different, then the page containing P violates the range constraint of P. We define the checkRange() function that computes the pages that violate this constraint. A detailed description of the checkRange function is given in Algorithm 3.

**Function** *checkRange (Property P)*

$VPS \leftarrow \{\}$; //set of violated pages ;
$R \leftarrow \text{Range(P)}$;
**if** *($\not\exists$ R)* **then**
  | return VPS;
**else**
    PGS $\leftarrow$ {page $\in$ Pages / [P::V] $\lor$ [P:=V'] $\in$ page};
    **if** *(PGS $\neq$ {})* **then**
        **for** *each page $\in$ PGS* **do**
            $PVS \leftarrow$ { V $\in$ Values / [P::V] $\lor$ [P:=V'] $\in$ page} ;
            **if** *(PVS $\neq$ {})* **then**
                **for** *each V $\in$ PVS* **do**
                    **if** *( isLiteral(V) $\land$ Range(V) $\neq$ R)* **then**
                      | VPS $\leftarrow$ VPS $\cup$ {page} ;
                      | break;
                    **end**
                    **if** *(isURI(V))* **then**
                      $CP \leftarrow$ { C $\in$ Concepts/ [category::C] $\in$ V};
                      **if** *((CP $\neq$ {}) $\land$ (R $\notin$ CP))* **then**
                        | $VPS \leftarrow$ VPS $\cup$ {page} ;
                        | break ;
                      **end**
                  **end**
                **end**
            **end**
        **end**
    **end**
    return VPS;
**end**
**end**

**Algorithm 3.** The checkRange function

The SIDM was implemented using PHP and JQuery as programming languages, WAMP as the Web server, and ARC2 as the triple store. The implementation is a simulation of a P2PSW peer. The prototype can be downloaded and tested at this address: https://sites.google.com/site/charbelrahhal/home/developed-softwares.

## 5 Integrate the Semantic Inconsistency Detection Mechanism in the First Generation of P2PSW

In this section, I present how the developed SIDM can be integrated in SWOOKI and DSMW. There are two possible cases, either the users on the peers build the semantic inconsistency rules incrementally or the set of rules is fixed and is the same on all the peers.

## 5.1  Variable Set of Semantic Consistency Rules

On every peer, the user can create and edit two types of special semantic wiki pages: concepts and properties. These pages will contain semantic annotations that represent the semantic consistency rules. Once the changes are saved, the pages will be replicated and the annotations will be extracted and stored in the triple store of the peer. These will be used as an input to the SIDM and later on to check the semantic inconsistency of the wiki pages on the user's peer. In this case, the set of semantic consistency rules will diverge on the peers and will be handled differently in SWOOKI and in DSMW.

– **In SWOOKI:** when the user specifies the semantic consistency rules locally in a concept or a property and saves. These will be integrated locally, propagated through the network, and integrated on the other peers. Hence, the concepts and the properties will be replicated on the peers (see Fig. 8). A user on a peer can check if there are changes occurred in the semantic consistency rules before running the SIDM. Either he agrees with these changes and starts the checker or he can undo them. Undoing changes exist in SWOOKI. Thanks to its optimistic replication algorithm, SWOOKI ensures that eventually after integrating all the changes, the semantic consistency rules will converge on the peers.

– **In DSMW:** every user can specify its semantic consistency rules and publishes them when he is ready. Other peers can create pull feeds and pull the rules specified by that user (see Fig. 9). The process of publishing and pulling among the peers can continue until an agreement is reached or stops when the users decide to. The SIDM can be run at any time. In case of an agreement, the semantic consistency rules will be same on the peers. DSMW also supports an undo mechanism. An advantage DSMW has over SWOOKI is that users can be aware when a change occurs in the pushfeed and pull it afterwards.

## 5.2  Same Set of Semantic Consistency Rules

Another alternative is to use a fixed set of semantic consistency rules on all the peers before to start running SIDM (see Fig. 10). First, the users on the peers will select the same specification/ ontology from a list. An ontology specifies the semantic consistency rules to be created. The list could be a special semantic wiki page or interface. It refers to a set of specifications that can be imported from different locations. Once the ontology is selected, the corresponding concept and property pages will be created with their semantic annotations. To ensure a fixed set of rules, these pages could not be directly editable; they are read only pages. Finally, the annotations are mapped into RDF statements and stored in the triple store. As a result, the semantic consistency rules will be the same on all the peers and the SIDM will have the same input everywhere. This process can apply on both SWOOKI and DSMW.

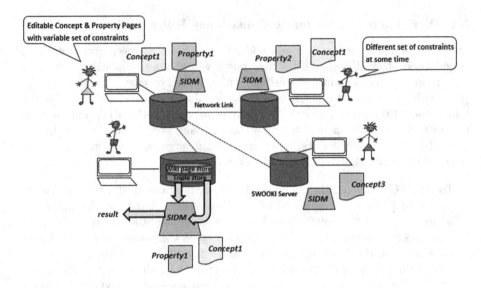

**Fig. 8.** Different semantic rules on SWOOKI

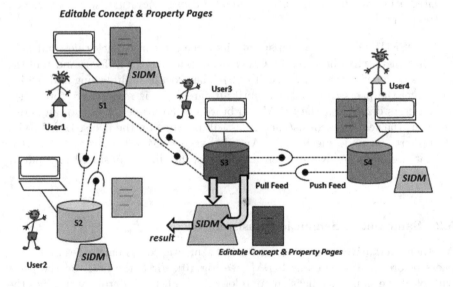

**Fig. 9.** Different semantic rules on DSMW

# 6    Running SIDM

This section presents two ways to check the semantic inconsistency either directly on a semantic wiki page or on a property/concept level. In the later one, it checks whether there are one or many semantic wiki pages that violate the constraints on a property or a concept.

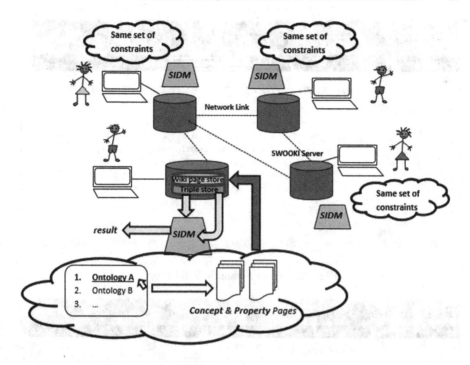

**Fig. 10.** Same set of semantic rules in SWOOKI

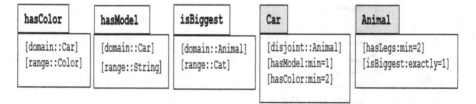

| hasColor | hasModel | isBiggest | Car | Animal |
|---|---|---|---|---|
| [domain::Car]<br>[range::Color] | [domain::Car]<br>[range::String] | [domain::Animal]<br>[range::Cat] | [disjoint::Animal]<br>[hasModel:min=1]<br>[hasColor:min=2] | [hasLegs:min=2]<br>[isBiggest:exactly=1] |

**Fig. 11.** Property and Concept Pages with their constraints

## 6.1   Check Consistency on a Semantic Wiki Page Level

Consider that in the P2PSW there are only one semantic wiki page "Jaguar", three property pages "hasColor", "hasModel" and "isBiggest", and two concept pages "Animal" and "Car". The property and concept pages are shown in Fig. 11. We want to check the semantic consistency of the "Jaguar" page. The annotations in "Jaguar" indicate that Jaguar is at the same time a car and an animal. This is could be obtained by the edition of "Jaguar" page on two different peers and the current wiki page content is the result of the automatic changes merge.

First, we click on "Check Consistency" tab (see Fig. 12) on the "Jaguar" page. When the tab is clicked, the SIDM is executed and the result is displayed in a check consistency page (see Fig. 13). It shows that the "Jaguar" page is inconsis-

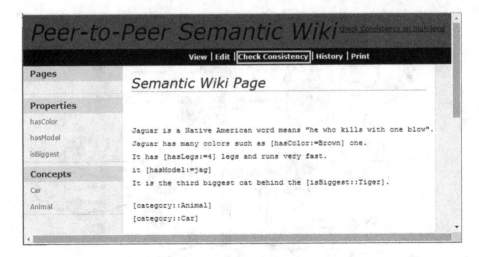

**Fig. 12.** Jaguar Semantic Wiki Page

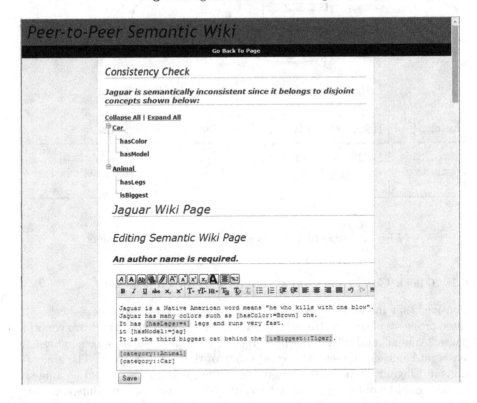

**Fig. 13.** Highlighted annotations in the check consistency page

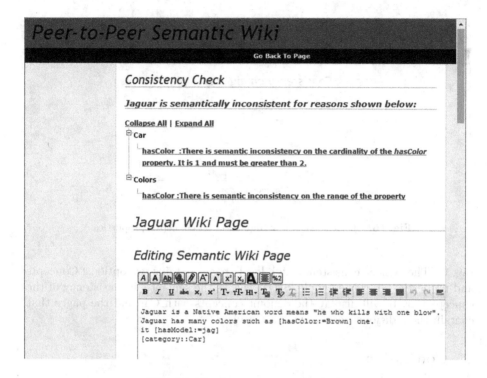

**Fig. 14.** The Jaguar page rechecked

tent since it belongs to two disjoint concepts Car and Animal. The inconsistent concepts are visualized via a treeview. The nodes in the treeview show these concepts along with their properties, they can be expanded or collapsed. We can choose to remove all the annotations in the page related to animal. By clicking on the Animal tree node, all the concerned annotations will be highlighted and can be easily removed. We can copy the deleted lines into another wiki page that can be called Jaguar Animal.

Another check of the page consistency (see Fig. 14) shows that the page is still inconsistent. It points to two types of inconsistency found in the page. The "Jaguar" page is a Car and has only one color property. However, the semantic consistency rules in Car Concept page specify that every car should have at least two colors. In addition, the range of hasColor property is a literal in the "Jaguar" page ([hasColor:=Brown]) which violates the semantic consistency rule in Color Property page that determines the range of hasColor property as an instance of a Color concept. In this case, we can make the necessary changes in the "Jaguar" page. A last check on the page will show that "Jaguar" is semantically consistent.

## 6.2   Check Consistency on a Concept/Property Level

We associated with every semantic wiki page a "Check Consistency on high level" link (see Fig. 12) which will open a special wiki page in the browser that looks like

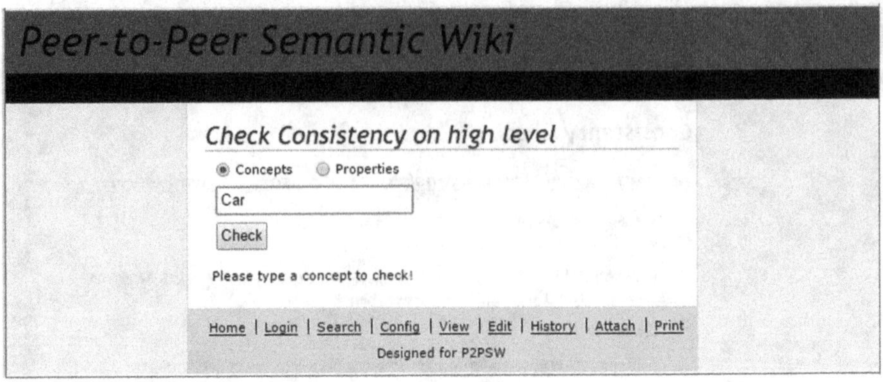

**Fig. 15.** Check consistency high level on concepts/properties

Fig. 15. The "Check consistency high level" page contains two options: Concepts and properties. In this example, SIDM checks the semantic inconsistency of the concept Car. It will display the disjoint concepts with Car and the pages that contain these disjoint concepts via a treeview.

## 7  Conclusion

This section gives an evaluation of the approach and points to perspectives and future works. The research work conducted focused on building a second generation of P2PSW by providing them with a semantic inconsistency detection mechanism. The SIDM improves the quality of the structured data in P2PSW, and consequently their functionality and the knowledge extraction.

The development of SIDM followed many steps: (1) defining the semantic inconsistency in the context of P2PSW, (2) defining the semantic rules and the way they can be integrated in the wiki, and (3) developing an algorithm for the detection of the semantic inconsistency on different levels. As a result, we can detect the inconsistency of the entire P2PSW. The SIDM not only detects the inconsistency existence but also specifies the inconsistent annotations. At the end, SIDM was implemented and tests were ran to remove any bugs and optimize SIDM algorithm.

SIDM is designed for P2PSW but it can be integrated in any semantic wiki that manipulates the annotations as typed links such as Semantic MediaWiki. This is can be done easily since SIDM was implemented in PHP which is used in Semantic MediaWiki.

The complexity of the inconsistency detection algorithm depends on the number of the annotations in the wiki pages and on the number of semantic wiki pages checked at the same time. To detect the inconsistency, SIDM can extract first the required information from the store using a graph in one pass and make the check on it. It means that every check requires only one request to the triple store. Triple stores were designed to be very scalable. They can store billions of triples, handle a large number of requests and answer them in very short time since they use different indexations. Currently, we are conducting user studies to evaluate our approach. These studies will help us to enhance the approach and the functionality in the P2PSW in general.

# References

1. Skaf-Molli, H., Rahhal, C., Molli, P.: Peer-to-peer semantic wikis. In: Bhowmick, S.S., Küng, J., Wagner, R. (eds.) DEXA 2009. LNCS, vol. 5690, pp. 196–213. Springer, Heidelberg (2009). doi:10.1007/978-3-642-03573-9_16
2. Meilender, T., Jay, N., Lieber, J., Palomares, F.: Semantic wiki engines: a state of the art. Semantic Web J. (2010)
3. Rahhal, C., Yactin, H.: Semantic wikis distributed on structured peer-to-peer networks. In: CSCEET 2017: The Fourth International Conference on Computer Science, Computer Engineering, and Education Technologies, 26–28 April 2017
4. Saito, Y., Shapiro, M.: Optimistic replication. ACM Comput. Surv. **37**, 42–81 (2005). doi:10.1145/1057977.1057980
5. Oster, G., Urso, P., Molli, P., Imine, A.: Data consistency for P2P Collaborative editing. In CSCW'06: ACM Conference on Computer Supported Cooperative Work, pp. 259–268, 4–8 November (2006). doi:10.1145/1180875.1180916
6. Weiss, S., Urso, P., Molli, P.: Logoot: a scalable optimistic replication algorithm for collaborative editing on P2P networks. In: ICDCS 2009: 29th IEEE International Conference on Distributed Computing Systems, pp. 404–412, 22–26 June 2009. doi:10.1109/ICDCS.2009.75
7. Buffa, M., Gandon, F., Ereteo, G., Sander, P., Faron, C.: SweetWiki: a semantic wiki. J. Web Semant. **6**, 84–97 (2008). doi:10.1016/j.websem.2007.11.003
8. Hoehndorf, R., et al.: BOWiki: an ontology-based wiki for annotation of data and integration of knowledge in biology. J. BMC Bioinf. **10**, May 2009. doi:10.1186/1471-2105-10-S5-S5
9. Rahhal, C., Skaf-Molli, H., Molli, P.: Swooki, un wiki sémantique sur réseau pair-à-pair. Journal Ingénierie des Systèmes d'Information (ISI) **14**(1), 117–140 (2009). doi:10.3166/isi.14.1.117-140, Lavoisier
10. Rahhal, C., Skaf-Molli, H., Molli, P., Weiss, S.: Multi-synchronous collaborative semantic wikis. In: Vossen, G., Long, D.D.E., Yu, J.X. (eds.) WISE 2009. LNCS, vol. 5802, pp. 115–129. Springer, Heidelberg (2009). doi:10.1007/978-3-642-04409-0_17
11. OWL working group: Web Ontology Language (OWL), 11 December 2012. https://www.w3.org/OWL,
12. Yang, S., Tan, H., Jinzhao, W.: Semantic Consistency Checking in Building Ontology from Heterogeneous Sources. J. Appl. Math. vol. 2014 (2014). doi:10.1155/2014/181938
13. Han, X., Sun, L.: Semantic consistency: a local subspace based method for distant supervised relation extraction. In: Proceedings of the 52nd Annual Meeting of the Association for Computational Linguistics, Baltimore, MD, USA, 22–27 June 2014
14. Harris, S., Seaborne, A.: SPARQL 1.1 Query Language. W3C recommendation, 21 March 2013. https://www.w3.org/TR/sparql11-query/

# Formalizing a Paraconsistent Logic in the Isabelle Proof Assistant

Jørgen Villadsen[(⊠)] and Anders Schlichtkrull

DTU Compute, Technical University of Denmark,
2800 Kongens Lyngby, Denmark
jovi@dtu.dk

**Abstract.** We present a formalization of a so-called paraconsistent logic that avoids the catastrophic explosiveness of inconsistency in classical logic. The paraconsistent logic has a countably infinite number of non-classical truth values. We show how to use the proof assistant Isabelle to formally prove theorems in the logic as well as meta-theorems about the logic. In particular, we formalize a meta-theorem that allows us to reduce the infinite number of truth values to a finite number of truth values, for a given formula, and we use this result in a formalization of a small case study.

**Keywords:** Paraconsistent logic · Many-valued logic · Formalization · Isabelle proof assistant · Inconsistency · Paraconsistency

## 1 Introduction

Proof assistants are computer programs that assist users in conducting proofs. In general, proof assistants are useful tools both for clarifying concepts and for catching mistakes [14]. In addition, proof assistants are often able to perform calculations in different ways using rewriting rules or code generation. We use the Isabelle proof assistant [28,29], more precisely Isabelle's default higher-order logic called Isabelle/HOL, which includes powerful specification tools for advanced datatypes, inductive definitions and recursive functions.

### 1.1 Formalization in Proof Assistants

Today's proof assistants use proof systems with axioms and rules as famously characterized in the beginning of Kurt Gödel's seminal paper from 1931 on the Incompleteness Theorems [15]:

> The development of mathematics toward greater precision has led, as is well known, to the formalization of large tracts of it, so that one can prove any theorem using nothing but a few mechanical rules.

A. Hameurlain et al. (Eds.): TLDKS XXXIV, LNCS 10620, pp. 92–122, 2017.
https://doi.org/10.1007/978-3-662-55947-5_5

Modern computers are indeed excellent at following such mechanical rules used in proof systems. A book about "the seventeen provers of the world" included formalizations of a proof of the irrationality of $\sqrt{2}$ from researchers using various proof assistants and automatic theorem provers [48]. Arguably the two most used proof assistants with large mathematical libraries are Coq [4] and Isabelle [28,29] — both the results of more than 30 years of research in automated reasoning.

The creator of Isabelle, Lawrence C. Paulson, states in a recent paper on the first formalization of Gödel's Incompleteness Theorems [30]:

> Note that this paper contains no definitions or proofs as conventionally understood in mathematics; rather, it describes definitions and formal proofs that have been conducted in Isabelle/HOL, and lessons learned from them.

A formalization can catch mistakes, small or big, in definitions, theorems and proofs. Furthermore formalizations bring attention to vague specifications and make it easier to experiment with variants of definitions and theorems.

We return to the ins and outs of formalization in Isabelle in a moment.

## 1.2 Paraconsistency

In brief, paraconsistency is about handling contradictions in a coherent way, and many approaches have been investigated [1,2,9,11,31,32,46]. In classical logic there are only two truth values and everything follows from a contradiction, but in a paraconsistent logic not everything follows from a contradiction.

In the present paper we formalize the syntax and semantics of a many-valued paraconsistent logic with a countably infinite number of truth values [20,40–43]. We do not consider any proof systems for our particular paraconsistent logic, but we can prove theorems and non-theorems using the semantics like it is done with truth tables for classical propositional logic. However, since our paraconsistent logic has infinitely many truth values, it is far from obvious that finite truth tables suffice.

Although we in the present paper formalize a particular many-valued paraconsistent logic, the logic can be changed or even replaced in the formalization. Isabelle would then show which formal theorems and proofs need to be adapted.

It is helpful to distinguish between weak and strong paraconsistency, quoting Weber [46]:

> Roughly, weak paraconsistency is the cluster concept that
> - any apparent contradictions are always due to human error;
> - classical logic is preferable, and in a better world where humans did not err, we would use classical logic;
> - no true theory would ever contain an inconsistency.

This is our view on the matter, however, there is another view, again quoting Weber [46]:

On the other side, strong paraconsistency includes ideas like
- Some contradictions may not be errors;
- classical logic is wrong in principle;
- some true theories may actually be inconsistent.

The proof assistant Isabelle uses classical logic and it seems hard to adhere to strong paraconsistency then.

The standard definition of paraconsistency is in terms of non-explosion [46]:

A logic is paraconsistent iff it is not the case for all sentences $A$, $B$ that $A, \neg A \vdash B$.

However, in our paraconsistent logic we have nothing on the left-hand side of the turnstile ($\vdash$) so we instead consider the following statement:

$$\vdash A \wedge \neg A \rightarrow B$$

In order to illustrate the notion of entailment we introduce a small case study. Classical logic is problematic in, for example, multi-agent systems, since the belief base of an agent very well could contain contradictory beliefs and thus be inconsistent. For example, as a small case study, consider an agent with a set of atomic beliefs (item 0) and a few simple rules:

0. $P \wedge Q \wedge \neg R$
1. $P \wedge Q \rightarrow R$
2. $R \rightarrow S$

This leaves the agent with contradictory beliefs, namely $R$ and $\neg R$, so the agent might start behaving in an undesirable way if it uses classical logic. It could now believe that $\neg P$, or $\neg Q$ — or even $\varphi$ for any formula $\varphi$. Using our paraconsistent logic this is not the case [20]. We return to the case study in Sect. 8.

In multi-agent systems where agents have to take into account the beliefs of other agents, it can be difficult to use other approaches like belief revision [17] because belief revision seems to be a rather strong assumption about the capabilities of other agents whereas our many-valued paraconsistent logic is "just" a generalization of classical logic with respect to both syntax (new operators) and semantics (more truth values). Think of a judge who has conflicting arguments of the prosecutor and the defender of a culprit. Such a reasoner needs to take an unbiased, impartial point of view without the possibility of coercing neither the prosecutor nor the defender to change their belief in favor of the counterparty.

## 1.3   Formalization of Logic

We formally prove theorems in the logic as well as theorems about the logic. The proofs are checked by the Isabelle proof assistant [28, 29]. By submission to the online Archive of Formal Proofs we make sure that the proofs are maintained continuously against the current stable release of Isabelle [37]:

http://isa-afp.org/browser_info/current/AFP/Paraconsistency

The above link provides PDF documents with or without proofs and the theory file can be browsed online. The Archive of Formal Proofs has mid 2017 almost 100,000 theorems and lemmas in total and covers numerous advanced topics in mathematics, logic and computer science:

http://isa-afp.org/statistics.shtml

Since the start in 2004 more than 250 authors have contributed. There are 42 entries in the logic category. For example, Paulson's formalization of Gödel's Incompleteness Theorems is in the Archive of Formal Proofs [30] and so are two recent formalizations of proof systems:

1. Jensen, Schlichtkrull and Villadsen [19] formalize a declarative first-order prover with equality based on John Harrison's *Handbook of Practical Logic and Automated Reasoning* and the entire prover can be executed within Isabelle as a very simple interactive proof assistant.
2. Michaelis and Nipkow [25] formalize proof systems for classical propositional logic and prove the most important meta-theoretic results about semantics and proofs: compactness, soundness, completeness, translations between proof systems, cut-elimination, interpolation and model existence.

These formalizations as well as our work on paraconsistency are in the repository IsaFoL, Isabelle Formalization of Logic, with the goal to develop lemma libraries and methodology for formalizing modern research in automated reasoning:

https://bitbucket.org/isafol/isafol/

The repository gives an overview of recent formalizations of logics in the Isabelle proof assistant. A state-of-the-art approach to the formalization of soundness and completeness results for logics has been developed by Blanchette, Popescu and Traytel [6] and the formalization is available in the Archive of Formal Proofs, but paraconsistent and/or many-valued logics are not considered.

## 1.4   The Isabelle Proof Assistant

One of Isabelle's central components is the Isar language for writing proofs [47]. The language bears resemblance to logical systems, handwritten mathematical proofs and programming languages.

It is similar to logical systems, in particular natural deduction, in that formulas can be proved by breaking them down into smaller parts using appropriate inference rules.

It is similar to mathematical paper proofs because an Isar-proof can be written as a sequence of sentences, each one following from the previous ones, that leads us towards a goal. In particular it is very similar to the structured proof style that Lamport [22,23] recommends for the 21st century.

It is similar to a programing language in that its syntax is structured and consists of various commands — these commands instruct Isabelle on how to prove the desired theorems.

Another important feature of Isar is that it allows one to mix this structured reasoning with state-of-the-art automatic theorem provers.

We illustrate the language with a simple proof of a — perhaps — surprising theorem called the drinker's paradox. The theorem states that in a bar there is a person such that if he is drinking then everybody is drinking (we use predicate $D$ for drinking). We have the following Isar proof:

```
theorem "∃x. D x ⟶ (∀x. D x)"
proof cases
    assume "∀x. D x"
    then have "P ⟶ (∀x. D x)" for P ..
    then show ?thesis ..
next
    assume "¬ (∀x. D x)"
    then have "∃x. ¬ D x" by simp
    then obtain a where nda: "¬ D a" ..
    have "D a ⟶ (∀x. D x)"
    proof
        assume "D a"
        then show "∀x. D x" using nda by metis
    qed
    then show ?thesis ..
qed
```

Even for the uninitiated the proof should be at least somewhat readable because keywords such as **theorem, proof, assume, then** and **have** are well known from mathematical literature. Furthermore, each sentence is written in Isabelle/HOL, which has a similar notation to e.g. first-order logic (FOL).

Let us describe the Isar-proof in detail. After we state the theorem comes a proof block starting with **proof** *cases* and ending with the **qed** on the very last line. This proof block allows us to do proof by cases on whether $\forall x. D\ x$ is true or not and in both cases we are obliged to prove the theorem. One can easily imagine a classical proof system with such a rule.

We start by proving the first case $\forall x. D\ x$. This proof starts with **assume** $\forall x. D\ x$ and ends with **then show** *?thesis* .. two lines below. The proof is similar to a paper proof of a sequence of three sentences – each line corresponding to a sentence. Here *?thesis* refers to the theorem we are proving.

Next comes the second case $\neg(\forall x. D\ x)$. Again the proof is a sequence of sentences. To convince Isabelle that the first sentence follows from the second, we apply the proof method called *simp*, which does simplifications, by writing **by** *simp*. Next we use the **obtain** command to obtain the element $a$ that the previous sentence proved exists. After this we prove an implication using an inner proof block. Notice how the inner proof block is nested in the outer proof block. In this inner proof block we prove the implication by breaking it down structurally using the implication introduction rule from natural deduction, which states that to prove an implication we assume the antecedent and prove the consequent. Notice also that in the inner proof block we use another proof method called *metis* and additionally allow it to use the previously labelled sentence *nda*. The *metis* proof method is an automatic theorem prover.

Note that Isabelle/HOL is written in a curried style. This means that function application is written without parentheses unless necessary. An example is $D\,x$ as we saw above. Additionally $n$-argument functions are typically given a type

$$'a_1 \Rightarrow ('a_2 \Rightarrow ('a_3 \Rightarrow (\cdots \Rightarrow ('a_n \Rightarrow 'b)\cdots)))$$

or, if we drop the parentheses

$$'a_1 \Rightarrow 'a_2 \Rightarrow 'a_3 \Rightarrow \cdots \Rightarrow 'a_n \Rightarrow 'b$$

instead of

$$('a_1 \times \cdots \times 'a_n) \Rightarrow 'b.$$

Therefore, an application of, e.g., a binary function $R$ to two arguments $x$ and $y$ is written as $R\,x\,y$.

You can try to write the above proof in Isabelle. You will notice that it is easy to accidentally introduce some mistake that makes Isabelle unable to finish the proof. This is the advantage of proving theorems in Isabelle — the system is very good at catching small and big mistakes.

### 1.5  Contributions and Overview

All formulas in the present paper have been checked by the Isabelle proof assistant except for the informal presentation in Sect. 2. We must emphasize that the proofs in the paper are not generated by Isabelle or any other computer program. All proofs in the paper are word for word authored by us. Our proofs can — at least in principle — be read and checked by other Isabelle users and can also be read and checked by the Isabelle proof assistant — and have therefore been accepted for the Archive of Formal Proofs.

Our main contributions are as follows.

– In Sect. 3: A formalization of the syntax and semantics of the many-valued paraconsistent logic with many new definitions.
– In Sects. 4 and 5: A series of theorems and non-theorems of which only a few have been considered in our previous publications.
– In Sect. 6: A new analysis of the required number of truth values for counterexamples.

- In Sect. 7: A reduction theorem that was originally mentioned without proof in our extended abstract [20].
- In Sect. 8: A proposal for entailment and verification of the results for the case study presented in the present section — these results were also mentioned without proof in our extended abstract [20].

We describe related work in Sect. 9 and conclude in Sect. 10.

## 2  The Paraconsistent Logic — An Informal Presentation

By "informal" we here mean that we provide a mathematical presentation of the logic but the formalization in the Isabelle proof assistant is provided in the following sections. We describe the propositional fragment of our higher-order many-valued paraconsistent logic [43]. We follow the concise presentation in our extended abstract [20] but with some additional abbreviations.

### 2.1  Semantic Clauses and Key Equalities

We have the two classical determinate truth values $\{\bullet, \circ\}$ for truth and falsity and a countably infinite set of indeterminate truth values $\{I, II, III, \ldots\}$.

The indeterminate truth values are not ordered with respect to truth content. The only designated truth value is $\bullet$ and hence only this truth value yields the logical truths.

This use of $\bullet$ and $\circ$ for the classical truth values goes back to our previous publications [41–43] and the references therein. Note that as usual the corresponding operators are $\top$ and $\bot$ (see below).

The logic is a generalization of Łukasiewicz's three-valued logic — originally proposed 1920–30 — with the intermediate value duplicated many times and ordered such that none of the copies of this value imply other ones, but the logic differs from Łukasiewicz's many-valued logics as well as from logics based on bilattices [16].

The motivation for the logical operators is based on key equalities shown to the right of the semantic clauses. We also have $\varphi \Leftrightarrow \neg\neg\varphi$ as a key equality. Negation does not change indeterminate truth values since they are not ordered with respect to truth content. In the higher-order paraconsistent logic [41–43] the key equalities are proper equalities = corresponding to $\Leftrightarrow$ here. The key equalities do not provide an axiomatization as such but rather they provide for each logical operator the semantic clauses except for the default case.

Note that in the semantic clauses several cases may apply if and only if they agree on the result and that the semantic clauses work for classical logic too. Atoms are interpreted by the basic semantic clause and $\top$ by $[\![\top]\!] = \bullet$.

$$[\![\neg\varphi]\!] = \begin{cases} \bullet & \text{if } [\![\varphi]\!] = \circ \\ \circ & \text{if } [\![\varphi]\!] = \bullet \\ [\![\varphi]\!] & \text{otherwise} \end{cases} \qquad \begin{array}{c} \top \Leftrightarrow \neg\bot \\ \bot \Leftrightarrow \neg\top \end{array}$$

$$[\![\varphi \wedge \psi]\!] \;=\; \begin{cases} [\![\varphi]\!] & \text{if } [\![\varphi]\!] = [\![\psi]\!] \\ [\![\psi]\!] & \text{if } [\![\varphi]\!] = \bullet \\ [\![\varphi]\!] & \text{if } [\![\psi]\!] = \bullet \\ \circ & \text{otherwise} \end{cases} \qquad \begin{aligned} \varphi &\Leftrightarrow \varphi \wedge \varphi \\ \psi &\Leftrightarrow \top \wedge \psi \\ \varphi &\Leftrightarrow \varphi \wedge \top \end{aligned}$$

Abbreviations:

$$\bot \equiv \neg\top \qquad\qquad \varphi \vee \psi \equiv \neg(\neg\varphi \wedge \neg\psi)$$

We continue with biimplication (and we then simply obtain implication and modality as abbreviations). The semantic clauses for $\leftrightarrow$ extend the clauses for $\Leftrightarrow$, which always give a determinate truth value.

$$[\![\varphi \Leftrightarrow \psi]\!] \;=\; \begin{cases} \bullet & \text{if } [\![\varphi]\!] = [\![\psi]\!] \\ \circ & \text{otherwise} \end{cases}$$

$$[\![\varphi \leftrightarrow \psi]\!] \;=\; \begin{cases} \bullet & \text{if } [\![\varphi]\!] = [\![\psi]\!] \\ [\![\psi]\!] & \text{if } [\![\varphi]\!] = \bullet \\ [\![\varphi]\!] & \text{if } [\![\psi]\!] = \bullet \\ [\![\neg\psi]\!] & \text{if } [\![\varphi]\!] = \circ \\ [\![\neg\varphi]\!] & \text{if } [\![\psi]\!] = \circ \\ \circ & \text{otherwise} \end{cases} \qquad \begin{aligned} \top &\Leftrightarrow \varphi \leftrightarrow \varphi \\ \psi &\Leftrightarrow \top \leftrightarrow \psi \\ \varphi &\Leftrightarrow \varphi \leftrightarrow \top \\ \neg\psi &\Leftrightarrow \bot \leftrightarrow \psi \\ \neg\varphi &\Leftrightarrow \varphi \leftrightarrow \bot \end{aligned}$$

Abbreviations:

$$\Box\varphi \equiv \varphi \Leftrightarrow \top \qquad \neg\varphi \equiv \Box\neg\varphi \qquad \nabla\varphi \equiv \neg\Box(\varphi \vee \neg\varphi)$$

$$\varphi \Rightarrow \psi \equiv \varphi \Leftrightarrow \varphi \wedge \psi \qquad\qquad \varphi \rightarrow \psi \equiv \varphi \leftrightarrow \varphi \wedge \psi$$

$$\varphi \mathbin{⋏} \psi \equiv \Box(\varphi \wedge \psi) \qquad\qquad \varphi \mathbin{W} \psi \equiv \Box(\varphi \vee \psi)$$

## 2.2 Truth Tables

Although we have a countably infinite set of truth values we can investigate the logic by truth tables since the indeterminate truth values are not ordered with respect to truth content.

In order to grasp the main properties of the operators we need just the two indeterminate truth values I and II as in the following truth tables.

| □ | |
|---|---|
| • | • |
| ∘ | ∘ |
| I | ∘ |

| ∧ | • | ∘ | I | II |
|---|---|---|---|---|
| • | • | ∘ | I | II |
| ∘ | ∘ | ∘ | ∘ | ∘ |
| I | I | ∘ | I | ∘ |
| II | II | ∘ | ∘ | II |

| ∨ | • | ∘ | I | II |
|---|---|---|---|---|
| • | • | • | • | • |
| ∘ | • | ∘ | I | II |
| I | • | I | I | • |
| II | • | II | • | II |

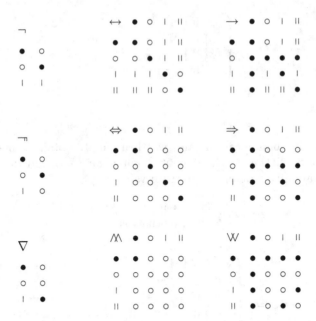

Observe that with respect to validity, viz. the classical determinate truth value •
for truth, the operators ¬ and ⊣ behave the same and likewise for the operators
⇔ and ↔ and ⇒ and →, respectively.

The truth tables are obtained from the semantic clauses. The formalization
includes features for this calculation but since the truth tables are solely for
informal presentation purposes we have typeset them using the same symbols
as used in the semantics clauses. However, Sect. 6 contains a few truth tables
calculated by Isabelle. The theory file for the formalization includes all calculated
truth tables.

## 3    Syntax and Semantics

We formalize the syntax and semantics of the many-valued paraconsistent logic
as follows. For the syntax we first define the propositional symbols (*id*) as a
simple abbreviation for text strings and the formulas (*fm*) as a recursive datatype
(almost as the productions for a context-free grammar).

**type-synonym** *id* = *string*

**datatype** *fm* =
                *Pro id* |
                *Truth* |
                *Neg′ fm* |
                *Con′ fm fm* |
                *Eql fm fm* |
                *Eql′ fm fm*

We then define the remaining operators as abbreviations. We do this with Isabelle's **abbreviation** command by giving the name of the abbreviated operator, e.g. *Falsity*, and thereafter its type, e.g. *fm*. After the **where** keyword we write the equality that defines the abbreviation, e.g. *Falsity* $\equiv$ *Neg' Truth*.

**abbreviation** *Falsity* :: *fm* **where** *Falsity* $\equiv$ *Neg' Truth*

**abbreviation** *Dis'* :: *fm* $\Rightarrow$ *fm* $\Rightarrow$ *fm*
  **where** *Dis' p q* $\equiv$ *Neg' (Con' (Neg' p) (Neg' q))*

**abbreviation** *Imp* :: *fm* $\Rightarrow$ *fm* $\Rightarrow$ *fm* **where** *Imp p q* $\equiv$ *Eql p (Con' p q)*

**abbreviation** *Imp'* :: *fm* $\Rightarrow$ *fm* $\Rightarrow$ *fm* **where** *Imp' p q* $\equiv$ *Eql' p (Con' p q)*

**abbreviation** *Box* :: *fm* $\Rightarrow$ *fm* **where** *Box p* $\equiv$ *Eql p Truth*

**abbreviation** *Neg* :: *fm* $\Rightarrow$ *fm* **where** *Neg p* $\equiv$ *Box (Neg' p)*

**abbreviation** *Con* :: *fm* $\Rightarrow$ *fm* $\Rightarrow$ *fm* **where** *Con p q* $\equiv$ *Box (Con' p q)*

**abbreviation** *Dis* :: *fm* $\Rightarrow$ *fm* $\Rightarrow$ *fm* **where** *Dis p q* $\equiv$ *Box (Dis' p q)*

**abbreviation** *Cla* :: *fm* $\Rightarrow$ *fm* **where** *Cla p* $\equiv$ *Dis (Box p) (Eql p Falsity)*

**abbreviation** *Nab* :: *fm* $\Rightarrow$ *fm* **where** *Nab p* $\equiv$ *Neg (Cla p)*

The truth values are the two determinate truth values and the countably infinite number of indeterminate truth values. We also define a useful abbreviation for negation (*eval-neg*). This function turns *Det False* into *Det True* and vice versa, but does not change the value of indeterminate truth values. The function is defined by a case-expression that matches $x$ with the patterns *Det False*, *Det True* and *Indet n* (where $n$ can be any value), and returns the value to the right of the corresponding arrow. Finally, we define the semantics as a recursive function on the structure of the given formula (*eval*) using the **fun** command. The function is defined by a number of equations. In one of the equations we again use a case expression. This time the case expression contains a number of dummy variables (wildcard patterns), which are typeset as dashes (-). Each one of these will independently match with anything.

**datatype** *tv* = *Det bool* | *Indet nat*

**abbreviation** (*input*) *eval-neg* :: *tv* $\Rightarrow$ *tv*
**where**
  *eval-neg x* $\equiv$
    (
    *case x of*
      *Det False* $\Rightarrow$ *Det True* |
      *Det True* $\Rightarrow$ *Det False* |
      *Indet n* $\Rightarrow$ *Indet n*

)

**fun** *eval* :: (*id* ⇒ *tv*) ⇒ *fm* ⇒ *tv*
**where**
  *eval i* (*Pro s*) = *i s* |
  *eval i Truth* = *Det True* |
  *eval i* (*Neg' p*) = *eval-neg* (*eval i p*) |
  *eval i* (*Con' p q*) =
    (
      *if eval i p* = *eval i q then eval i p else*
      *if eval i p* = *Det True then eval i q else*
      *if eval i q* = *Det True then eval i p else Det False*
    ) |
  *eval i* (*Eql p q*) =
    (
      *if eval i p* = *eval i q then Det True else Det False*
    ) |
  *eval i* (*Eql' p q*) =
    (
      *if eval i p* = *eval i q then Det True else*
        (
          *case* (*eval i p*, *eval i q*) *of*
          (*Det True*, -) ⇒ *eval i q* |
          (-, *Det True*) ⇒ *eval i p* |
          (*Det False*, -) ⇒ *eval-neg* (*eval i q*) |
          (-, *Det False*) ⇒ *eval-neg* (*eval i p*) |
          - ⇒ *Det False*
        )
    )

We prove a few useful results about the semantics. We first prove a formulation of the semantics for *Eql'* and *Neg'* without the *eval-neg* abbreviation. We then prove that a double negation with *Neg'* does not change the semantics.

  **theorem** *eval-equality*:
    *eval i* (*Eql' p q*) =
      (
        *if eval i p* = *eval i q then Det True else*
        *if eval i p* = *Det True then eval i q else*
        *if eval i q* = *Det True then eval i p else*
        *if eval i p* = *Det False then eval i* (*Neg' q*) *else*
        *if eval i q* = *Det False then eval i* (*Neg' p*) *else*
        *Det False*
      )
    **by** (*cases eval i p*; *cases eval i q*) *simp-all*

  **theorem** *eval-negation*:
    *eval i* (*Neg' p*) =
      (
        *if eval i p* = *Det False then Det True else*

> *if eval i p = Det True then Det False else*
> *eval i p*
> )
> **by** (*cases eval i p*) *simp-all*

**corollary** *eval i* (*Cla p*) = *eval i* (*Box* (*Dis' p* (*Neg' p*)))
  **using** *eval-negation*
  **by** *simp*

**lemma** *double-negation*: *eval i p* = *eval i* (*Neg'* (*Neg' p*))
  **using** *eval-negation*
  **by** *simp*

We define the notion of valid formulas by quantifying over all interpretations.

**definition** *valid* :: *fm* ⇒ *bool*
**where**
  *valid p* ≡ ∀ *i*. *eval i p* = *Det True*

**proposition** *valid Truth* **and** ¬ *valid Falsity*
  **unfolding** *valid-def*
  **by** *simp-all*

The last proposition shows that the logic is consistent in the sense that there is a formula which is a theorem and not all formulas are theorems. The proof is explained in the next section.

# 4    Various Theorems and Proof Styles

We prove a series of theorems and non-theorems most of which are schemata. The purpose of the following quite long list is twofold: to investigate our paraconsistent logic, and secondly, to show a number of proof styles.

The first seven propositions are proved by unfolding the definition of validity and then simplifying the result to a true atomic proposition. The next two propositions are proved by the *metis* proof method as explained in Sect. 1. We let *metis* use a number of lemmas including *eval-equality*, *eval-negation* and two lemmas about respectively truth values and evaluation, that Isabelle proved implicitly when we defined these notions. Isabelle's powerful Sledgehammer tool has been used to obtain the proofs [5].

The next proposition — *P* is not valid — is proved by the *auto* proof method, which does a combination of simplification and classical reasoning. The following proposition — ¬*P* is not valid — is proved by manually providing a counterexample – unfortunately Sledgehammer cannot find a proof for this proposition. The counterexample is the interpretation that maps everything to *True*. It is written as a λ-expression as known from the λ-calculus. In general, a λ-expression λx.F x represents the function that takes any x as input and returns F x.

Hereafter comes a proposition stating that the validity of $p$ implies the non-validity of $Neg'\,p$. This is written using keywords **assumes** and **shows**, which logically is the same as if we had explicitly written an implication $\longrightarrow$, but will make theorems easier to read when there are many assumptions. Several of the following propositions are written in the same style.

The remaining propositions are proved using more or less the same proof methods (one proposition requires the so-called *force* proof method that can prove some propositions where *auto* gives up).

Some propositions have assumptions and in the proof the special fact *assms* can be used to refer to the assumptions.

In Isabelle there is no technical difference between the keywords **theorem**, **corollary**, **proposition** and **lemma**. We have found it useful to always name theorems and simply take propositions to be unnamed theorems. Lemmas are stepping stones and must of course have names in order to be used later in proofs. A corollary is taken to be readily proved from a theorem; see the theorem named *conjunction* (after 14 propositions).

> **proposition** *valid* (*Cla* (*Box p*)) **and** ¬ *valid* (*Nab* (*Box p*))
> **unfolding** *valid-def*
> **by** *simp-all*

> **proposition** *valid* (*Cla* (*Cla p*)) **and** ¬ *valid* (*Nab* (*Nab p*))
> **unfolding** *valid-def*
> **by** *simp-all*

> **proposition** *valid* (*Cla* (*Nab p*)) **and** ¬ *valid* (*Nab* (*Cla p*))
> **unfolding** *valid-def*
> **by** *simp-all*

> **proposition** *valid* (*Box p*) $\longleftrightarrow$ *valid* (*Box* (*Box p*))
> **unfolding** *valid-def*
> **by** *simp*

> **proposition** *valid* (*Neg p*) $\longleftrightarrow$ *valid* (*Neg'\,p*)
> **unfolding** *valid-def*
> **by** *simp*

> **proposition** *valid* (*Con p q*) $\longleftrightarrow$ *valid* (*Con'\,p q*)
> **unfolding** *valid-def*
> **by** *simp*

> **proposition** *valid* (*Dis p q*) $\longleftrightarrow$ *valid* (*Dis'\,p q*)
> **unfolding** *valid-def*
> **by** *simp*

> **proposition** *valid* (*Eql p q*) $\longleftrightarrow$ *valid* (*Eql'\,p q*)
> **unfolding** *valid-def*
> **using** *eval.simps tv.inject eval-equality eval-negation*
> **by** (*metis* (*full-types*))

**proposition** *valid* (*Imp p q*) ⟷ *valid* (*Imp′ p q*)
  **unfolding** *valid-def*
  **using** *eval.simps tv.inject eval-equality eval-negation*
  **by** (*metis* (*full-types*))

**proposition** ¬ *valid* (*Pro ″p″*)
  **unfolding** *valid-def*
  **by** *auto*

**proposition** ¬ *valid* (*Neg′* (*Pro ″p″*))
**proof** –
  **have** *eval* (λ*s. Det True*) (*Neg′* (*Pro ″p″*)) = *Det False*
    **by** *simp*
  **then show** *?thesis*
    **unfolding** *valid-def*
    **using** *tv.inject*
    **by** *metis*
**qed**

**proposition assumes** *valid p* **shows** ¬ *valid* (*Neg′ p*)
  **using** *assms*
  **unfolding** *valid-def*
  **by** *simp*

**proposition assumes** *valid* (*Neg′ p*) **shows** ¬ *valid p*
  **using** *assms*
  **unfolding** *valid-def*
  **by** *force*

**proposition** *valid* (*Neg′* (*Neg′ p*)) ⟷ *valid p*
  **unfolding** *valid-def*
  **using** *double-negation*
  **by** *simp*

**theorem** *conjunction*: *valid* (*Con′ p q*) ⟷ *valid p* ∧ *valid q*
  **unfolding** *valid-def*
  **by** *auto*

**corollary assumes** *valid* (*Con′ p q*) **shows** *valid p* **and** *valid q*
  **using** *assms conjunction*
  **by** *simp-all*

**proposition assumes** *valid p* **and** *valid* (*Imp p q*) **shows** *valid q*
  **using** *assms eval.simps tv.inject*
  **unfolding** *valid-def*
  **by** (*metis* (*full-types*))

**proposition assumes** *valid p* **and** *valid* (*Imp′ p q*) **shows** *valid q*
  **using** *assms eval.simps tv.inject eval-equality*

**unfolding** *valid-def*
**by** (*metis* (*full-types*))

The key equalities from Sect. 2 can also be proved but they are omitted here. The theory file for the formalization has the details.

The preceding propositions show that our paraconsistent logic is well-behaved in many ways. For example, the last propositions prove the rule of modus ponens for both kinds of implication.

## 5    Counterexamples for Non-theorems

We introduce the possibility for restricting the domain of truth values and use it for stating counterexamples.

We first define a function *domain* that, for any given set of natural numbers, constructs the corresponding domain in our logic. It does so by turning the natural numbers in the set into indeterminate truth values using *Indet* and additionally adding the determinate truth values to the set.

We then prove the theorem *universal-domain* where the first universal set $\{n.\,True\}$ has type *nat set* and the second universal set $\{x.\,True\}$ has type *tv set*. The function *domain* provides the correspondence.

**definition** *domain* :: *nat set* $\Rightarrow$ *tv set*
**where**
    *domain* $U \equiv \{Det\ True,\ Det\ False\} \cup Indet\ `\ U$

**theorem** *universal-domain*: *domain* $\{n.\ True\} = \{x.\ True\}$
**proof** $-$
    **have** $\forall x.\ x = Det\ True \vee x = Det\ False \vee x \in range\ Indet$
        **using** *range-eqI* *tv.exhaust* *tv.inject*
        **by** *metis*
    **then show** *?thesis*
        **unfolding** *domain-def*
        **by** *blast*
**qed**

We define the notion of valid formulas restricted to a given set of indeterminate truth values. We say that a formula $p$ is valid in $U$ if it is valid considering not all indeterminate truth values, but only those from $U$. Or more precisely, if $p$ always evaluates to true in any interpretation $i$ that has *domain* $U$ as function range. In the formalization we use Isabelle/HOL's *range* function to get the range of $i$.

**definition** *valid-in* :: *nat set* $\Rightarrow$ *fm* $\Rightarrow$ *bool*
**where**
    *valid-in* $U\ p \equiv \forall i.\ range\ i \subseteq domain\ U \longrightarrow eval\ i\ p = Det\ True$

**abbreviation** *valid-boole* :: *fm* $\Rightarrow$ *bool* **where** *valid-boole* $p \equiv valid\text{-}in\ \{\}\ p$

**proposition** *valid* $p \longleftrightarrow valid\text{-}in\ \{n.\ True\}\ p$

**unfolding** *valid-def valid-in-def*
**using** *universal-domain*
**by** *simp*

**theorem** *valid-valid-in*: **assumes** *valid p* **shows** *valid-in U p*
  **using** *assms*
**unfolding** *valid-in-def valid-def*
**by** *simp*

**theorem** *transfer*: **assumes** ¬ *valid-in U p* **shows** ¬ *valid p*
  **using** *assms valid-valid-in*
**by** *blast*

In particular the above theorem (*transfer*) is useful in order to prove that a formula is not valid. As a particular example we will show that $P \wedge \neg P \to Q$ is not valid. First we show that it is valid in the boolean logic. Next we show that it is not valid in *domain* {1}. We do this by providing a counterexample. With the **let** command we define the counterexample *?i* (the **let** command requires that we have this question mark). The counterexample is first defined as returning *Indet 1* on any input, and is then modified (using :=) to return *Det False* on input *q*. The proof uses the **moreover** and **ultimately** commands. This works in the way that the statements just before each of the moreover commands are collected and used to prove the statement after the **ultimately** command. After proving this result, we use it together with *transfer* to prove that the formula is not valid.

**abbreviation** (*input*) *Explosion* :: *fm* ⇒ *fm* ⇒ *fm*
**where**
  *Explosion p q* ≡ *Imp'* (*Con' p* (*Neg' p*)) *q*

**proposition** *valid-boole* (*Explosion* (*Pro* ''p'') (*Pro* ''q''))
  **unfolding** *valid-in-def*
**proof** (*rule*; *rule*)
  **fix** *i* :: *id* ⇒ *tv*
  **assume** *range i* ⊆ *domain* {}
  **then have**
    *i* ''p'' ∈ {*Det True, Det False*}
    *i* ''q'' ∈ {*Det True, Det False*}
    **unfolding** *domain-def*
  **by** *auto*
  **then show** *eval i* (*Explosion* (*Pro* ''p'') (*Pro* ''q'')) = *Det True*
    **by** (*cases i* ''p''; *cases i* ''q'') *simp-all*
**qed**

**lemma** *explosion-counterexample*:
  ¬ *valid-in* {1} (*Explosion* (*Pro* ''p'') (*Pro* ''q''))
**proof** −
  **let** *?i* = (λ*s. Indet 1*)(''q'' := *Det False*)
  **have** *range ?i* ⊆ *domain* {1}

    **unfolding** *domain-def*
    **by** (*simp add: image-subset-iff*)
   **moreover have** *eval ?i* (*Explosion* (*Pro* ''*p*'') (*Pro* ''*q*'')) = *Indet 1*
    **by** *simp*
   **moreover have** *Indet 1 $\neq$ Det True*
    **by** *simp*
   **ultimately show** *?thesis*
    **unfolding** *valid-in-def*
    **by** *metis*
  **qed**

  **theorem** *explosion-not-valid*: ¬ *valid* (*Explosion* (*Pro* ''*p*'') (*Pro* ''*q*''))
   **using** *explosion-counterexample transfer*
   **by** *simp*

The last theorem shows that the many-valued logic is a paraconsistent logic since $P \wedge \neg P \to Q$ is not valid.

# 6   On the Number of Truth Values

For the normal two-value boolean propositional logic we can decide if a formula is valid or not by enumerating all interpretations and checking if they satisfy our formula. This approach will clearly not work for our many-valued logic since there are infinitely many truth values and thus also infinitely many interpretations.

However, it turns out that we do not need to consider all possibilities of truth values. For any formula there is a finite subset that it suffices to check. In this section we will argue for a lower bound on the size of this subset. Specifically we will argue that for an arbitrary formula containing $n$ different propositional symbols, we need to consider interpretations with $n$ different indeterminate truth values.

We first consider the simple case of formulas with one propositional symbol. In order to conduct the analysis, we first prove that if the range of an interpretation is a subset of *domain U*, then any formula will evaluate to a value in *domain U* under this interpretation. Then we consider the example of *Cla p* where *Cla* is the unary operator that evaluates to true when its operand evaluates to a *Cla*ssical truth value. Let us introduce the informal notation $\Delta$ for *Cla*. We prove that $\Delta p$ is valid in all boolean interpretations. Next we prove that it is not valid in *domain* {1}. Therefore we can conclude that considering 0 indeterminate truth values is not enough – we need to consider at least 1. We have also printed its truth table for illustration. In the calculated truth table below * is used for • and *o* is used for ◦. The functions *unary* and *binary* return truth tables as strings for unary and binary operators, respectively, and the theory file for the formalization has the details (about 50 lines of code, cf. [45]). The proof method *code-simp* performs the calculations of the truth table strings.

**lemma** *ranges:* **assumes** *range i ⊆ domain U* **shows** *eval i p ∈ domain U*
  **using** *assms*
  **unfolding** *domain-def*
  **by** *(induct p) auto*

**proposition**
  *unary (Cla (Pro "p")) [Det True, Det False, Indet 1] = ''*
  \*
  \*
  *o*
*''*

  **by** *code-simp*

**proposition** *valid-boole (Cla p)*
  **unfolding** *valid-in-def*
**proof** *(rule; rule)*
  **fix** *i :: id ⇒ tv*
  **assume** *range i ⊆ domain {}*
  **then have**
    *eval i p ∈ {Det True, Det False}*
  **using** *ranges[of i {}]*
  **unfolding** *domain-def*
  **by** *auto*
  **then show** *eval i (Cla p) = Det True*
  **by** *(cases eval i p) simp-all*
**qed**

**proposition** ¬ *valid-in {1} (Cla (Pro "p"))*
**proof** −
  **let** *?i = λs. Indet 1*
  **have** *range ?i ⊆ domain {1}*
  **unfolding** *domain-def*
  **by** *(simp add: image-subset-iff)*
  **moreover have** *eval ?i (Cla (Pro "p")) = Det False*
  **by** *simp*
  **moreover have** *Det False ≠ Det True*
  **by** *simp*
  **ultimately show** *?thesis*
  **unfolding** *valid-in-def*
  **by** *metis*
**qed**

We repeat the exercise for a formula with two propositional symbols. This time we consider the formula $\Delta_2$, which is $(\Delta p \vee \Delta q) \vee (p \Leftrightarrow q)$. We prove it valid in all boolean interpretations as well as in all interpretations with *domain* $\{1\}$. Next we prove that it is not valid in *domain* $\{1, 2\}$. Therefore it is not enough to consider 1 indeterminate truth value – we need to consider at least 2.

**abbreviation** (*input*) *Cla2* :: *fm* ⇒ *fm* ⇒ *fm*
**where**
　*Cla2 p q* ≡ *Dis* (*Dis* (*Cla p*) (*Cla q*)) (*Eql p q*)

**proposition**
　*binary* (*Cla2* (*Pro "p"*) (*Pro "q"*))
　　[*Det True, Det False, Indet 1, Indet 2*] = *"*
　\*\*\*\*
　\*\*\*\*
　\*\*\*0
　\*\*0\*
*"*

　**by** *code-simp*

**proposition** *valid-boole* (*Cla2 p q*)
　**unfolding** *valid-in-def*
**proof** (*rule; rule*)
　**fix** *i* :: *id* ⇒ *tv*
　**assume** *range*: *range i* ⊆ *domain* {}
　**then have**
　　*eval i p* ∈ {*Det True, Det False*}
　　*eval i q* ∈ {*Det True, Det False*}
　　**using** *ranges*[*of i* {}]
　　**unfolding** *domain-def*
　　**by** *auto*
　**then show** *eval i* (*Cla2 p q*) = *Det True*
　　**by** (*cases eval i p*; *cases eval i q*) *simp-all*
**qed**

**proposition** *valid-in* {*1*} (*Cla2 p q*)
　**unfolding** *valid-in-def*
**proof** (*rule; rule*)
　**fix** *i* :: *id* ⇒ *tv*
　**assume** *range*: *range i* ⊆ *domain* {*1*}
　**then have**
　　*eval i p* ∈ {*Det True, Det False, Indet 1*}
　　*eval i q* ∈ {*Det True, Det False, Indet 1*}
　　**using** *ranges*[*of i* {*1*}]
　　**unfolding** *domain-def*
　　**by** *auto*
　**then show** *eval i* (*Cla2 p q*) = *Det True*
　　**by** (*cases eval i p*; *cases eval i q*) *simp-all*
**qed**

**proposition** ¬ *valid-in* {*1, 2*} (*Cla2* (*Pro "p"*) (*Pro "q"*))
**proof** −
　**let** *?i* = (λ*s. Indet 1*)(*"q"* := *Indet 2*)
　**have** *range ?i* ⊆ *domain* {*1, 2*}
　　**unfolding** *domain-def*
　　**by** (*simp add*: *image-subset-iff*)

**moreover have** *eval ?i* (*Cla2* (*Pro* ''*p*'') (*Pro* ''*q*'')) = *Det False*
  **by** *simp*
**moreover have** *Det False* $\neq$ *Det True*
  **by** *simp*
**ultimately show** *?thesis*
  **unfolding** *valid-in-def*
  **by** *metis*
**qed**

We repeat the exercise for a formula with three propositional symbols. This time we consider the formula $\Delta_3$, which is $(\Delta p \lor \Delta q \lor \Delta r) \lor ((p \Leftrightarrow q) \lor (p \Leftrightarrow r) \lor (q \Leftrightarrow r))$. We prove it valid in all boolean interpretations as well as in all interpretations with *domain* $\{1\}$ and *domain* $\{1, 2\}$. Next we prove that it is not valid in *domain* $\{1, 2, 3\}$. Therefore it is not enough to consider 2 indeterminate truth values – we need to consider at least 3.

**abbreviation** (*input*) *Cla3* :: *fm* $\Rightarrow$ *fm* $\Rightarrow$ *fm* $\Rightarrow$ *fm*
**where**
  *Cla3 p q r* $\equiv$ *Dis* (*Dis* (*Cla p*) (*Dis* (*Cla q*) (*Cla r*)))
  (*Dis* (*Eql p q*) (*Dis* (*Eql p r*) (*Eql q r*)))

**proposition** *valid-boole* (*Cla3 p q r*)
  **unfolding** *valid-in-def*
**proof** (*rule*; *rule*)
  **fix** *i* :: *id* $\Rightarrow$ *tv*
  **assume** *range i* $\subseteq$ *domain* {}
  **then have**
    *eval i p* $\in$ {*Det True*, *Det False*}
    *eval i q* $\in$ {*Det True*, *Det False*}
    *eval i r* $\in$ {*Det True*, *Det False*}
    **using** *ranges*[*of i* {}]
    **unfolding** *domain-def*
    **by** *auto*
  **then show** *eval i* (*Cla3 p q r*) = *Det True*
    **by** (*cases eval i p*; *cases eval i q*; *cases eval i r*) *simp-all*
**qed**

**proposition** *valid-in* {*1*} (*Cla3 p q r*)
  **unfolding** *valid-in-def*
**proof** (*rule*; *rule*)
  **fix** *i* :: *id* $\Rightarrow$ *tv*
  **assume** *range i* $\subseteq$ *domain* {*1*}
  **then have**
    *eval i p* $\in$ {*Det True*, *Det False*, *Indet 1*}
    *eval i q* $\in$ {*Det True*, *Det False*, *Indet 1*}
    *eval i r* $\in$ {*Det True*, *Det False*, *Indet 1*}
    **using** *ranges*[*of i* {*1*}]
    **unfolding** *domain-def*
    **by** *auto*
  **then show** *eval i* (*Cla3 p q r*) = *Det True*

    **by** (*cases eval i p*; *cases eval i q*; *cases eval i r*) *simp-all*
**qed**

**proposition** *valid-in* {*1*, *2*} (*Cla3 p q r*)
  **unfolding** *valid-in-def*
**proof** (*rule*; *rule*)
  **fix** *i* :: *id* ⇒ *tv*
  **assume** *range i* ⊆ *domain* {*1*, *2*}
  **then have**
      *eval i p* ∈ {*Det True*, *Det False*, *Indet 1*, *Indet 2*}
      *eval i q* ∈ {*Det True*, *Det False*, *Indet 1*, *Indet 2*}
      *eval i r* ∈ {*Det True*, *Det False*, *Indet 1*, *Indet 2*}
    **using** *ranges*[*of i* {*1*, *2*}]
    **unfolding** *domain-def*
    **by** *auto*
  **then show** *eval i* (*Cla3 p q r*) = *Det True*
    **by** (*cases eval i p*; *cases eval i q*; *cases eval i r*) *auto*
**qed**

**proposition** ¬ *valid-in* {*1*, *2*, *3*} (*Cla3* (*Pro "p"*) (*Pro "q"*) (*Pro "r"*))
**proof** −
  **let** ?*i* = (λ*s*. *Indet 1*)(*"q"* := *Indet 2*, *"r"* := *Indet 3*)
  **have** *range* ?*i* ⊆ *domain* {*1*, *2*, *3*}
    **unfolding** *domain-def*
    **by** (*simp add: image-subset-iff*)
  **moreover have** *eval* ?*i* (*Cla3* (*Pro "p"*) (*Pro "q"*) (*Pro "r"*)) = *Det False*
    **by** *simp*
  **moreover have** *Det False* ≠ *Det True*
    **by** *simp*
  **ultimately show** ?*thesis*
    **unfolding** *valid-in-def*
    **by** *metis*
**qed**

You might have noticed that there is a pattern in $\Delta$, $\Delta_2$ and $\Delta_3$. Let us now study that pattern.

$\Delta$ can be read as follows: its operand evaluates to a classical value. It is easy to realize that this holds when we have only classical values. It is also clear that it is not valid already if we allow a single indeterminate value since then the operand might evaluate to that.

$\Delta_2$ can be read as follows: Either $p$ or $q$ evaluates to a classical value, or they evaluate to the same value. It is easy to realize that this holds when we have only one indeterminate value since if none of them evaluate to a classical value then they must both evaluate to the indeterminate one. It is also clear that this does not hold if we allow two indeterminate values since then $p$ and $q$ might respectively evaluate to these two values.

$\Delta_3$ can be read as follows. Either $p$, $q$ or $r$ evaluates to a classical value, or two of them evaluate to the same value. It is easy to realize that this holds when we only have two indeterminate values, by a similar argument to the one we saw for $\Delta_2$. It is also clear that this does not hold if we allow three indeterminate values, again by a similar argument.

It should be clear that this pattern can be extended as necessary for any number of truth values.

Thus, we now know that in order to check if a formula is valid, we need to consider interpretations with at least as many indeterminate truth values as there are propositional symbols in the formula – otherwise we might have missed an interpretation that falsified the formula. Thus we have found a lower bound on the number of needed indeterminate truth values. In the next section we will find an upper bound on the number of needed indeterminate truth values.

## 7   A Reduction Theorem

We obtain a reduction theorem by considering the number of propositional symbols in a given formula. Several of the proofs are long — about 250 lines — and are therefore omitted. The theory file for the formalization has the details.

We define a function *props* that returns the set of identifiers for a formula. We then prove that only the propositional symbols in the formula are relevant for the semantics (*relevant-props*).

> **fun** *props* :: *fm* ⇒ *id set*
> **where**
>   *props Truth* = {} |
>   *props* (*Pro s*) = {*s*} |
>   *props* (*Neg′ p*) = *props p* |
>   *props* (*Con′ p q*) = *props p* ∪ *props q* |
>   *props* (*Eql p q*) = *props p* ∪ *props q* |
>   *props* (*Eql′ p q*) = *props p* ∪ *props q*
>
> **lemma** *relevant-props*:
> **assumes** ∀ *s* ∈ *props p*. *i1 s* = *i2 s*
> **shows** *eval i1 p* = *eval i2 p*
> **using** *assms*
>   **by** (*induct p*) (*simp-all, metis*)

The proof is by induction over formulas (*induct*) followed by simplifications of all cases (*simp-all*) — one case is left over and requires the powerful resolution proof method (*metis*).

We define a function *change-tv* that applies a function to the number in an indeterminate truth value. We then prove that if *f* is an injection then *change-tv f* is also an injection (*change-tv-injection*).

> **fun** *change-tv* :: (*nat* ⇒ *nat*) ⇒ *tv* ⇒ *tv*
> **where**
>   *change-tv f* (*Det b*) = *Det b* |
>   *change-tv f* (*Indet n*) = *Indet* (*f n*)
>
> **lemma** *change-tv-injection*: **assumes** *inj f* **shows** *inj* (*change-tv f*)
> — Proof omitted

The above proof and the next two proofs are available online.

We define a function *change-int* that takes a function and applies it to an interpretation to get a new interpretation. We then prove that if we replace each indeterminate truth value in an interpretation with another one, then it just changes the result of the formula accordingly (*eval-change*).

> **definition**
> *change-int* :: $(nat \Rightarrow nat) \Rightarrow (id \Rightarrow tv) \Rightarrow (id \Rightarrow tv)$
> **where**
> *change-int* $f\ i \equiv \lambda s.\ change\text{-}tv\ f\ (i\ s)$
>
> **lemma** *eval-change*:
> **assumes** *inj f*
> **shows** *eval* (*change-int* $f\ i$) $p = change\text{-}tv\ f$ (*eval* $i\ p$)
> — Proof omitted

We prove that if our formula is valid when we have at least one indeterminate value in our domain for each propositional symbol, then it is valid in general (*valid-in-valid*).

> **theorem** *valid-in-valid*: **assumes** *card* $U \geq card$ (*props p*) **and** *valid-in* $U\ p$
> **shows** *valid p*
> — Proof omitted

We reformulate the theorem as follows.

> **theorem** *reduce*: *valid* $p \longleftrightarrow valid\text{-}in$ $\{1..card\ (props\ p)\}$ $p$
> **using** *valid-in-valid transfer*
> **by** *force*

We prove in the final reduction theorem (*reduce*) that we can decide the validity of a given formula by considering as many indeterminacies as the number of propositional symbols in the formula. This also means that the logic is weakened when additional indeterminate truth values are added. For the atomic formula $P$ it is clear that ı suffices. To see this we use the fact that indeterminate truth values are not ordered with respect to truth content. If $[\![P]\!] = $ ı and we replace the truth value with ıı then the truth value is still indeterminate.

## 8    Entailment — A Case Study

We propose a definition of entailment and verify the results for the case study presented in Sect. 1.

The following abbreviation *Entail* takes a list of formulas (the assumptions) and a single formula (the conclusion) and returns an equivalent formula with implication and possibly conjunctions.

**abbreviation** (*input*) *Entail* :: *fm list* ⇒ *fm* ⇒ *fm*
**where**
  *Entail l p* ≡ *Imp* (*if l* = [] *then Truth else fold Con'* (*butlast l*) (*last l*)) *p*

**theorem** *entailment-not-chain*:
  ¬ *valid* (*Eql* (*Entail* [*Pro* ″*p*″, *Pro* ″*q*″] (*Pro* ″*r*″))
    (*Box* ((*Imp'* (*Pro* ″*p*″) (*Imp'* (*Pro* ″*q*″) (*Pro* ″*r*″)))))))
**proof** −
  **let** *?i* = (λ*s. Indet 1*)(″*r*″ := *Det False*)
  **have** *eval ?i* (*Eql* (*Entail* [*Pro* ″*p*″, *Pro* ″*q*″] (*Pro* ″*r*″))
    (*Box* ((*Imp'* (*Pro* ″*p*″) (*Imp'* (*Pro* ″*q*″) (*Pro* ″*r*″))))))) = *Det False*
    **by** *simp*
  **moreover have** *Det False* ≠ *Det True*
    **by** *simp*
  **ultimately show** *?thesis*
    **unfolding** *valid-def*
    **by** *metis*
**qed**

Recall the formulas $P \wedge Q \wedge \neg R$, $P \wedge Q \rightarrow R$ and $R \rightarrow S$. We introduce *B0*, *B1* and *B2* as the corresponding abbreviations.

  **abbreviation** (*input*) *B0* :: *fm*
    **where** *B0* ≡ *Con'* (*Con'* (*Pro* ″*p*″) (*Pro* ″*q*″)) (*Neg'* (*Pro* ″*r*″))

  **abbreviation** (*input*) *B1* :: *fm*
    **where** *B1* ≡ *Imp'* (*Con'* (*Pro* ″*p*″) (*Pro* ″*q*″)) (*Pro* ″*r*″)

  **abbreviation** (*input*) *B2* :: *fm*
    **where** *B2* ≡ *Imp'* (*Pro* ″*r*″) (*Pro* ″*s*″)

From *B0* and *B1* we have explosion in classical logic (in the following theorem *p* is an arbitrary formula in our paraconsistent logic; however, in the proof of the theorem the *p* in double quotes corresponds to the particular *p* in *B0* and *B1*).

  **theorem** *classical-logic-is-not-usable*: *valid-boole* (*Entail* [*B0, B1*] *p*)
    **unfolding** *valid-in-def*
  **proof** (*rule; rule*)
    **fix** *i* :: *id* ⇒ *tv*
    **assume** *range i* ⊆ *domain* {}
    **then have**
        *i* ″*p*″ ∈ {*Det True, Det False*}
        *i* ″*q*″ ∈ {*Det True, Det False*}
        *i* ″*r*″ ∈ {*Det True, Det False*}
      **unfolding** *domain-def*
      **by** *auto*
    **then show** *eval i* (*Entail* [*B0, B1*] *p*) = *Det True*
      **by** (*cases i* ″*p*″; *cases i* ″*q*″; *cases i* ″*r*″) *simp-all*
  **qed**

**corollary** *valid-boole* (*Entail* [*B0, B1*] (*Pro* ''*r*''))
  **by** (*rule classical-logic-is-not-usable*)

**corollary** *valid-boole* (*Entail* [*B0, B1*] (*Neg'* (*Pro* ''*r*'')))
  **by** (*rule classical-logic-is-not-usable*)

**proposition** ¬ *valid* (*Entail* [*B0, B1*] (*Pro* ''*r*''))
**proof** −
  **let** *?i* = (λ*s. Indet* 1)(''*r*'' := *Det False*)
  **have** *eval ?i* (*Entail* [*B0, B1*] (*Pro* ''*r*'')) = *Det False*
    **by** *simp*
  **moreover have** *Det False* ≠ *Det True*
    **by** *simp*
  **ultimately show** *?thesis*
    **unfolding** *valid-def*
    **by** *metis*
**qed**

When we consider the full paraconsistent logic, however, everything does not follow. We illustrate this by showing that the negations of $p$, $q$ and $s$ do not follow. Of these three results that use counterexamples we only include the proof of the last one as they are very similar, but the two others are available in the theory file.

**proposition** ¬ *valid* (*Entail* [*B0, Box B1, Box B2*] (*Neg'* (*Pro* ''*p*'')))
— Proof omitted

**proposition** ¬ *valid* (*Entail* [*B0, Box B1, Box B2*] (*Neg'* (*Pro* ''*q*'')))
— Proof omitted

**proposition** ¬ *valid* (*Entail* [*B0, Box B1, Box B2*] (*Neg'* (*Pro* ''*s*'')))
**proof** −
  **let** *?i* = (λ*s. Indet* 1)(''*s*'' := *Det True*)
  **have** *eval ?i* (*Entail* [*B0, Box B1, Box B2*] (*Neg'* (*Pro* ''*s*''))) = *Det False*
    **by** *simp*
  **moreover have** *Det False* ≠ *Det True*
    **by** *simp*
  **ultimately show** *?thesis*
    **unfolding** *valid-def*
    **by** *metis*
**qed**

We do want something to follow − otherwise we would be unable to reason. Indeed something does follow namely $r$, its negation and $s$. Of the three results that use proof by cases and the reduction theorem (*reduce*) we only include the proof of the last one as they are very similar, but the two others are available in the theory file.

**proposition** *valid (Entail [B0, Box B1, Box B2] (Pro "r"))*
— Proof omitted

**proposition** *valid (Entail [B0, Box B1, Box B2] (Neg' (Pro "r")))*
— Proof omitted

**proposition** *valid (Entail [B0, Box B1, Box B2] (Pro "s"))*
**proof** −
  **have** {*1..card (props (Entail [B0, Box B1, Box B2] (Pro "s")))*} =
    {*1, 2, 3, 4*}
    **by** *code-simp*
  **moreover have** *valid-in* {*1, 2, 3, 4*}
    *(Entail [B0, Box B1, Box B2] (Pro "s"))*
    **unfolding** *valid-in-def*
  **proof** (*rule; rule*)
    **fix** *i :: id* ⇒ *tv*
    **assume** *range i* ⊆ *domain* {*1, 2, 3, 4*}
    **then have** *icase*:
      *i "p"* ∈ {*Det True, Det False, Indet 1, Indet 2, Indet 3, Indet 4*}
      *i "q"* ∈ {*Det True, Det False, Indet 1, Indet 2, Indet 3, Indet 4*}
      *i "r"* ∈ {*Det True, Det False, Indet 1, Indet 2, Indet 3, Indet 4*}
      *i "s"* ∈ {*Det True, Det False, Indet 1, Indet 2, Indet 3, Indet 4*}
      **unfolding** *domain-def*
      **by** *auto*
    **show** *eval i (Entail [B0, Box B1, Box B2] (Pro "s"))* = *Det True*
      **using** *icase*
      **by** (*cases i "p"; cases i "q"; cases i "r"; cases i "s"*) *simp-all*
  **qed**
  **ultimately show** *?thesis*
    **using** *reduce*
    **by** *simp*
**qed**

We hence obtain the following results for the agent using the turnstile symbol (⊢) for the entailment given the set of beliefs and rules.

$$\nvdash \neg P \quad \nvdash \neg Q \quad \nvdash \neg S$$

$$\vdash R \quad \vdash \neg R \quad \vdash S$$

For comparison, due to the catastrophic explosiveness of classical logic, the following results are obtained using classical logic:

$$\vdash \neg P \quad \vdash \neg Q \quad \vdash \neg S$$

$$\vdash R \quad \vdash \neg R \quad \vdash S$$

## 9   Related Work

Paraconsistent and/or many-valued logics are occasionally considered in the proof assistant Isabelle. Krauss [21] considers, in a tutorial for Isabelle/HOL, a very small example of a three-valued logic only to illustrate pattern matching in Isabelle/HOL. Brucker, Tuong and Wolff [8] formalize, in Isabelle/HOL, the four-valued logic OCL, which complements the UML software modelling language. Georgescu, Leustean and Preoteasa [13] take an algebraic approach and formalize, in Isabelle/HOL, the theory of pseudo hoops, which is a generalization of the BL-algebra and the many-valued BL-logic [10]. Steen and Benzmüller [39] present a semantic embedding of a many-valued logic in Isabelle/HOL. The truth values are encoded as particular functions and Isabelle/HOL's proof methods are then used directly.

There are several implementations of Dana Scott's Logic of Computable Functions (LCF) [26,38]. HOLCF [33] extends Isabelle/HOL with ideas from LCF, and allows reasoning about functional programs, including programs that never complete successfully due to errors or non-termination. Regensburger [34] formalizes, in HOLCF, the type of lifted booleans, which consists of true, false and a bottom value. The bottom value of the lifted booleans thus represents a computation of a boolean value that never completes successfully. The type of lifted booleans in HOLCF is also described by Müller, Nipkow, Oheimb and Slotosch [27] as well as by Huffman [18].

We deal with a formalization in a proof assistant of the syntax and semantics of a many-valued paraconsistent logic. Marcos [24] considers another kind of many-valued logic and describes a special computer program in the functional programming language ML. This computer program automatically generates proof tactics to be used by Isabelle. We do not use any computer programs (well, except Isabelle itself, of course). And we do not generate proof tactics. We have ourselves authored all proofs. Furthermore our proofs are in higher-order logic, Isabelle/HOL, which is the default logic in Isabelle. In [24] the default higher-order logic is not used. Instead it is replaced by certain finite-valued logics. This is possible since Isabelle is a generic proof assistant but we do not use this feature at all. More precisely, we formalize the syntax and semantics of the logic, and this is not done in [24]. We can prove theorems in the logic as well as meta-theorems about the logic, but in [24] only theorems in the logic can be proved. Since the logics are rather different it is not possible to compare the efficiency of the two approaches when it comes to proving theorems.

Here, we have only considered the formalization of propositional logic, but the formalization of first-order logic or even higher-order logic is also possible. Several proof systems for classical first-order logic have been proved sound and complete:

- Sequent calculus [6,35].
- Natural deduction [3,7,12,44].
- Resolution [36].

But even without developing a proof system we can obtain many theorems and meta-theorems by formalizing the syntax and semantics in a proof assistant like Isabelle.

# 10    Conclusion

In this paper we considered a logic with infinitely many truth values (cf. Sect. 3 on the syntax and semantics of the logic). Specifically, we investigated how many truth values we need to consider in order to decide if a formula is valid or not. In Sect. 6 we explained that in order to check the validity of a formula with $n$ different propositional symbols we should consider interpretations that use $n$ different indeterminate truth values. The reason was that the formula might be true in any interpretation that uses only $n - 1$ different indeterminate truth values but false in one that uses $n$ of them. We gave concrete examples of such formulas for $n = 1, 2, 3$. The formulas showed a pattern that we argued would generalize to any $n$. Future work includes a formalization of this argument.

Our main theoretic result is the reduction theorem from Sect. 7:

> **proposition** *valid p* $\longleftrightarrow$ *valid-in* $\{1 .. card\ (props\ p)\}$ *p*
> **using** *reduce* .

In the above formulation of the reduction theorem, the right-hand side *valid p* means that a formula $p$ is true in all interpretations — of which there are infinitely many. The left-hand side *valid-in* $\{1 .. card\ (props\ p)\}$ *p* means that $p$ is true in all the interpretations whose domains are restricted to a finite set consisting of true, false and a number of indeterminate truth values as small as the number of propositional symbols in $p$. This important result allows us to reduce the infinite number of truth values to a finite number of truth values, for a given formula, and in our case study we use this result. Future work includes further investigations of the practical applications of the reduction theorem.

Using a proof assistant like Isabelle makes it possible to clarify concepts and to catch mistakes. However, we have not found errors in our extended abstract [20]. The formalization of the case study shows the limits since using straightforward proof techniques the results can take up to half a minute for Isabelle to prove using a standard computer. It has been a pleasure to use the Isabelle proof assistant for the formalization of our paraconsistent logic. We plan to make a similar formalization in the Coq proof assistant [4] in order to compare the two systems.

In our extended abstract [20] several of these results were mentioned without proof and we now have precise definitions and formal proofs. The reduction theorem was the most difficult proof and large parts of the 1582-lines theory file for Isabelle2016-1 are omitted in the present paper. After the initial successful proofs we spent a lot of time improving the definitions, theorems and proofs; this also involved discussions with other Isabelle users as well as with our students in order to obtain the most elegant and general results.

**Acknowledgements.** Thanks to Andreas Halkjær From, Alexander Birch Jensen and John Bruntse Larsen for comments on drafts of the paper. Also thanks to Hendrik Decker and the anonymous reviewers for many constructive comments.

# References

1. Akama, S. (ed.): Towards Paraconsistent Engineering. Intelligent Systems Reference Library, vol. 110. Springer, Cham (2016). doi:10.1007/978-3-319-40418-9
2. Batens, D., Mortensen, C., Priest, G., Van-Bendegem, J. (eds.): Frontiers in Paraconsistent Logic. Research Studies Press, Philadelphia (2000)
3. Berghofer, S.: First-Order Logic According to Fitting. Archive of Formal Proofs (2007). http://isa-afp.org/entries/FOL-Fitting.shtml
4. Bertot, Y., Castéran, P.: Interactive Theorem Proving and Program Development – Coq'Art: The Calculus of Inductive Constructions. EATCS Texts in Theoretical Computer Science. Springer, Heidelberg (2004). doi:10.1007/978-3-662-07964-5
5. Blanchette, J.C., Böhme, S., Paulson, L.C.: Extending Sledgehammer with SMT solvers. J. Autom. Reason. **51**(1), 109–128 (2013)
6. Blanchette, J.C., Popescu, A., Traytel, D.: Soundness and completeness proofs by coinductive methods. J. Autom. Reason. **58**(1), 149–179 (2017)
7. Breitner, J., Lohner, D.: The Meta Theory of the Incredible Proof Machine. Archive of Formal Proofs (2016). http://isa-afp.org/entries/Incredible_Proof_Machine.shtml
8. Brucker, A.D., Tuong, F., Wolff, B.: Featherweight OCL: A Proposal for a Machine-Checked Formal Semantics for OCL 2.5. Archive of Formal Proofs (2014). http://isa-afp.org/entries/Featherweight_OCL.shtml
9. Carnielli, W.A., Coniglio, M.E., D'Ottaviano, I.M.L. (eds.): Paraconsistency: The Logical Way to the Inconsistent. Marcel Dekker, New York (2002)
10. Ciungu, L.C.: Non-commutative Multiple-Valued Logic Algebras. Springer Monographs in Mathematics. Springer, Cham (2014). doi:10.1007/978-3-319-01589-7
11. Decker, H., Villadsen, J., Waragai, T. (eds.) International Workshop on Paraconsistent Computational Logic, vol. 95. Roskilde University, Computer Science, Technical reports (2002)
12. From, A.H.: Formalized First-Order Logic. B.Sc. thesis, Technical University of Denmark (2017)
13. Georgescu, G., Leustean, L., Preoteasa, V.: Pseudo Hoops. Archive of Formal Proofs (2011). http://isa-afp.org/entries/PseudoHoops.shtml
14. Geuvers, H.: Proof assistants: history, ideas and future. Sadhana **34**(1), 3–25 (2009). Springer
15. Gödel, K.: On formally undecidable propositions of principia mathematica and related systems. In: van Heijenoort, J. (ed.) From Frege to Gödel. Harvard University Press (1967)
16. Gottwald, S.: A Treatise on Many-Valued Logics. Research Studies Press, Baldock (2001)
17. Hansson, S.O.: Logic of belief revision. In: Zalta, E.N. et al. (eds.) Stanford Encyclopedia of Philosophy (2016). http://plato.stanford.edu/entries/logic-belief-revision/. Winter Edition
18. Huffman, B.: Reasoning with Powerdomains in Isabelle/HOLCF. In: Mohamed, O.A., Muñoz, C., Tahar, S. (eds.) TPHOLs 2008. Emerging Trends Proceedings, pp. 45–56. Technical report, Concordia University (2008)
19. Jensen, A.B., Schlichtkrull, A., Villadsen, J.: First-Order Logic According to Harrison. Archive of Formal Proofs (2017). http://isa-afp.org/entries/FOL_Harrison.shtml
20. Jensen, A.S., Villadsen, J.: Paraconsistent computational logic. In: Blackburn, P., Jørgensen, K.F., Jones, N., Palmgren, E. (eds.) 8th Scandinavian Logic Symposium: Abstracts, pp. 59–61. Roskilde University (2012)

21. Krauss, A.: Defining Recursive Functions in Isabelle/HOL. Isabelle Distribution (2017). http://isabelle.in.tum.de/doc/functions.pdf
22. Lamport, L.: How to write a proof. Am. Math. Mon. **102**(7), 600–608 (1995)
23. Lamport, L.: How to write a 21st century proof. J. Fixed Point Theor. Appl. **11**(1), 43–63 (2012)
24. Marcos, J.: Automatic generation of proof tactics for finite-valued logics. In: Proceedings of Tenth International Workshop on Rule-Based Programming, pp. 91–98 (2009)
25. Michaelis, J., Nipkow, T.: Propositional Proof Systems. Archive of Formal Proofs (2017). http://isa-afp.org/entries/Propositional_Proof_Systems.shtml
26. Milner, R.: Logic for computable functions: description of a machine implementation. Stanford University (1972)
27. Müller, O., Nipkow, T., Oheimb, D., Slotosch, O.: HOLCF = HOL + LCF. J. Funct. Program. **9**(2), 191–223 (1999)
28. Nipkow, T., Paulson, L.C., Wenzel, M.: Isabelle/HOL — A Proof Assistant for Higher-Order Logic. LNCS, vol. 2283. Springer, Heidelberg (2002). doi:10.1007/3-540-45949-9
29. Nipkow, T., Klein, G.: Concrete Semantics — With Isabelle/HOL. Springer, Cham (2014). doi:10.1007/978-3-319-10542-0
30. Paulson, L.C.: A machine-assisted proof of Gödel's incompleteness theorems for the theory of hereditarily finite sets. Rev. Symb. Log. **7**(3), 484–498 (2014)
31. Priest, G., Routley, R., Norman, J. (eds.): Paraconsistent Logic: Essays on the Inconsistent. Philosophia Verlag, Munich (1989)
32. Priest, G., Tanaka, K., Weber, Z.: Paraconsistent logic. In: Zalta, E.N. et al. (eds.) Stanford Encyclopedia of Philosophy (2016). http://plato.stanford.edu/entries/logic-paraconsistent. Winter Edition
33. Regensburger, F.: HOLCF: higher order logic of computable functions. In: Schubert, E.T., Windley, P.J., Alves-Foss, J. (eds.) TPHOLs 1995. LNCS, vol. 971, pp. 293–307. Springer, Heidelberg (1995). doi:10.1007/3-540-60275-5_72
34. Regensburger, F.: The type of lifted booleans. Isabelle Distribution (2017). http://isabelle.in.tum.de/library/HOL/HOLCF/Tr.html
35. Ridge, T.: A Mechanically Verified, Efficient, Sound and Complete Theorem Prover for First Order Logic. Archive of Formal Proofs (2004). http://isa-afp.org/entries/Verified-Prover.shtml
36. Schlichtkrull, A.: The Resolution Calculus for First-Order Logic. Archive of Formal Proofs (2016). http://isa-afp.org/entries/Resolution_FOL.shtml
37. Schlichtkrull, A., Villadsen, J.: Paraconsistency. Archive of Formal Proofs (2017). http://isa-afp.org/entries/Paraconsistency.shtml
38. Scott, D.S.: A type-theoretical alternative to ISWIM, CUCH, OWHY. Theor. Comput. Sci. **121**, 411–440 (1993). Annotated version of an unpublished manuscript from 1969
39. Steen, A., Benzmüller, C.: Sweet SIXTEEN: automation via embedding into classical higher-order logic. Log. Log. Philos. **25**(4), 535–554 (2016)
40. Villadsen, J.: Combinators for paraconsistent attitudes. In: de Groote, P., Morrill, G., Retoré, C. (eds.) LACL 2001. LNCS, vol. 2099, pp. 261–278. Springer, Heidelberg (2001). doi:10.1007/3-540-48199-0_16
41. Villadsen, J.: Paraconsistent assertions. In: Lindemann, G., Denzinger, J., Timm, I.J., Unland, R. (eds.) MATES 2004. LNCS, vol. 3187, pp. 99–113. Springer, Heidelberg (2004). doi:10.1007/978-3-540-30082-3_8

42. Villadsen, J.: A paraconsistent higher order logic. In: Buchberger, B., Campbell, J.A. (eds.) AISC 2004. LNCS, vol. 3249, pp. 38–51. Springer, Heidelberg (2004). doi:10.1007/978-3-540-30210-0_5

43. Villadsen, J.: Supra-logic: using transfinite type theory with type variables for paraconsistency. J. Appl. Non Class. Log. **15**(1), 45–58 (2005). Logical approaches to paraconsistency

44. Villadsen, J., Jensen, A.B., Schlichtkrull, A.: NaDeA: a natural deduction assistant with a formalization in Isabelle. IFCoLog J. Log. Appl. **4**(1), 55–82 (2017)

45. Villadsen, J., Schlichtkrull, A.: Formalization of many-valued logics. In: Christiansen, H., Jiménez-López, M.D., Loukanova, R., Moss, L.S. (eds.) Partiality and Underspecification in Information, Languages, and Knowledge, Chap. 7. Cambridge Scholars Publishing (2017)

46. Weber, Z.: Paraconsistent Logic. The Internet Encyclopedia of Philosophy (2017). http://www.iep.utm.edu/para-log

47. Wenzel, M.: Isar — a generic interpretative approach to readable formal proof documents. In: Bertot, Y., Dowek, G., Théry, L., Hirschowitz, A., Paulin, C. (eds.) TPHOLs 1999. LNCS, vol. 1690, pp. 167–183. Springer, Heidelberg (1999). doi:10. 1007/3-540-48256-3_12

48. Wiedijk, F. (ed.): The Seventeen Provers of the World. LNCS (LNAI), vol. 3600. Springer, Heidelberg (2006)

# A Proximity-Based Understanding
# of Conditionals

Ricardo Queiroz de Araujo Fernandes[1,2(✉)], Edward Hermann Haeusler[1,2],
and Luiz Carlos Pinheiro Dias Pereira[1,2]

[1] Systems Development Center, Brazilian Army, Brasília, DF, Brazil
ricardo.fernandes@eb.mil.br
[2] Pontifícia Universidade Católica do Rio de Janeiro, Rio de Janeiro, RJ, Brazil
{hermann,luiz}@inf.puc-rio.br

**Abstract.** The aim of the present paper is to introduce a new logic, PUC-Logic, which will be used to give a systematic account of well-known counterfactuals conditionals on the basis of a concept of *proximity*. We will formulate a natural deduction system for PUC-Logic, the system PUC-ND, that will be shown to be sound and complete with respect to the semantics of PUC-Logic. We shall also prove that PUC-Logic is decidable and that the system PUC-ND satisfies the normalization theorem.

**Keywords:** Conditionals · Counterfactual logic · Natural deduction

## 1 Introduction

Let us consider the following two sentences:

- If Oswald did not kill Kennedy, then someone else did.
- If Oswald had not killed Kennedy, then someone else would have [1].

The first sentence is a clear instance of an indicative conditional while the second sentence is a clear instance of a subjunctive conditional. In logic, the indicative conditional is usually associated to material implication, whereas the natural language subjunctive construction is traditionally studied in philosophy and logic by means of counterfactual conditionals [1,2]. Conditional propositions involve two components, the antecedent and the consequent. Counterfactual conditionals differ from material implication in a subtle and important way. The truth of material implication is based on actual state-of-affairs[1]. Given

---

R.Q. de Araujo Fernandes—We would like to thank PUC-Rio for the VRac sponsorship and DAAD (Germany) for the Specialist Literature Programme.

[1] The expression state-of-affairs is here used in an intuititive and very general sense as a kind of "truth-maker", as that piece of reality that is responsible for the truth of a proposition (as Michael Dummett [16] would put it). There's a long and important discussion in Philosophy as to the true nature of state-of-affairs, but to get into this discussion is clearly beyond the scope of the presente paper.

A. Hameurlain et al. (Eds.): TLDKS XXXIV, LNCS 10620, pp. 123–152, 2017.
https://doi.org/10.1007/978-3-662-55947-5_6

that Kennedy was killed, we can accept the first sentence as true. On the other hand, a counterfactual conditional should take into account the truth of the antecedent, even if this is not the case. The truth of the antecedent is mandatory in this kind of analysis. Some approaches to counterfactuals entail belief revision, particularly those based on Ramsey's *test evaluation* [8]. In this type of analysis, the truth value of a counterfactual is considered in the context of a minimal change generated by admitting the truth of the antecedent [2]. A possible way to circumvent belief revision mechanisms is to consider alternative (possible) state-of-affairs, considered here as worlds, and some accessibility relation between state-of-affairs that can be used to choose the closest world among the worlds that satisfy the antecedent. If the consequent is true with respect to this closest world, then the counterfactual is also true [1]. Both conditionals have false antecedents and false consequents in the current state-of-affairs. However, the second conditional is false, since we find no reason to accept that, in the closest worlds in which Kennedy is not killed by Oswald, Kennedy is killed by someone else. We have chosen Lewis' [1] approach to inference systems for counterfactuals because his accessibility relation leaves out the discussion concerning the definition of similarity among worlds, which is considered as given in his analysis. Lewis' analysis also opens the way for another kind of contribution, which runs in a certain sense in the reverse direction: if we can find some general properties of his accessibility relation, with respect to the evaluation of formulas in counterfactual reasoning, maybe we could also find some interesting similarity properties.

Counterfactual reasoning can be very useful as a purely logical approach to hypothetical queries in deductive databases. A hypothetical query in a deductive database $D$ is made under the assumption that an additional fact $A$ holds in $D$. *Additional* means here that one does not derive this fact solely on the basis of $D$. The set of answers for this query is computed in $D \cup \{A\}$. Standard logic programming languages (PLs) that are used in these tasks are based on material implication and negation-as-failure. Through the use of negation-as-failure, as in Datalog or Prolog, typical examples of PLs, $\neg A$ can be derived from $D$, and hence $D \cup \{A\}$ is inconsistent. The usual implementation is based on revisions of $D$ in order to obtain a consistent subset of $D$ which is relevant and sufficient to derive a meaningful answer-set to the query. When $D$ is sufficiently big, the process is computationally quite expensive, due to the algorithmic complexity of proof-methods. We believe PUC-Logic and its natural deduction system PUC-ND can contribute to a better understanding of hypothetical queries in deductive databases as well as to a better implementation of hypothetical reasoning in deductive databases. As already said, PUC-Logic can express some counterfactuals conditionals that can be found in the literature and it may help us to reason in knowledge bases (deductive databases) without any need to perform revisions on the base. This seems to be our most promising practical contribution. Any further application is beyond the scope of the present paper.

In this paper we (1) define the logic PUC-Logic for counterfactuals; (2) discuss Lewis' counterfactuals from the unified perspectve of PUC-Logic; (3) define the natural deduction system PUC-ND for PUC-Logic; (4) show that PUC-ND is sound and complete with respect to the semantics of PUC-Logic; (5) prove the normalization theorem for PUC-ND; and (6) we show that PUC-Logic is decidable. The paper is organized as follows: in Sect. 2 we present in very general terms Lewis' counterfactual analysis. In Sect. 3 we discuss some counterfactual applications to computer science and the main contribution of the present work in this area. In Sect. 4 we describe (1) the syntax and semantics of PUC-Logic and (2) the natural deduction system PUC-ND. In Sect. 6 we prove (i) that the system PUC-ND is sound and complete for PUC-Logic, (ii) we indicated how to prove the normalization theorem for PUC-ND, and (iii) we prove the decidability of PUC-Logic. In Sect. 7 we refer to some related work, and in the final Sect. 8 we present our conclusions and some future work.

## 2 Lewis' Counterfactual Analysis

"*If kangaroos had no tails, they would topple over*, seems to me to mean something like this: in any possible state-of-affairs in which kangaroos have no tails, and which resembles our actual state-of-affairs as much as kangaroos having no tails permits it to, the kangaroos topple over." [1]

The expression "resembles" that occurs in the quotation may be seen as a reference to a concept of *similarity* between possible state-of-affairs and the actual state-of-affairs, and the expression "as much as", that also occurs in the quotation, may be understood as a comparison of *similarities* among different possible states-of-affairs and the actual state-of-affairs (even though Lewis himself did not give any formal definition of *similarity* in his book [1]). Lewis' definition for the basic counterfactual conditional operators is as follows:

- $A \mathbin{\Box\!\!\rightarrow} B$: If it were the case that $A$, then it would be the case that $B$;
- $A \mathbin{\Diamond\!\!\rightarrow} B$: If it were the case that $A$, then it might be the case that $B$.
- $A \preccurlyeq B$: It is as possible that $A$ as it is that $B$.

The *comparative possibility* operator $\preccurlyeq$ was shown to act as a kind of primitive notion for counterfactuals and, as we shall see later, this operator will simplify several proofs in the present work. Lewis' semantical framework is the usual possible world semantics for intensional logics, with state-of-affairs being treated as *worlds*. In order to express the relation of similarity between worlds, he used some notions of *proximity*: a world is closer to the actual world in comparison to other worlds if it is more similar to the actual world than these other considered worlds. Lewis called the world set to be considered for an evaluation, the *conditional strictness*, and pointed out that a counterfactual conditional strictness is based on world similarities. He also showed that counterfactuals can not be treated by the usual modal operators, because the conditional strictness can not be given before all evaluations. Lewis constructed examples of connected sequences of counterfactuals in a single English sentence for which the conditional strictness cannot be given for the evaluation, as in the sentence below:

"If Otto had come, it would have been a lively party, but if both Otto and Anna had come it would have been a dreary party; but if Waldo had come as well, it would have been lively; but..."

Counterfactual strictness cannot be defined by the context because this sentence provides a single context for all counterfactual evaluations. If we try to fix a strictness which makes one counterfactual true, then the next counterfactual becomes false. Lewis proposed a variable strictness conditional in which different strictness degrees are given for every world before any counterfactual evaluation. In order to express this concept, the accessibility relation is defined by a *sphere system* which is provided for every world by a nesting function $ which has as domain a world set $\mathcal{W}$. The nested function attributes a set of non-empty world sets to each world, and this set of sets is ordered by the inclusion relation. Sphere systems of any kind are central in most of traditional analysis of counterfactuals logics. Given that the systems of spheres are also used in other logics, if we manage to handle systems of spheres in a satisfactory manner, we will be able to use our formal system in a broader class of logics. We decided to denote the spheres by the term *neighborhood* because it reinforces the connection with the notion of proximity. In Lewis' definitions [1], the nesting function is a primitive notion:

$\phi \mathrel{\Box\!\!\!\rightarrow} \psi$ is true at a world $i$ (according to a sphere system $) if and only if either no $\phi$-world belongs to any sphere $S$ in $\$_i{}^2$, or some sphere $S$ in $\$_i$ does contain at least one $\phi$-world and $\phi \rightarrow \psi$ holds at every world in $S$.

$\phi \preccurlyeq \psi$ is true at a world $i$ (according to a sphere system $) if and only if for every sphere $S$ in $\$_i$, if $S$ contains any $\psi$-world, then $S$ contains a $\phi$-world.

Lewis also provided a set of conditions which may be applied to the nesting function $. Every combination of these conditions corresponds to a different counterfactual logic:

- **Normality (N):** $ is normal iff $\forall w \in \mathcal{W}, \$(w) \neq \emptyset$;
- **Total reflexivity (T):** $ is totally reflexive iff $\forall w \in \mathcal{W}, w \in \bigcup \$(w)$;
- **Weak centering (W):** $ is weakly centered iff $\forall w \in \mathcal{W}, \$(w) \neq \emptyset$ and $\forall N \in \$(w), w \in N$;
- **Centering (C):** $ is centered iff $\forall w \in \mathcal{W}, \{w\} \in \$(w)$;
- **Limit Assumption (L):** $ satisfies the Limit Assumption condition iff for any world $w$ and any formula $\phi$, if there is some $\phi$-world[3] in $\bigcup \$(w)$, then there is some smallest sphere of $\$(w)$ which contains a $\phi$-world;
- **Stalnaker's Assumption (A):** $ satisfies Stalnaker's Assumption iff for any world $w$ and any formula $\phi$, if there is some $\phi$-world in $\bigcup \$(w)$, then there is some sphere of $\$(w)$ which contains exactly one $\phi$-world;

---

[2] $\$_i$ gives the neighborhoods around the world $i$. They are the available strictness to evaluate counterfactuals at $i$.

[3] A $\phi$-world is a world in which $\phi$ holds.

- **Local Uniformity (U-):** $ is locally uniform iff for any world $w$ and any $v \in \bigcup \$(w)$, $\bigcup \$(w)$ and $\bigcup \$(v)$ are the same;
- **Uniformity (U):** $ is uniform iff for any worlds $w$ and $v$, $\bigcup \$(w)$ and $\bigcup \$(v)$ are the same;
- **Local absoluteness (A-):** $ is locally absolute iff for any world $w$ and any $v \in \bigcup \$(w)$, $\$(w)$ and $\$(v)$ are the same;
- **Absoluteness (A):** $ is absolute iff for any worlds $w$ and $v$, $\$(w)$ and $\$(v)$ are the same.

Lewis classified his counterfactual logics on the basis of these conditions on the $ function. If there is no condition on $, then we have the **V**-logic, which is the most basic counterfactual logic presented by Lewis, where "V" stands for *variable strictness conditional*. If, for example, we accept the centering condition (**C**), then we have the **VC**-logic. Lewis showed in his book a chart of 26 non-equivalent **V**-logics that arise from combinations of these conditions. We prefer to call the spheres *neighborhoods* because this terminology represents more closely the concept of *proximity* that Lewis used to express similarity. Neighborhoods provide a relative way to compare distance: the world which is contained in a neighborhood is closer to the actual world than another world that is not contained in the same neighborhood. As far as we know, our deductive system is the only one in the literature which deals with all counterfactual logics considered by Lewis, starting from the **V**-logic. In comparison to other approaches, we avoid using modalities in the syntax to benefit from well-known results from propositional logic. It is important to emphasize that the notion of closeness is a topological notion provided by the work of Lewis. The system of spheres is used to express when a world $w$ is closer to a world $v$ than to a world $u$. Namely, $w$ is closer to $v$ than to $u$ if and only if every neighborhood that contains $w$ and $v$ contains $u$.

# 3 A Brief Discussion on the Applications of Counterfactuals in Computer Science

A counterfactual $A \mathbin{\square\!\!\rightarrow} B$ holds in a given state-of-affairs whenever $A$ is false in this state-of-affairs and $B$ holds in some of its closest[4] state-of-affairs, and different counterfactual conditionals can be produced depending on the way "closest" and "some" are defined.

Hypothetical reasoning can be quite useful in computer science and technology: knowledge representation, data modelling and agents modelling are good examples of areas that may require this kind of reasoning. In fact, we find in these areas the most popular applications of counterfactuals. In this section we will discuss in more detail one kind of application of this mode of reasoning in computer science.

---

[4] The notion of closeness or proximity is based on the work of Lewis; it is a topological notion explained in the end of Sect. 2 and formally defined in Sect. 4.

One of the most popular applications of counterfactual reasoning is in the area of hypothetical queries answering over a deductive database (DDB). The expression "hypothetic" query refers here to queries of the form *What if John was not in the city would he go to the meeting?* This kind of query is widely used in scientific practice: for example, [9] describes a very sophisticated application of hypothetical queries answering over deductive databases in order to discover, from scientific texts, knowledge correlating the presence of certain proteins to the Alzheimer disease. In [14], we can find a quite interesting similar application in business intelligence.

In order to make our discussion more objective, we will compare ordinary and deductive databases and their respective queries with respect to the potential use of counterfactuals. Hypothetical queries constitute a key issue for understanding the difference between databases and deductive databases, A deductive database is a database which stores a finite set of facts and rules, and from this stock of information one should be able to derive new facts, i.e., implicit knowledge, from queries. It can be based on logic programming languages (Prolog, Datalog, for example) and in these cases it uses *negation-as-failure* as the only "logical" negation. The main feature of a DDB is its ability to answer queries of the kind "what-if." Besides DDBs that are based on logic programming, we can also mention DDBs [13,25] that are based on higher-order logic and that do have a genuine negation. The main difference between databases and DDBs is that the former can be seen as models and the later cannot.

A relational database $\mathcal{B}$ is a tuple $\langle B, \gamma \rangle$. $\gamma$ is a set of first-order logical sentences, and $B$ is a finite first-order model of $\gamma$, i.e., $B \models \gamma$[5]. The set of formulas $\Gamma$ is the integrity constraints of $\mathcal{B}$, in the terminology of databases. From a logician point of view, a query regarding $\mathcal{B}$ can be seen as a formula $\alpha(x_1, \ldots, x_n)$ with free variables $x_1, \ldots, x_n$. An answer for this query is a set $s$ of tuples $(b_1, \ldots, b_n)$, $b_i \in B, i = 1, n$, such that, $B \models \alpha(b_1, \ldots, b_n)$[6]. In the relational model, queries are first-order formulas, with some restrictions to ensure safeness, which is a discussion out of this article scope. Queries answering may represent the derivation of new facts from the database. This is a consequence of the fact that an ordinary database is essentially a first-order logic model and the queries represent relations/concepts defined using formulas with free-variables in the first-order language of the model. The answering set of a query/formula is the set of tuples for which the query/formula holds. It should be noted that $\Gamma$ is used only when some updating (changing) in $\mathcal{B}$ is necessary. Any evolution of $\mathcal{B}$ in time has to satisfy $\Gamma$. There is no feasible room inside this approach to perform hypothetical reasoning. A deductive database, for the purposes of the level of the present discussion, is a database system that it is able to make deductions from its facts and rules. In a certain sense it is similar to a logic program or to a knowledge base.

---

[5] This definition of database which includes a first-order model $B$ and not only the integrity constraints is similar to the definition of a relational database in [17].

[6] $\alpha(b_1, \ldots, b_n)$ is an abuse of notation; it means that $b_i$ is assigned to $x_i$ by means of some assignment function.

Let us consider a DDB that represents knowledge on hazard assessment on chemical research laboratories. This could be modelled by having actions that must be taken in a laboratory organized according risks, safeness and so on. Examples of such actions are "clean air", "exhaust chemicals", "wash cabinet", "control spilling, and etc. The predicate Must(someaction) is used to infer which action(s) has(have) to be taken. Consider a what-if question such as: "What if glassware breaks during the reaction?" A way to implement this what-if question as a (hypothetical) query in the DDB is to obtain the answering set for $P \mathbin{\square\!\!\rightarrow} Q$, where $P$ is "glassware breaks" and $Q$ be "Must(x)", i.e., "what-if" query is mapped into a hypothetical query of the form $P \mathbin{\square\!\!\rightarrow} Q$. In this case, the query could derive $Must(controlspilling)$ providing "control spilling" as the answering set for the query. Notice that the use of a counterfactual conditional is important, for $P$ is not derivable/provable from the knowledge base $\mathcal{B}$ of the DDB - it is in general false. Seminal work on this are [4, 26]. As a matter of comparison, let us consider an implementation of this hypothetical query that uses the classical material implication.

It takes knowledge to update, and revision to remove inconsistencies. Given that $P$ is not derivable from $\mathcal{B}$, we have two possibilities: either $\neg P$ is not derivable from $\mathcal{B}$ too, or $\neg P$ is derivable from $\mathcal{B}$. The first alternative is simpler than the second in the attempt to answer the conditional query. Using the material implication we *assert* $p$ in $\mathcal{B}$ and try to derive $q$. This case is performed in a consistent $\mathcal{B}$. The second alternative involves fixing the inconsistent knowledge base $\mathcal{B} \cup \{P\}$. [6] is one of the first works to describe the operations which can be applied in the knowledge base to remove facts from it and consistently allow a (possible) derivation of $Q$. The operations described by [6] suggests to deal with counterfactual reasoning that uses material implication and involves removing and updating operations in the knowledge base. It is known as the *logic programming approach* to deductive and hypothetical databases. A logic programming mechanism supporting hypothetical updates together with integrity constraints is the kernel of this approach. It allows updating using sets of atom, and it uses a kind of revision method to recover consistency whenever some integrity constraint is violated. *Negation as failure* is well-known to be the only negation in logic programming. Thus inside logic programming, when we have a query $P \rightarrow Q$ and neither $P$ nor $\neg P$ are derivable, the first alternative plus negation as failure implies that $\neg P$ is derivable from $\mathcal{B}$. Thus, both cases involve updating the knowledge base. Summing up, if $P$ is derivable, then we must perform updates and if $P$ is not derivable, then we must also perform updates in the DDBs.

Given the main differences between databases and DDBs, one can see how the research on the implementation of a logic capable to express counterfactual reasoning is important for the fields of deductive databases and artificial intelligence in general. Consider we have to deal with big deductive databases (or knowledge bases). In this case, the recovery of a consistent set of facts/rules after sequences of updates can be a very hard computational task; we just have to remember that this task involves testing for tautological consequence, which is a very expensive computational task.

One of the main practical PUC-Logic contributions is to make it possible to deal with counterfactual queries and updates in a purely logical way. The fact that PUC-Logic is decidable logic and that PUC-ND satisfies good proof-theoretical properties clearly indicate that one should try to implement a counterfactual language for hypothetical deductive databases.

Finally, we would like to mention that there is a vast literature on the use of counterfactuals in modeling agents in a multi-agent system. They are used to represent (counterfactual) knowledge as well as counterfactual emotions and morality (see [21]).

## 4  A Proximity-Based Understanding of Conditionals

In [15] we presented a sequent calculus for counterfactual logic based on Local Set Theory [3]. In the present work, we avoid the direct use of counterfactual operators in the inference system. We introduce labels[7] in our language to *syntactically* represent quantifications over two specific domains: neighborhoods and world and, for this reason a label may be a neighborhood label or a world label. For example, the (labeled) formula $A^{\circledast,\bullet}$, where $A$ is a propositional variable, means that there is some neighborhood of the current state-of-affairs such that in every world in this neighborhood $A$ holds. The label $\bullet$ quantifies over neighborhoods and the label $\circledast$ quantifies over worlds in this neighborhood. Definition 13 formalizes the semantics of any (labeled) formula. This type of semantics is called *sphere semantics* in the literature on conditionals. We take Lewis [1] as our main reference for the kind of sphere semantics we propose for PUC-Logic. The main contribution of PUC-Logic is its ability to express sphere semantics as defined in Definition 13. PUC-Logic defines the many counterfactual conditionals considered in [1]. Our goal is to perform logic programming using conditional counterfactuals. To obtain such logic programming approach, we define a deductive system for PUC-Logic. PUC-ND is a Natural Deduction deductive system. It plays the role of an inference system which deals with quantification of worlds and neighborhoods using an interplay between formula labels and inference contexts. These quantifications appear in every definition of counterfactual operators given by Lewis [1]. In our approach, counterfactual operators become syntactic sugar of the inference system. As it will be shown, it is necessary to introduce the total order of set inclusion among neighborhoods in the inference system, because the inclusion relation has an impact on semantics. The use of **labels** is essential for obtaining a Natural Deduction with so nice proof-theoretical properties such as normalization of proofs and sub-formula property. The later being important regarding the implementation of counterfactuals in an automatic theorem prover to be built.

---

[7] We are going to use labels in the spirit of labelled deductive systems, as it is used by Gabbay and Negri. Labels help us to push down semantic notions into the syntax (see, for example, [22]).

**Definition 1.** *Given a non-empty set $\mathcal{W}$ that will be taken as the world set, we define a nesting function $ which assigns to each world in $\mathcal{W}$ a set of nested subsets of $\mathcal{W}$. A set of nested sets is a set of sets in which the inclusion relation among sets is a total order.*

**Definition 2.** *A frame is a tuple $\mathcal{F} = \langle \mathcal{W}, \$, \mathcal{V} \rangle$ where $\mathcal{V}$ is a (truth assignment) function that assigns to each atomic formula a subset of $\mathcal{W}$. A model is a pair $\mathcal{M} = \langle \mathcal{F}, \chi \rangle$, where $\mathcal{F}$ is a frame and $\chi$ a world in $\mathcal{W}$, called the reference world of the model. A template is a pair $\mathcal{T} = \langle \mathcal{M}, N \rangle$, where $N \in \$(\chi)$. N is called the reference neighborhood of the template.*

Intead of the notion of template, we could have used two types of models: one for worlds and another for neighborhoods. In the sequel, whenever we present the components of models and templates, we will use the notations $\mathcal{M} = \langle \mathcal{W}, \$, \mathcal{V}, \chi \rangle$ and $\mathcal{T} = \langle \mathcal{W}, \$, \mathcal{V}, \chi, N \rangle$ for models and templates respectively. We shall use the term *structure* as a general term to refer to models and templates.

**Definition 3.** *A structure is finite iff its world set is finite.*

We now define a relation between structures in order to represent the pertinence of neighborhoods to a neighborhood system of a world and the pertinence of worlds to a given neighborhood.

**Definition 4.** *Given a model $\mathcal{M} = \langle \mathcal{W}, \$, \mathcal{V}, \chi \rangle$, then for any $N \in \$(\chi)$, the template $\mathcal{T} = \langle \mathcal{W}, \$, \mathcal{V}, \chi, N \rangle$ is in perspective relation to $\mathcal{M}$. We represent this by $\mathcal{M} \multimap \mathcal{T}$. Given a template $\mathcal{T} = \langle \mathcal{W}, \$, \mathcal{V}, \chi, N \rangle$, then, for any $w \in N$, the model $\mathcal{M} = \langle \mathcal{W}, \$, \mathcal{V}, w \rangle$ is in perspective relation to $\mathcal{T}$. We represent this by $\mathcal{T} \multimap \mathcal{M}$.*

As the nesting function evaluation may be different for different worlds, each world may produce different conclusions. For this reason we use the term *perspective* to denote the relation between structures (models and templates), if they are connected by the local evaluation of the nesting function.

**Definition 5.** *The concatenation of n cases of the perspective relation is called a path of size n and is represented by the symbol $\multimap_n$. We consider $\multimap_0$ as the identity.*

Remark: if the size of a path is even, then a model is related to another model or a template is related to another template.

**Definition 6.** *The transitive closure of the perspective relation is called projective relation, which is represented by the symbol $\rightsquigarrow$.*

**Definition 7.** *Given a world $\chi$ and the nested neighborhood function $, we can build the following sequence of world sets:*

1. $\Delta_0^{\$}(\chi) = \{\chi\}$;     2. $\Delta_{k+1}^{\$}(\chi) = \bigcup_{w \in \Delta_k^{\$}(\chi)}(\bigcup \$(w))$, $k \geq 0$.

*Let*

$$\overbrace{\bigwedge_{n}^{\$}(\chi)}^{} = \bigcup_{0 \le m \le n} \bigwedge_{m}^{\$}(\chi)$$

*and*

$$\bigwedge_{n}^{\$}(\chi) = \bigcup_{n \in \mathbb{N}} \overbrace{\bigwedge_{n}^{\$}(\chi)}^{}.$$

By definition, we may notice that

$$\bigwedge^{\$}(\chi) = \{w \in \mathcal{W} \mid \langle \mathcal{W}, \$, \mathcal{V}, \chi \rangle \rightsquigarrow \langle \mathcal{W}, \$, \mathcal{V}, w \rangle\}.$$

We now introduce labels in our language in order to syntactically represent quantifications over two specific domains: neighborhoods and worlds. We have labels of two types: neighborhood labels or a world labels. We denote the set of neighborhood labels by $L_n$ and the set of world labels by $L_w$. We use the term *ns* as an abbreviation for the term neighborhood system.

– Neighborhood labels:
   (⊛) Universal quantifier over neighborhoods of some ns;
   (⊙) Existential quantifier over neighborhoods of some ns;
   ($N$) Variables (capital letters) which denote some neighborhood of some ns.
– World labels:
   ($*$) Universal quantifier over worlds of some neighborhood;
   (•) Existential quantifier over worlds of some neighborhood;
   ($u$) Variables (lower case) which denote some world of some neighborhood.

**Definition 8.** *The language of PUC-Logic consists of:*

– *countably many neighborhood variables:* $N, M, L, \ldots$;
– *countably many world variables:* $w, z, \ldots$;
– *countably many propositional symbols:* $p_0, p_1, \ldots$;
– *countably many propositional constants:* $\uparrow N, \downarrow N, \uparrow M, \downarrow M, \ldots$;
– *the propositions* $\top_n, \perp_n, \top_w, \perp_w$;
– *connectives:* $\wedge, \vee, \rightarrow, \neg$;
– *neighborhood labels:* $\circledast, \odot$;
– *world labels:* $*, \bullet$;
– *auxiliary symbols:* $(,)$.

As in the case of labels, we want to separate the set of well-formed formulas into two disjoint sets, according to the type of label attached to the formula. We denote the set of neighborhood formulas by $F_n$ and the set of world formulas by $F_w$.

**Definition 9.** *The sets $F_n$ and $F_w$ of well-formed formulas[8] are constructed by:*

1. $\top_n, \bot_n \in F_n$;
2. $\top_w, \bot_w \in F_w$;
3. $\alpha \in F_n$, *for every propositional symbol $\alpha$;*
4. $\uparrow N, \downarrow N \in F_w$, *for every neighborhood variable $N$;*
5. *if $\alpha \in F_n$, then $\neg\alpha \in F_n$;*
6. *if $\alpha \in F_w$, then $\neg\alpha \in F_w$;*
7. *if $\alpha, \beta \in F_n$, then $\alpha \wedge \beta, \alpha \vee \beta, \alpha \to \beta \in F_n$;*
8. *if $\alpha, \beta \in F_w$, then $\alpha \wedge \beta, \alpha \vee \beta, \alpha \to \beta \in F_w$;*
9. *if $\alpha \in F_n$ and $\phi \in L_w$, then $\alpha^\phi \in F_w$;*
10. *if $\alpha \in F_w$ and $\phi \in L_n$, then $\alpha^\phi \in F_n$.*

We introduced two different formulas for true and false, one pair of true and false formulas for the set $F_w$ and another pair for the set $F_n$. This is intended to make $F_w$ and $F_n$ disjoint sets of formulas. The formula $\uparrow N$ is introduced to represent a neighborhood which contains the neighborhood $N$ and the formula $\downarrow N$ represents a neighborhood which is contained in $N$. The last two rules of Definition 9 introduce the labeled formulas. Moreover, since we can label a labeled formula, every formula has a stack of labels which represents nested labels. We call it the *attribute* of the formula. The top label of the stack is the *index* of the formula. We represent a formula attribute as a letter which appears to the right of the formula. If the attribute is empty, we may omit it, and the formula has no index. The attribute of some formula will always be empty if the last rule used to build the formula is not one of the labeling rules, as in the case of $((\alpha \to \alpha)^{\circledast, \bullet}) \vee (\gamma^{\odot, *})$. In order to read a labeled formula, it is necessary to read its index first and then the rest of the formula. For example, $(\alpha \to \alpha)^{\circledast, \bullet}$ should be read as there is some world, in all neighborhoods of the considered neighborhood system, in which it is the case $\alpha \to \alpha$. We may concatenate stacks of labels and labels using commas to produce a stack of labels which is obtained by respecting the order of the labels in the stacks and the order of the concatenation, like $\alpha^{\Sigma, \Delta}$, where $\alpha$ is a formula, and $\Sigma$ and $\Delta$ are stacks of labels. But we admit no nesting of attributes and this means that $(\alpha^\Sigma)^\Delta$ is the same as $\alpha^{\Sigma, \Delta}$.

**Definition 10.** *Given a stack of labels $\Sigma$, we define $\overline{\Sigma}$ to be the stack of labels which is obtained from $\Sigma$ by reversing the order of the labels in the stack.*

**Definition 11.** *Given a stack of labels $\Sigma$, its size $s(\Sigma)$ is the number of labels in $\Sigma$.*

**Definition 12.** *Given a world set $\mathcal{W}$, a set of world variables and a set of neighborhood variables, an assignment-function $\sigma$ is a function that assigns a world in $\mathcal{W}$ to each world variable, and a non-empty set of $\mathcal{W}$ to each neighborhood variable.*

---

[8] We use the term wff to denote both the singular and the plural form of the expression *well-formed formula*.

**Definition 13.** *Given an assignment-function $\sigma$, the relation $\models$ of satisfaction between formulas, models and templates is given by:*

1. *If $\alpha$ is atomic, $\langle \mathcal{W}, \$, \mathcal{V}, \chi \rangle \models \alpha$ iff: $\chi \in \mathcal{V}(\alpha)$.*
2. *For every world $w \in \mathcal{W}$, $w \in \mathcal{V}(\top_n)$ and $w \notin \mathcal{V}(\bot_n)$;*
3. *$\langle \mathcal{W}, \$, \mathcal{V}, \chi \rangle \models \neg (\alpha^{\Sigma})$ iff: $\neg (\alpha^{\Sigma}) \in \mathbf{F}_n$ and $\langle \mathcal{W}, \$, \mathcal{V}, \chi \rangle \not\models \alpha^{\Sigma}$;*
4. *$\langle \mathcal{W}, \$, \mathcal{V}, \chi \rangle \models \alpha^{\Sigma} \wedge \beta^{\Omega}$ iff: $\alpha^{\Sigma} \wedge \beta^{\Omega} \in \mathbf{F}_n$ and*
   *( $\langle \mathcal{W}, \$, \mathcal{V}, \chi \rangle \models \alpha^{\Sigma}$ and $\langle \mathcal{W}, \$, \mathcal{V}, \chi \rangle \models \beta^{\Omega}$;*
5. *$\langle \mathcal{W}, \$, \mathcal{V}, \chi \rangle \models \alpha^{\Sigma} \vee \beta^{\Omega}$ ) iff: $\alpha^{\Sigma} \vee \beta^{\Omega} \in \mathbf{F}_n$ and*
   *( $\langle \mathcal{W}, \$, \mathcal{V}, \chi \rangle \models \alpha^{\Sigma}$ or $\langle \mathcal{W}, \$, \mathcal{V}, \chi \rangle \models \beta^{\Omega}$ );*
6. *$\langle \mathcal{W}, \$, \mathcal{V}, \chi \rangle \models \alpha^{\Sigma} \rightarrow \beta^{\Omega}$ iff: $\alpha^{\Sigma} \rightarrow \beta^{\Omega} \in \mathbf{F}_n$ and*
   *( $\langle \mathcal{W}, \$, \mathcal{V}, \chi \rangle \models \neg(\alpha^{\Sigma})$ or $\langle \mathcal{W}, \$, \mathcal{V}, \chi \rangle \models \beta^{\Omega}$ );*
7. *$\langle \mathcal{W}, \$, \mathcal{V}, \chi \rangle \models \alpha^{\Sigma, \circledast}$ iff: $\forall N \in \$(\chi) : \langle \mathcal{W}, \$, \mathcal{V}, \chi, N \rangle \models \alpha^{\Sigma}$;*
8. *$\langle \mathcal{W}, \$, \mathcal{V}, \chi \rangle \models \alpha^{\Sigma, \circledcirc}$ iff: $\exists N \in \$(\chi) : \langle \mathcal{W}, \$, \mathcal{V}, \chi, N \rangle \models \alpha^{\Sigma}$;*
9. *$\langle \mathcal{W}, \$, \mathcal{V}, \chi \rangle \models \alpha^{\Sigma, N}$ iff: $\langle \mathcal{W}, \$, \mathcal{V}, \chi, \sigma(N) \rangle \models \alpha^{\Sigma}$;*
10. *$\langle \mathcal{W}, \$, \mathcal{V}, \chi, N \rangle \models \uparrow M$ iff: $\sigma(M) \in \$(\chi)$ and $\sigma(M) \subset N$;*
11. *$\langle \mathcal{W}, \$, \mathcal{V}, \chi, N \rangle \models \downarrow M$ iff: $\sigma(M) \in \$(\chi)$ and $N \subset \sigma(M)$;*
12. *$\langle \mathcal{W}, \$, \mathcal{V}, \chi, N \rangle \models \alpha^{\Sigma, *}$ iff: $\forall w \in N : \langle \mathcal{W}, \$, \mathcal{V}, w \rangle \models \alpha^{\Sigma}$;*
13. *$\langle \mathcal{W}, \$, \mathcal{V}, \chi, N \rangle \models \alpha^{\Sigma, \bullet}$ iff: $\exists w \in N : \langle \mathcal{W}, \$, \mathcal{V}, w \rangle \models \alpha^{\Sigma}$;*
14. *$\langle \mathcal{W}, \$, \mathcal{V}, \chi, N \rangle \models \alpha^{\Sigma, u}$ iff: $\sigma(u) \in N$ and $\langle \mathcal{W}, \$, \mathcal{V}, \sigma(u) \rangle \models \alpha^{\Sigma}$;*
15. *$\langle \mathcal{W}, \$, \mathcal{V}, \chi, N \rangle \models \neg (\alpha^{\Sigma})$ iff: $\neg (\alpha^{\Sigma}) \in \mathbf{F}_w$ and $\langle \mathcal{W}, \$, \mathcal{V}, \chi, N \rangle \not\models \alpha^{\Sigma}$;*
16. *$\langle \mathcal{W}, \$, \mathcal{V}, \chi, N \rangle \models \alpha^{\Sigma} \wedge \beta^{\Omega}$ iff: $\alpha^{\Sigma} \wedge \beta^{\Omega} \in \mathbf{F}_w$ and*
    *( $\langle \mathcal{W}, \$, \mathcal{V}, \chi, N \rangle \models \alpha^{\Sigma}$ and $\langle \mathcal{W}, \$, \mathcal{V}, \chi, N \rangle \models \beta^{\Omega}$ );*
17. *$\langle \mathcal{W}, \$, \mathcal{V}, \chi, N \rangle \models \alpha^{\Sigma} \vee \beta^{\Omega}$ iff: $\alpha^{\Sigma} \vee \beta^{\Omega} \in \mathbf{F}_w$ and*
    *( $\langle \mathcal{W}, \$, \mathcal{V}, \chi, N \rangle \models \alpha^{\Sigma}$ or $\langle \mathcal{W}, \$, \mathcal{V}, \chi, N \rangle \models \beta^{\Omega}$ );*
18. *$\langle \mathcal{W}, \$, \mathcal{V}, \chi, N \rangle \models \alpha^{\Sigma} \rightarrow \beta^{\Omega}$ iff: $\alpha^{\Sigma} \rightarrow \beta^{\Omega} \in \mathbf{F}_w$ and*
    *( $\langle \mathcal{W}, \$, \mathcal{V}, \chi, N \rangle \models \neg(\alpha^{\Sigma})$ or $\langle \mathcal{W}, \$, \mathcal{V}, \chi, N \rangle \models \beta^{\Omega}$ );*
19. *$\langle \mathcal{W}, \$, \mathcal{V}, \chi, N \rangle \models \top_w$ and $\langle \mathcal{W}, \$, \mathcal{V}, \chi, N \rangle \not\models \bot_w$, for every template.*

The relation of satisfaction will also be used between models, templates and sets of formulas.

**Definition 14.** *Given $\Gamma \in \mathbf{F}_n$ and a model $\mathcal{M}$, $\mathcal{M} \models \Gamma$ iff $\mathcal{M}$ satisfies every formula of $\Gamma$. Likewise for templates and subsets of $\mathbf{F}_w$ and templates.*

**Definition 15.** *Given $\alpha^{\Sigma}, \beta^{\Omega} \in \mathbf{F}_n$, we say the relation of logical consequence $\alpha^{\Sigma} \models \beta^{\Omega}$ holds iff $\mathcal{M} \models \alpha^{\Sigma}$ implies $\mathcal{M} \models \beta^{\Omega}$, for any model $\mathcal{M}$. Likewise for $\alpha^{\Sigma}, \beta^{\Omega} \in \mathbf{F}_w$ and templates.*

The relation of logical consequence will also be used between formulas and sets of formulas.

**Definition 16.** *Given $\Gamma \cup \{\alpha^{\Sigma}\} \subset \mathbf{F}_n$, the relation $\Gamma \models \alpha^{\Sigma}$ is defined iff for any model $\mathcal{M}$, $\mathcal{M} \models \Gamma$ implies $\mathcal{M} \models \alpha^{\Sigma}$. Likewise for subsets of $\mathbf{F}_w$.*

**Definition 17.** *$\alpha^{\Sigma} \in \mathbf{F}_n$ is a n-tautology iff $\mathcal{M} \models \alpha^{\Sigma}$, for every model $\mathcal{M}$. $\alpha^{\Sigma} \in \mathbf{F}_w$ is a w-tautology iff $T \models \alpha^{\Sigma}$, for every template $T$.*

**Lemma 1.** $\alpha^\Sigma$ *is a n-tautology iff* $\alpha^{\Sigma,*,\circledast}$ *is a n-tautology.*

*Proof.* If $\alpha^\Sigma$ is a n-tautology, $\forall z \in \mathcal{W}$, $\langle \mathcal{W}, \$, \mathcal{V}, z \rangle \models \alpha^\Sigma$. In particular, given a world $\chi \in \mathcal{W}$, $\forall N \in \$(\chi) : \forall w \in N : \langle \mathcal{W}, \$, \mathcal{V}, w \rangle \models \alpha^\Sigma$ and, by definition, $\langle \mathcal{W}, \$, \mathcal{V}, \chi \rangle \models \alpha^{\Sigma,*,\circledast}$ for every world of $\mathcal{W}$ and $\alpha^{\Sigma,*,\circledast}$ is also a n-tautology. Conversely, if $\alpha^{\Sigma,*,\circledast}$ is a n-tautology, then $\forall N \in \$(\chi) : \forall w \in N : \langle \mathcal{W}, \$, \mathcal{V}, w \rangle \models \alpha^\Sigma$ for every choice of $\mathcal{W}$, $\$$, $\mathcal{V}$ and $w$. So, given $\mathcal{W}$, $\mathcal{V}$ and $w$, we can choose $\$$ to be the constant function $\{\mathcal{W}\}$. So, $\forall z \in \mathcal{W}$, $\langle \mathcal{W}, \$, \mathcal{V}, z \rangle \models \alpha^\Sigma$ and $\alpha^\Sigma$ must also be a n-tautology.

The relation defined below is motivated by the fact that, if a model $\mathcal{M}$ satisfies a formula like $\alpha^{\circledast,*}$, then for every template $\mathcal{T}$ such that $\mathcal{M} \multimap \mathcal{T}$, $\mathcal{T}$ satisfies $\alpha^\circledast$ by definition. In the same way we have that for every model $\mathcal{H}$ such that $\mathcal{M} \multimap_2 \mathcal{H}$, $\mathcal{H}$ satisfies $\alpha$ by definition.

**Definition 18.** *Given a model* $\mathcal{M}$, *called the reference model, the relation of referential consequence* $\alpha^\Sigma \models_{\mathcal{M}:i} \beta^\Omega$ *is defined iff* $\mathcal{M} \models \alpha^\Sigma$ *implies* $\mathcal{H} \models \beta^\Omega$, *for any structure* $\mathcal{M} \multimap_i \mathcal{H}$.

We will also use the referential consequence between formulas and sets of formulas.

**Definition 19.** *Given* $\Gamma \cup \{\alpha^\Sigma\} \subset \mathbf{F}_n$, $\Gamma \models_{\mathcal{M}:i} \alpha^\Sigma$ *iff* $\mathcal{M} \models \Gamma$ *implies* $\mathcal{H} \models \alpha^\Sigma$, *for any structure* $\mathcal{M} \multimap_i \mathcal{H}$ *which* $\mathcal{H} \models \Gamma$.

We shall now start the definition of the natural deduction system *PUC-ND* for PUC-Logic. Every PUC-ND rule has a stack of labels, called its *context*. The scope is represented by a Greek capital letter at the right of each rule. The *scope* of a rule is the top label of its context. Given a context $\Delta$, we denote its scope by $!\Delta$. If the context is empty, then there is no scope. As in the case of labels and formulas, we want to separate the contexts into two disjoint sets: $\Delta \in \mathbf{C}_n$ if $!\Delta \in \mathbf{L}_n$; $\Delta \in \mathbf{C}_w$ if $\Delta$ is empty or $!\Delta \in \mathbf{L}_w$. The rules are numbered from 1 to 30. In some rules, we have scopes, namely the Greek capital letter on the right side of the inference bar. It is worth observing that *PUC-ND* is clearly not a logic programming inference system, but it is just an inferential basis for the development of a logic programming language. The rules in Fig. 1 constitute the Natural System PUC-ND and the restrictions imposed on the application of each rule are explicitly presented. The last inference bar of each rule separates premises and deductions of premises from the conclusion. As in traditional natural deduction systems, each connective in PUC-ND has a set of introduction and elimination rules. The other rules in PUC-ND concerns the manipulation of labels in a logically based way. The formulas have contexts, which are stacks of labels, while inference rules have only scopes, which are only labels, instead of stacks. In fact, the scope is the topmost label.

$$1:\ \cfrac{\cfrac{\Pi}{\alpha^\Sigma \wedge \beta^\Omega}\ \Delta}{\alpha^\Sigma}\ \Delta \qquad\quad 2:\ \cfrac{\cfrac{\Pi}{\alpha^\Sigma \wedge \beta^\Omega}\ \Delta}{\beta^\Omega}\ \Delta \qquad\quad 3:\ \cfrac{\cfrac{\Pi_1}{\alpha^\Sigma}\ \Delta \qquad \cfrac{\Pi_2}{\beta^\Omega}\ \Delta}{\alpha^\Sigma \wedge \beta^\Omega}\ \Delta$$

$$4:\ \cfrac{\cfrac{\Pi}{\alpha^\Sigma}\ \Delta}{\alpha^\Sigma \vee \beta^\Omega}\ \Delta \qquad\qquad 5:\ \cfrac{\cfrac{\Pi_1}{\alpha^\Sigma \vee \beta^\Omega}\ \Delta \qquad \cfrac{\overset{[\alpha^\Sigma]}{\Pi_2}}{\gamma^\Lambda}\ \Delta\atop \gamma^\Lambda \ \Theta \qquad \cfrac{\overset{[\beta^\Omega]}{\Pi_3}}{\gamma^\Lambda}\ \Delta\atop \gamma^\Lambda \ \Theta}{\gamma^\Lambda}\ \Theta$$

$$6:\ \cfrac{\cfrac{\Pi}{\beta^\Omega}\ \Delta}{\alpha^\Sigma \vee \beta^\Omega}\ \Delta \qquad\quad 7:\ \cfrac{\cfrac{\overset{[\neg(\alpha^\Sigma)]}{\Pi}}{\bot}\ \Delta}{\alpha^\Sigma}\ \Delta \qquad\quad 8:\ \cfrac{\cfrac{\Pi}{\bot}\ \Delta}{\alpha^\Sigma}\ \Delta$$

$$9:\ \cfrac{\cfrac{\Pi}{\bot}\ \Delta}{\bot_n} \qquad\qquad 10:\ \cfrac{\alpha^\Sigma}{\alpha^\Sigma}\ \Delta \qquad\qquad 11:\ \cfrac{\cfrac{\overset{[\alpha^\Sigma]}{\Pi}}{\beta^\Omega}\ \Delta}{\alpha^\Sigma \to \beta^\Omega}\ \Delta$$

$$12:\ \cfrac{\cfrac{\Pi_1}{\alpha^\Sigma}\ \Delta \qquad \cfrac{\Pi_2}{\alpha^\Sigma \to \beta^\Omega}\ \Delta}{\beta^\Omega}\ \Delta \qquad 13:\ \cfrac{\cfrac{\Pi}{\alpha^{\Sigma,\phi}}\ \Delta}{\alpha^\Sigma}\ \Delta,\phi \qquad 14:\ \cfrac{\cfrac{\Pi}{\alpha^\Sigma}\ \Delta,\phi}{\alpha^{\Sigma,\phi}}\ \Delta$$

$$15:\ \cfrac{\cfrac{\Pi}{\alpha^\Sigma}\ \Delta,u}{\alpha^\Sigma}\ \Delta,* \qquad\qquad 16:\ \cfrac{\cfrac{\Pi}{\alpha^\Sigma}\ \Delta,*}{\alpha^\Sigma}\ \Delta,u \qquad\qquad 17:\ \cfrac{\cfrac{\Pi}{\alpha^\Sigma}\ \Delta,u}{\alpha^\Sigma}\ \Delta,\bullet$$

$$18:\ \cfrac{\cfrac{\Pi_1}{\alpha^\Sigma}\ \Delta,\bullet \qquad \cfrac{\overset{[\alpha^\Sigma]}{\Pi_2}}{\beta^\Omega}\ \Delta,u\atop \Theta}{\beta^\Omega}\ \Theta \qquad\qquad 19:\ \cfrac{\cfrac{\Pi_1}{\alpha^\Sigma}\ \Delta,N \qquad \cfrac{\Pi_2}{\beta^\Omega}\ \Delta,\odot}{\alpha^\Sigma}\ \Delta,\odot$$

$$20:\ \cfrac{\cfrac{\Pi_1}{\alpha^\Sigma}\ \Delta,\odot \qquad \cfrac{\overset{[\alpha^\Sigma]}{\Pi_2}}{\beta^\Omega}\ \Delta,N\atop \Theta}{\beta^\Omega}\ \Theta \qquad 21:\ \cfrac{\cfrac{\Pi}{\alpha^\Sigma}\ \Delta,N}{\alpha^\Sigma}\ \Delta,\circledast \qquad 22:\ \cfrac{\cfrac{\Pi_1}{\alpha^\Sigma}\ \Delta,\circledast \qquad \cfrac{\Pi_2}{\beta^\Omega}\ \Delta,N}{\alpha^\Sigma}\ \Delta,N$$

$$23:\ \cfrac{\cfrac{\Pi_1}{\alpha^{\Sigma,\bullet}}\ \Delta,N \qquad \cfrac{\Pi_2}{\uparrow N}\ \Delta,M}{\alpha^{\Sigma,\bullet}}\ \Delta,M \qquad\qquad 24:\ \cfrac{\cfrac{\Pi_1}{\alpha^{\Sigma,*}}\ \Delta,N \qquad \cfrac{\Pi_2}{\downarrow N}\ \Delta,M}{\alpha^{\Sigma,*}}\ \Delta,M$$

$$25:\ \cfrac{\cfrac{\Pi_1}{\uparrow M}\ \Delta,N \qquad \cfrac{\Pi_2}{\uparrow P}\ \Delta,M}{\uparrow P}\ \Delta,N \qquad\qquad 26:\ \cfrac{\cfrac{\Pi_1}{\downarrow M}\ \Delta,N \qquad \cfrac{\Pi_2}{\downarrow P}\ \Delta,M}{\downarrow P}\ \Delta,N$$

$$27:\ \cfrac{\cfrac{\overset{[\uparrow M]}{\Pi_1}}{\alpha^\Sigma}\ \Delta,N\atop \Theta \qquad \cfrac{\overset{[\uparrow N]}{\Pi_2}}{\alpha^\Sigma}\ \Delta,M\atop \Theta}{\alpha^\Sigma}\ \Theta \qquad\qquad 28:\ \cfrac{\cfrac{\overset{[\downarrow M]}{\Pi_1}}{\alpha^\Sigma}\ \Delta,N\atop \Theta \qquad \cfrac{\overset{[\downarrow N]}{\Pi_2}}{\alpha^\Sigma}\ \Delta,M\atop \Theta}{\alpha^\Sigma}\ \Theta$$

$$29:\ \cfrac{\cfrac{\overset{[\uparrow N]}{\Pi_1}}{\alpha^\Sigma}\ \Delta,M\atop \Theta \qquad \cfrac{\overset{[\downarrow N]}{\Pi_2}}{\alpha^\Sigma}\ \Delta,M\atop \Theta}{\alpha^\Sigma}\ \Theta \qquad\qquad 30:\ \cfrac{}{\top}\ \Delta$$

**Fig. 1.** Natural deduction system for PUC-Logic (PUC-ND)

**Definition 20.** *We say a wff $\alpha^\Sigma$ fits in a context $\Delta$ iff $\alpha^{\Sigma,\overline{\Delta}} \in \boldsymbol{F}_n$.*

The wff $\alpha^\bullet \to \beta^\bullet$ and $\gamma^{u,\circledast,*}$ fit in the context $\{\odot\}$, because $(\alpha^\bullet \to \beta^\bullet)^\odot \in \boldsymbol{F}_n$ and $\gamma^{u,\circledast,*,\odot} \in \boldsymbol{F}_n$. The wff $\alpha^\bullet \vee \beta^*$ and $\gamma^{*,N,u}$ do not fit in the context $\{\odot,*\}$, because $(\alpha^\bullet \vee \beta^*)^{*,\odot}$ and $\gamma^{*,N,u,*,\odot}$ are not wff and therefore cannot be in $\boldsymbol{F}_n$. There is no wff which fits in the context $\{*\}$, because the label $* \in \boldsymbol{L}_w$ and the rule of labeling can only include the resulting formula into $\boldsymbol{F}_w$. We can conclude that if a wff is in $\boldsymbol{F}_n$, then the context must be in $\boldsymbol{C}_w$ (the same holds for $\boldsymbol{F}_w$ and $\boldsymbol{C}_n$). The *fit* restriction ensures that the conclusion of a rule is always a wff. Moreover, the definition of *fit* resembles the *attribute grammar* approach for context free languages [5]. This is the main reason to name the stack of labels of a formula as the attribute of the formula. We present below the names of the inference rules of PUC-ND and their respective restrictions.

1. $\wedge$-**elimination:** (a) $\alpha^\Sigma$ and $\beta^\Omega$ must fit in the context; (b) $\Delta$ has no existential quantifier; The existential quantifier is excluded to make it possible to distribute the context over the $\wedge$ operator, what is shown in Lemma 8.
2. $\wedge$-**elimination:** (a) $\alpha^\Sigma$ and $\beta^\Omega$ must fit in the context; (b) $\Delta$ has no existential quantifier; The existential quantifier is excluded to make it possible to distribute the context over the $\wedge$ operator, what is shown in Lemma 8.
3. $\wedge$-**introduction:** (a) $\alpha^\Sigma$ and $\beta^\Omega$ must fit in the context; (b) $\Delta$ has no existential quantifier; The existential quantifier is excluded because the existence of some world (or neighborhood) in which some wff $A$ holds and the existence of some world in which $B$ holds do not implies there is some world in which $A$ and $B$ holds.
4. $\vee$-**introduction:** (a) $\alpha^\Sigma$ and $\beta^\Omega$ must fit in the context; (b) $\Delta$ has no universal quantifier; The universal quantifier is excluded to make it possible to distribute the context over the $\vee$ operator, what is shown in Lemma 8.
5. $\vee$-**elimination:** (a) $\alpha^\Sigma$ and $\beta^\Omega$ must fit in the context $\Delta$; (b) $\Delta$ has no universal quantifier; The universal quantifier is excluded because of the fact that for all worlds (or neighborhoods) $A \vee B$ holds does not implies for all worlds $A$ holds or for all worlds $B$ holds.
6. $\vee$-**introduction:** (a) $\alpha^\Sigma$ and $\beta^\Omega$ must fit in the context; (b) $\Delta$ has no universal quantifier;
   The universal quantifier is excluded to make it possible to distribute the context over the $\vee$ operator, what is shown in Lemma 8.
7. $\perp$-**classical:** (a) $\alpha^\Sigma$ and $\perp$ must fit in the context;
8. $\perp$-**intuitionistic:** (a) $\alpha^\Sigma$ and $\perp$ must fit in the context;
9. **absurd expansion:** (a) $\Delta$ must have no occurrence of $\circledast$; (b) $\perp$ must fit in the context; (c) $\Delta$ must be non empty.
   The symbol $\perp$ is used to denote a formula that may only be $\perp_n$ or $\perp_w$. In the occurrence of $\circledast$, we admit the possibility of an empty neighborhood system. In that context, the absurd does not mean that we actually reach an absurd in our world. $\Delta$ must be non empty to avoid unnecessary detours, like the conclusion of $\perp_n$ from $\perp_n$ in the empty context;

10. **hypothesis-injection:** (a) $\alpha^\Sigma$ must fit in the context.
    This rule permits a change of scope before any formula change. It also avoids combinatorial definitions of rules with hypothesis and formulas inside a given context;
11. **→-introduction:** (a) $\alpha^\Sigma$ and $\beta^\Omega$ must fit in the context;
12. **→-elimination (modus ponens):** (a) $\alpha^\Sigma$ and $\beta^\Omega$ must fit in the context; (b) $\Delta$ has no existential quantifier; (c) the premises may be in reverse order; The existential quantifier is excluded because the existence of some world (or neighborhood) in which some wff $A$ holds and the existence of some world in which $A \to B$ holds do not implies there is some world in which $B$ holds.
13. **context-introduction:** (a) $\alpha^{\Sigma,\phi}$ and $\alpha^\Sigma$ must fit in their contexts;
14. **context-elimination:** (a) $\alpha^{\Sigma,\phi}$ and $\alpha^\Sigma$ must fit in their contexts;
15. **world universal introduction:** (a) $\alpha^\Sigma$ must fit in the context; (b) $u$ must not occur in any hypothesis on which $\alpha^\Sigma$ depends; (c) $u$ must not occur in the context of any hypothesis on which $\alpha^\Sigma$ depends;
16. **world universal elimination:** (a) $\alpha^\Sigma$ must fit in the context; (b) $u$ must not occur in $\alpha^\Sigma$ or $\Delta$;
17. **world existential introduction:** (a) $\alpha^\Sigma$ must fit into the context;
18. **world existential elimination:** (a) the formula $\alpha^\Sigma$ must fit in the context; (b) $u$ must not occur in $\alpha^\Sigma$, $\Delta$, $\Theta$ or any open hypothesis on which $\beta^\Omega$ depends; (c) $u$ must not occur in the context of any open hypothesis on which $\beta^\Omega$ depends; (d) the premises may be in reverse order;
19. **neighborhood existential introduction:** (a) $\alpha^\Sigma$ must fit in the context; (b) the premises may be in reverse order;
20. **neighborhood existential elimination:** (a) the formula $\alpha^\Sigma$ must fit in the context; (b) $N$ must not occur in $\alpha^\Sigma$, $\Delta$, $\Theta$ or any open hypothesis on which $\beta^\Omega$ depends; (c) $N$ must not occur in the context of any open hypothesis on which $\beta^\Omega$ depends; (d) the premises may be in reverse order;
21. **neighborhood universal introduction:** (a) the formula $\alpha^\Sigma$ must fit into the contexts; (b) $N$ must not occur in any open hypothesis on which $\alpha^\Sigma$ depends; (c) $N$ must not occur in the context of any open hypothesis on which $\alpha^\Sigma$ depends;
22. **neighborhood universal wild-card:** (a) the formulas $\alpha^\Sigma$ and $\beta^\Omega$ must fit in their contexts; (b) the premises may be in reverse order;
    This rule is necessary because a neighborhood system may be empty and every variable must denote some neighborhood, because of the variable assignment function $\sigma$. The wild-card rule may be seen as a permission to use some available variable as an instantiation, by making explicit the choice of the variable.
23. **world existential propagation:** (a) $\alpha^{\Sigma,\bullet}$ and $\uparrow N$ fit in their contexts; (b) the premises may be in reverse order;
24. **world universal propagation:** (a) $\alpha^{\Sigma,*}$ and $\downarrow N$ fit in their contexts; (b) the premises may be in reverse order;
25. **transitive neighborhood inclusion:** (a) $\uparrow M$ and $\uparrow P$ fit in their contexts; (b) the premises may be in reverse order;

26. **transitive neighborhood inclusion:** (a) $\downarrow M$ and $\downarrow P$ fit in their contexts; (b) the premises may be in reverse order;
27. **neighborhood total order:** (a) $\uparrow M$, $\uparrow N$ and $\alpha^\Sigma$ fit in their contexts; (b) the premises may be in reverse order;
28. **neighborhood total order:** (a) $\downarrow M$, $\downarrow N$ and $\alpha^\Sigma$ fit in their contexts; (b) the premises may be in reverse order;
29. **neighborhood total order:** (a) $\uparrow N$, $\downarrow N$ and $\alpha^\Sigma$ fit in their contexts. (b) the premises may be in reverse order;
30. **truth acceptance:** (a) $\Delta$ must have no occurrence of $\circledcirc$; (b) $\top$ must fit in the context. The symbol $\top$ is used to denote a formula which may only be $\top_n$ or $\top_w$. If we accepted the occurrence of $\circledcirc$, the existence of some neighborhood in every neighborhood system would be necessary and the logic expressed by PUC-ND should be normal according to Lewis classification [1]. $\Delta$ must be non empty to avoid unnecessary detours, like the conclusion of $\top_n$ from $\top_n$ in the empty context.

We present below an example of a proof in PUC-ND. If there is some neighborhood which has some $\beta^\Omega$-world but no $\alpha^\Sigma$-world, then, for all neighborhoods, having some $\alpha^\Sigma$-world implies having some $\beta^\Omega$-world. The reason is the total order for the inclusion relation among neighborhoods.

**Lemma 2.** *If $\Delta \in C_n$, then $s(\Delta)$ is odd. If $\Delta \in C_w$, then $s(\Delta)$ is even.*

*Proof.* By definition, if $\Delta$ is empty, then $\Delta \in C_w$ and $s(\Delta)$ is even. According to the PUC-ND rules, if $\Delta$ is empty, then $\{\Delta, \phi\} \in C_n$ and $s(\Delta)$ is odd. We conclude that changing the context from $C_w$ to $C_n$ and vice-versa always involves adding or subtracting one to the label size. As the empty context belongs to $C_w$, the even sizes are only for contexts in $C_w$.

## 5   Some PUC-Logic Properties

The proofs of soundness and completeness for PUC-Logic are given in [23]. In this section we give a sort of *road map* for these proofs. In the case of soundness, we prove that PUC-ND derivations preserve the relation of *resolution*, which generalizes the satisfiability relation.

**Definition 21.** *Given a model* $\mathcal{M}$*, a context* $\Delta$ *and a wff* $\alpha^\Sigma$*, the relation of resolution* $\mathcal{M} \models^\Delta \alpha^\Sigma$ *holds iff* $\alpha^\Sigma$ *fits in the context* $\Delta$ *and* $\mathcal{M} \models \alpha^{\Sigma,\overline{\Delta}}$*. Given* $\Gamma \subset F_n$ *or* $\Gamma \subset F_w$*, then* $\mathcal{M} \models^\Delta \Gamma$ *if the resolution relation holds for every formula of* $\Gamma$*.*

**Lemma 3.** *Given a model* $\mathcal{M} = \langle \mathcal{W}, \$, \mathcal{V}, \chi \rangle$*, if* $\mathcal{M} \models^\Delta \alpha^\Sigma$ *and* $\alpha^\Sigma \models_{\mathcal{M}:s(\Delta)} \beta^\Omega$*, then* $\mathcal{M} \models^\Delta \beta^\Omega$*.*

**Lemma 4.** *Given a model* $\mathcal{M} = \langle \mathcal{W}, \$, \mathcal{V}, \chi \rangle$*, if* $\mathcal{M} \models^\Delta \alpha^\Sigma$ *and* $\alpha^\Sigma \models \beta^\Omega$*, then* $\mathcal{M} \models^\Delta \beta^\Omega$*.*

**Lemma 5.** *Given a context* $\Delta$ *without universal quantifiers, if* $\alpha^{\Sigma,\overline{\Delta}} \vee \beta^{\Omega,\overline{\Delta}}$ *is wff, then* $\alpha^{\Sigma,\overline{\Delta}} \vee \beta^{\Omega,\overline{\Delta}} \equiv (\alpha^\Sigma \vee \beta^\Omega)^{\overline{\Delta}}$*.*

**Lemma 6.** *Given a context* $\Delta$ *without existential quantifiers, if* $\alpha^{\Sigma,\overline{\Delta}} \wedge \beta^{\Omega,\overline{\Delta}}$ *is wff, then* $\alpha^{\Sigma,\overline{\Delta}} \wedge \beta^{\Omega,\overline{\Delta}} \equiv (\alpha^\Sigma \wedge \beta^\Omega)^{\overline{\Delta}}$*.*

**Lemma 7.** *Given a context* $\Delta$ *without existential quantifiers, if* $(\alpha^\Sigma \to \beta^\Omega)^{\overline{\Delta}}$ *is wff, then it implies* $\alpha^{\Sigma,\overline{\Delta}} \to \beta^{\Omega,\overline{\Delta}}$*.*

**Lemma 8.** *PUC-ND without the rules* $5, 7, 11, 18, 20, 27, 28$ *and* $29$ *preserves resolution.*

**Lemma 9.** *Given a context* $\Delta$ *with no existential label, and a wff* $\alpha^\Sigma$ *which fits on* $\Delta$*, then, for any model,* $\mathcal{M} \models^\Delta \alpha^\Sigma \vee \neg(\alpha^\Sigma)$*.*

**Lemma 10.** *The rules of PUC-ND preserves resolution.*

**Definition 22.** *Given the formulas* $\alpha^\Sigma$ *and* $\beta^\Omega$*, the relation of derivability* $\alpha^\Sigma \vdash^\Delta_\Theta \beta^\Omega$ *holds iff there is a derivation with conclusion* $\beta^\Omega$ *in the context* $\Theta$ *such that the only open assumption in this derivation is* $\alpha^\Sigma$ *in the context* $\Delta$*. If* $\Gamma \subset F_n$ *or* $\Gamma \subset F_w$*, the relation* $\Gamma \vdash^\Delta_\Theta \alpha^\Sigma$ *of derivability is defined iff there is a derivation with conclusion* $\alpha^\Sigma$ *in the context* $\Theta$ *such that the open assumptions of this derivations are formulas of* $\Gamma$ *in the context* $\Delta$*.*

**Definition 23.** $\alpha^\Sigma$ *is a theorem iff* $\vdash \alpha^\Sigma$.

**Theorem 1.** $\Gamma \vdash \alpha^\Sigma$ *implies* $\Gamma \models \alpha^\Sigma$ *(Soundness)*.

*Proof.* The *fit* restriction on PUC-ND rules ensures $\alpha^\Sigma \in \boldsymbol{F}_n$, because it appears in the empty context. The same conclusion follows for every formula in $\Gamma$. The derivability assures there is a derivation with conclusion $\alpha^\Sigma$ whose open hypothesis form a subset of $\Gamma$, which we call $\Gamma'$. If we take a model $\mathcal{M}$ which satisfies every formula of $\Gamma$, then it also satisfies every formula of $\Gamma'$. So, $\mathcal{M} \models \gamma^\Theta$, for every $\gamma^\Theta \in \Gamma'$. But this means, by definition, for every wff of $\Gamma'$, the resolution relation holds with the empty context. Then, from Lemma 10 we know $\mathcal{M} \models \alpha^\Sigma$. So, every model which satisfies every formula of $\Gamma$, satisfies $\alpha^\Sigma$ and, by definition, $\Gamma \models \alpha^\Sigma$.

In order to prove the converse implication, we use the strategy of maximal consistent sets to prove completeness for the fragment $\{\wedge, \rightarrow, \bullet, \odot, \circledast\}$ of the language. The label $\odot$ is not definable from $\circledast$ and vice-versa, because the logic for neighborhoods is a free logic [18]. For the completeness proof we will restrict the formulas to *sentences*.

**Definition 24.** *Given* $\alpha^\Sigma \in \boldsymbol{F}_n$, *if* $\alpha^\Sigma$ *has no variables in the attributes of its subformulas, nor any subformula of the shape* $\uparrow N$ *or* $\downarrow N$, *then* $\alpha^\Sigma \in \boldsymbol{S}_n$. *By analogy, we can construct* $\boldsymbol{S}_w$ *from* $\boldsymbol{F}_w$.

**Definition 25.** *Given* $\Gamma \subset \boldsymbol{S}_n$ *(*$\Gamma \subset \boldsymbol{S}_w$*), we say* $\Gamma$ *is n-inconsistent (w-inconsistent) iff* $\Gamma \vdash \bot_n$ *(*$\Gamma \vdash_N^N \bot_w$, *where* $N$ *is a neighborhood variable which does not occur in* $\Gamma$*) and n-consistent (w-consistent) if* $\Gamma \nvdash \bot_n$ *(*$\Gamma \nvdash_N^N \bot_w$*)*.

**Lemma 11.** *Given* $\Gamma \subset \boldsymbol{S}_n$ *(*$\Gamma \subset \boldsymbol{S}_w$*), the three conditions are equivalent:*

1. $\Gamma$ *is n-inconsistent;*
2. $\Gamma \vdash \phi^\Theta$, *for any formula* $\phi^\Theta$ *which fits into the empty context;*
3. *There is at least a formula* $\phi^\Theta$, *such that* $\Gamma \vdash \phi^\Theta$ *and* $\Gamma \vdash \phi^\Theta \rightarrow \bot_n$.

**Lemma 12.** *Given* $\Gamma \subset \boldsymbol{S}_n$ *(*$\Gamma \subset \boldsymbol{S}_w$*), if there is a model (template) which satisfies every formula of* $\Gamma$, *then* $\Gamma$ *is n-consistent (w-consistent)*.

**Lemma 13.** *Given* $\Gamma \subset \boldsymbol{S}_n$: 1. *If* $\Gamma \cup \{\phi^\Theta \rightarrow \bot_n\} \vdash \bot_n$, *then* $\Gamma \vdash \phi^\Theta$; 2. *If* $\Gamma \cup \{\phi^\Theta\} \vdash \bot_n$, *then* $\Gamma \vdash \phi^\Theta \rightarrow \bot_n$. *Likewise for* $\Gamma \subset \boldsymbol{S}_w$.

**Lemma 14.** $\boldsymbol{S}_n$ *and* $\boldsymbol{S}_w$ *are denumerable*.

**Definition 26.** *A set* $\Gamma \subset \boldsymbol{S}_n$ *(*$\Gamma \subset \boldsymbol{S}_w$*) is maximally n-consistent (maximally w-consistent) iff* $\Gamma$ *is n-consistent (w-consistent) and it cannot be a proper subset of any other n-consistent (w-consistent) set*.

**Lemma 15.** *Every n-consistent (w-consistent) set is subset of a maximally n-consistent (w-consistent) set*.

**Lemma 16.** *If $\Gamma$ is maximally n-consistent (w-consistent) set, then $\Gamma$ is closed under derivability.*

**Lemma 17.** *If $\Gamma$ is maximally n-consistent (w-consistent), then:*

*(a) For all $\varphi^\Theta \in S_n$ ($\in S_w$), either $\varphi^\Theta \in \Gamma$ or $\varphi^\Theta \to \bot_n \in \Gamma$ ($\varphi^\Theta \to \bot_w$);*
*(b) For all $\varphi^\Theta, \psi^\Upsilon \in S_n$ ($\in S_w$), $\varphi^\Theta \to \psi^\Upsilon \in \Gamma$ iff $\varphi^\Theta \in \Gamma$ implies $\psi^\Upsilon \in \Gamma$.*

**Corollary 1.** *If $\Gamma$ is maximally n-consistent (w-consistent), then $\varphi^\Theta \in \Gamma$ iff $\varphi^\Theta \to \bot_n \notin \Gamma$.*

**Definition 27.** *Given the maximally n-consistent set $\Gamma \subset S_n$ and the maximally w-consistent set $\Lambda \subset S_w$, we say $\Gamma$ accepts $\Lambda$ ($\Gamma \propto \Lambda$) if $\alpha^\Sigma \in \Lambda$ implies $\alpha^{\Sigma,\odot} \in \Gamma$. If $\alpha^\Sigma \in \Gamma$ implies $\alpha^{\Sigma,\bullet} \in \Lambda$, then $\Lambda \propto \Gamma$.*

**Definition 28.** *Given maximally w-consistent sets $\Gamma$ and $\Lambda$, we say $\Gamma$ subordinates $\Lambda$ ($\Lambda \sqsubset \Gamma$) iff $\alpha^{\Sigma,\bullet} \in \Lambda$ implies $\alpha^{\Sigma,\bullet} \in \Gamma$ and $\alpha^{\Sigma,*} \in \Gamma$ implies $\alpha^{\Sigma,*} \in \Lambda$.*

**Lemma 18.** *If $\Gamma$ is n-consistent, then there is a model $\mathcal{M}$, such that $\mathcal{M} \models \alpha^\Sigma$, for every $\alpha^\Sigma \in \Gamma$.*

**Corollary 2.** *$\Gamma \nvdash \alpha^\Sigma$ iff there is a model $\mathcal{M}$, such that $\mathcal{M} \models \phi^\Theta$, for every $\phi^\Theta \in \Gamma$, and $\mathcal{M} \nvDash \alpha^\Sigma$.*

**Theorem 2.** *$\Gamma \models \alpha^\Sigma$ implies $\Gamma \vdash \alpha^\Sigma$ (Completeness).*

*Proof.* $\Gamma \nvdash \alpha^\Sigma$ implies $\Gamma \nvDash \alpha^\Sigma$, by the Corollary 2 and the logical consequence definition.

The proof of the normalization theorem for PUC-ND is based on the standard strategy employed in the case of classical propositional logic. In the case of maximum formulas in derivations with fixed contexts, we can use Prawitz [7] strategy to reduce applications of the classical absurd to atomic conclusions. In order to prove this result we must, as in [7], work with the fragment $\mathcal{L}_-$ which omits the operator $\vee$. After this preparatory result, we present the reductions for the remaining rules. We will follow the normalization algorithm proposed by van Dalen: given a derivation $\Pi$, we start from a subderivation $\Pi'$ of $\Pi$ which ends with an application of an elimination rule whose major premiss is a maximum formula of maximal rank and such that no maximum formula of maximal rank occurs above it or above a formula side-connected with it.

**Lemma 19.** *Let $\Pi$ be a derivation such that the only rules that occur in $\Pi$ are the rules from 1 to 8 and from 10 to 12. Then, $\Pi$ is normalizable.*

*Proof.* The system restricted to these rules can be seen as a natural deduction system for classical propositional logic, since the context is fixed and the formulas with labels are treated like atomic formulas. As we said above, we follow here Prawitz's strategy [7]. We present the $\wedge$-reductions and the $\to$-reduction in the case of fixed context and labels:

$$
\dfrac{\dfrac{\dfrac{\Pi_1}{\alpha}\Delta \quad \dfrac{\Pi_2}{\beta}\Delta}{\dfrac{\alpha \wedge \beta}{\dfrac{\alpha}{\Pi_3}\Delta}\Delta}\Delta}{} \quad \rhd \quad \dfrac{\dfrac{\Pi_1}{\alpha}\Delta}{\Pi_3}\Delta
\qquad
\dfrac{\dfrac{\dfrac{\Pi_1}{\alpha}\Delta \quad \dfrac{\Pi_2}{\beta}\Delta}{\dfrac{\alpha \wedge \beta}{\dfrac{\beta}{\Pi_3}\Delta}\Delta}\Delta}{} \quad \rhd \quad \dfrac{\dfrac{\Pi_2}{\beta}\Delta}{\Pi_3}\Delta
$$

$$
\dfrac{\dfrac{\Pi_1}{\alpha}\Delta \quad \dfrac{\dfrac{[\alpha]}{\dfrac{\Pi_2}{\beta}\Delta}\Delta}{\dfrac{\alpha \to \beta}{}\Delta}\Delta}{\dfrac{\beta}{\Pi_3}\Delta}
\quad \rhd \quad
\dfrac{\dfrac{\dfrac{\Pi_1}{\alpha}\Delta}{\dfrac{\Pi_2}{\beta}\Delta}\Delta}{\Pi_3}\Delta
$$

We first show that every application of the classical can be restricted to atomic conclusions. We introduce transformations on the derivation shown in the left according to the main logical operator of $\gamma$. We only present the transformation for $\wedge$ (see [7] for further details).

$$
\dfrac{\dfrac{[\neg\gamma]}{\dfrac{\Pi_1}{\dfrac{\bot}{\dfrac{\gamma}{\Pi_2}\Delta}\Delta}\Delta}\Delta}{}
\qquad
\dfrac{
\dfrac{\dfrac{{}^{1}[\alpha \wedge \beta]}{\alpha}\Delta \quad {}^{2}[\neg\alpha]}{1\,\dfrac{\dfrac{\bot}{[\neg(\alpha \wedge \beta)]}\Delta}{\dfrac{\Pi_1}{2\,\dfrac{\bot}{\alpha}\Delta}\Delta}\Delta}\Delta
\quad
\dfrac{\dfrac{{}^{3}[\alpha \wedge \beta]}{\alpha}\Delta \quad {}^{4}[\neg\beta]}{3\,\dfrac{\dfrac{\bot}{[\neg(\alpha \wedge \beta)]}\Delta}{\dfrac{\Pi_1}{4\,\dfrac{\bot}{\beta}\Delta}\Delta}\Delta}\Delta
}{\dfrac{\alpha \wedge \beta}{\Pi_2}\Delta}
$$

**Lemma 20.** *Given a derivation $\Pi$, if we exchange every occurrence of a world variable $u$ in $\Pi$ by a world variable $w$ which does not occur in $\Pi$, then the resulting derivation, which we represent by $\Pi(u \mid w)$, is also a derivation.*

*Proof.* By induction on the number of formula occurrences in $\Pi$.

Besides *maximum formulas*, derivations in PUC-ND may contain *detours*.

**Definition 29.** *A detour in a derivation $\Pi$ is any subderivation of $\Pi$ that has a formula in one context as hypothesis and which concludes with the same formula in the same context.*

**Theorem 3.** *Every derivation in PUC-ND is normalizable.*

*Proof.* We present the argument for the remaining rules. An application of rule 9 cannot produce maximum formulas, but it may produce *detours*, if we use it together with the rules 7 and 8, because the subderivation ($\Pi_2$ below) does not discharge any hypothesis of the upper subderivation ($\Pi_1$ below). But such detours may be replaced by an application of rule 8 as shown below:

$$\text{rule 9:}\ \cfrac{\cfrac{\dfrac{\Pi_1}{\bot}\,\Delta}{\bot_n}}{}\qquad\qquad\qquad \rhd\qquad \text{rule 8:}\ \dfrac{\dfrac{\Pi_1}{\bot}\,\Delta}{\beta^\Omega}\,\Delta\;\;\Delta$$

$$\text{rule 8:}\ \dfrac{\dfrac{\Pi_2}{\bot}\,\Delta}{\beta^\Omega}\,\Delta \qquad\qquad\qquad \dfrac{\Pi_3}{}\,\Delta$$

$$\dfrac{\Pi_3}{}\,\Delta$$

$$\text{rule 7:}\ \dfrac{\dfrac{\dfrac{[\neg(\beta^\Omega)]}{\neg(\beta^\Omega)}\,\Delta \quad \text{rule 9:}\ \dfrac{\dfrac{\Pi_1}{\bot}\,\Delta}{\bot_n}}{\dfrac{\Pi_2}{\bot}\,\Delta}}{\beta^\Omega}\,\Delta \qquad \rhd\qquad \text{rule 8:}\ \dfrac{\dfrac{\Pi_1}{\bot}\,\Delta}{\beta^\Omega}\,\Delta\;\;\Delta$$

$$\dfrac{\Pi_3}{}\,\Delta \qquad\qquad\qquad \dfrac{\Pi_3}{}\,\Delta$$

The rules 13 and 14 produce a detour only if the conclusion of one is taken as a hypothesis of the other rule for the same context and, as above, the considered subderivation does not discharge any hypothesis of the upper subderivation. In this case, if we eliminate such detour, we may produce a new maximum formula of the case of Lemma 19. We cannot produce new detours by doing this elimination because if there is any detour surrounding the formula $\alpha^\Sigma$, it must have existed before the elimination. If we start from the upper-leftmost detour, we eliminate the detours until we produce a derivation which contains only maximum formulas of the case of Lemma 19. The same argument works for the rules 15 and 16 and for the rules 21 and 22.

$$\text{rule 13:}\ \dfrac{\dfrac{\Pi_1}{\alpha^{\Sigma,\phi}}\,\Delta}{\alpha^\Sigma}\,\Delta,\phi$$

$$\text{rule 14:}\ \dfrac{\dfrac{\Pi_2}{\alpha^\Sigma}\,\Delta,\phi}{\alpha^{\Sigma,\phi}}\,\Delta \qquad \rhd\qquad \dfrac{\dfrac{\Pi_1}{\alpha^{\Sigma,\phi}}\,\Delta}{\Pi_3}\,\Delta$$

$$\dfrac{\Pi_3}{}\,\Delta$$

$$\text{rule 14:}\ \dfrac{\dfrac{\Pi_1}{\alpha^\Sigma}\,\Delta,\phi}{\alpha^{\Sigma,\phi}}\,\Delta$$

$$\text{rule 13:}\ \dfrac{\dfrac{\Pi_2}{\alpha^{\Sigma,\phi}}\,\Delta}{\alpha^\Sigma}\,\Delta,\phi \qquad \rhd\qquad \dfrac{\dfrac{\Pi_1}{\alpha^\Sigma}\,\Delta,\phi}{\Pi_3}\,\Delta,\phi$$

$$\dfrac{\Pi_3}{}\,\Delta,\phi$$

$$\text{rule 21: } \cfrac{\cfrac{\dfrac{\Pi_1}{\alpha^\Sigma}\,\Delta, N}{\alpha^\Sigma}\,\Delta, \circledast}{}\qquad\cfrac{}{\beta^\Omega}\,\Delta, N$$
$$\text{rule 22: }\cfrac{\qquad\qquad\qquad}{\alpha^\Sigma}\qquad\triangleright\qquad \dfrac{\Pi_1}{\alpha^\Sigma}\,\Delta, N$$

$$\text{rule 22: }\cfrac{\dfrac{\dfrac{\Pi_1}{\alpha^\Sigma}\,\Delta,\circledast}{\ }\qquad\dfrac{}{\beta^\Omega}\,\Delta, N}{\ }\,\Delta, N$$
$$\text{rule 21: }\cfrac{\alpha^\Sigma}{\alpha^\Sigma}\,\Delta,\circledast\qquad\triangleright\qquad \dfrac{\Pi_1}{\alpha^\Sigma}\,\Delta,\circledast$$

Rules 17 and 19 preserves normalization. These rules produce a detour only if the conclusion of one is taken as a hypothesis of the other rule for the same context. In this case, if we eliminate such detour, we may produce a new maximum formula of the case of Lemma 19. We cannot produce new detours by doing this elimination because if there is any detour surrounding the formula $\alpha^\Sigma$, it must have existed before the elimination. If we start from the upper-leftmost detour, we eliminate the detours until we produce a derivation which contains only maximum formulas of the case of Lemma 19. We used the representation $(u, v \mid w, u)$ for the substitution of all occurrences of the variable $u$ by the variable $w$ that do not occur in $\Pi_2$, $\Theta$ or $\beta^\Omega$, and the subsequent substitution of all occurrences of the variable $v$ by the variable $u$. The same argument works for the rules 18 and 20.

$$\text{rule 17: }\cfrac{\cfrac{\dfrac{\Pi_1}{\alpha^\Sigma}\,\Delta, N, u}{\alpha^\Sigma}\,\Delta, N, \bullet\quad \cfrac{\dfrac{[\alpha^\Sigma]}{\Pi_2}\,\Delta, N, v}{\beta^\Omega}\,\Theta}{\ }$$
$$\text{rule 19: }\cfrac{\qquad\qquad\qquad\qquad}{\beta^\Omega}\,\Theta\qquad\triangleright\qquad \cfrac{\cfrac{\dfrac{\Pi_1}{\alpha^\Sigma}\,\Delta, N, u}{\Pi_2(u, v \mid w, u)}\,\Delta, N, u}{\beta^\Omega(u, v \mid w, u)}\,\Theta(u, v \mid w, u)$$

$$\text{rule 17: }\cfrac{\dfrac{[\alpha^\Sigma]}{\alpha^\Sigma}\,\Delta, N, u}{\alpha^\Sigma}\,\Delta, N, \bullet$$
$$\text{rule 19: }\cfrac{\dfrac{\Pi_1}{\alpha^\Sigma}\,\Delta, N, \bullet\qquad\cfrac{\cfrac{\ }{\alpha^\Sigma}\ }{\Pi_2}\,\Theta}{\beta^\Omega}\,\Theta\qquad\triangleright\qquad \cfrac{\dfrac{\Pi_1}{\alpha^\Sigma}\,\Delta, N, \bullet}{\dfrac{\Pi_2}{\beta^\Omega}\,\Theta}$$

Although rules 23 to 26 cannot produce maximum formula, they can produce unnecessary detours. We repeat the above arguments to eliminate them. The reduction for the rule 24 is similar to the reduction for the rule 23, and the reductions for rule 26 are similar to the reductions for rule 25. For rules 25 and 26, the reductions depend on the size of the cycles built to recover the same formula in the same context. We present only the case for a cycle of size 3. The rules 27 to 30 produce no maximum formula nor any unnecessary detour.

$$\text{rule 23: } \cfrac{\cfrac{\Pi_1}{\alpha^{\Sigma,\bullet}}\,\Delta,N \qquad \cfrac{\Pi_2}{\uparrow N}\,\Delta,M}{\text{rule 23: } \cfrac{\alpha^{\Sigma,\bullet}\,\Delta,M \qquad \cfrac{\Pi_3}{\uparrow M}\,\Delta,N}{\cfrac{\alpha^{\Sigma,\bullet}}{\Pi_4}\,\Delta,N}} \qquad \rhd \qquad \cfrac{\cfrac{\Pi_1}{\alpha^{\Sigma,\bullet}}\,\Delta,N}{\Pi_4}\,\Delta,N$$

$$\text{rule 25: } \cfrac{\cfrac{\Pi_1}{\uparrow M}\,\Delta,N \qquad \cfrac{\Pi_2}{\uparrow P}\,\Delta,M}{\text{rule 25: } \cfrac{\uparrow P\,\Delta,N \qquad \cfrac{\Pi_3}{\uparrow Q}\,\Delta,P}{\text{rule 25: } \cfrac{\uparrow Q\,\Delta,N \qquad \cfrac{\Pi_4}{\uparrow M}\,\Delta,Q}{\cfrac{\uparrow M}{\Pi_5}\,\Delta,N}}} \qquad \rhd \qquad \cfrac{\cfrac{\Pi_1}{\uparrow M}\,\Delta,N}{\Pi_5}\,\Delta,N$$

**Definition 30.** *The label rank* $\aleph(\alpha^\Sigma)$ *of a wff* $\alpha^\Sigma$ *is the depth of label nesting:*

1. $\aleph(\alpha^\Sigma) = \aleph(\alpha) + s(\Sigma)/2$;
2. *If* $\alpha^\Sigma = \beta^\Omega \vee \gamma^\Theta$, *then* $\aleph(\alpha^\Sigma) = \max(\aleph(\beta^\Omega), \aleph(\gamma^\Theta))$;
3. *If* $\alpha^\Sigma = \beta^\Omega \wedge \gamma^\Theta$, *then* $\aleph(\alpha^\Sigma) = \max(\aleph(\beta^\Omega), \aleph(\gamma^\Theta))$;
4. *If* $\alpha^\Sigma = \beta^\Omega \to \gamma^\Theta$, *then* $\aleph(\alpha^\Sigma) = \max(\aleph(\beta^\Omega), \aleph(\gamma^\Theta))$;
5. *If* $\alpha^\Sigma = \neg\beta^\Omega$, *then* $\aleph(\alpha^\Sigma) = \aleph(\beta^\Omega)$;

Remark: by definition, the rank for a wff in $F_n$ must be a natural number.

**Lemma 21.** *Given a model* $\mathcal{M} = \langle W, \$, \mathcal{V}, \chi \rangle$ *and a* $\alpha^\Sigma \in F_n$, *if* $\aleph(\alpha^\Sigma) = k$, *then we only need to verify the worlds of* $\overbrace{\Delta_k^\$(\chi)}$ *to know if* $\mathcal{M} \models \alpha^\Sigma$ *holds.*

*Proof.* If $\aleph(\alpha^\Sigma) = 0$, then $\alpha^\Sigma$ is a propositional formula. In this case, we need only to verify that the formula holds at $\overbrace{\Delta_0^\$(\chi)} = \{\chi\}$. If $\aleph(\alpha^\Sigma) = k + 1$, then it must have a subformula of the form $(\beta^\Omega)^\phi$, where $\phi$ is a neighborhood label. In the worst case, we need to verify all neighborhoods of $\$(\chi)$ to assure the property described by $\beta^\Omega$ holds in all of them. $\beta^\Omega$ must have a subformula of the form $(\gamma^\Theta)^\psi$, where $\psi$ is a world label. In the worst case, we need to verify all worlds of $\$(\chi)$ to ensure the property described by $\gamma^\Theta$ holds in all of them. But $\aleph(\gamma^\Theta) = k$ and, by the induction hypothesis, we need only to verify in the worlds of $\overbrace{\Delta_k^\$(w)}$, for every $w \in \overbrace{\Delta_1^\$(\chi)}$. So we need, in the worst case, to verify the worlds of $\overbrace{\Delta_{k+1}^\$(w)}$.

**Lemma 22.** *If* $\mathcal{M} = \langle W, \$, \mathcal{V}, \chi \rangle \models \alpha^\Sigma$, *then there is a finite model* $\mathcal{M}' = \langle W', \$', \mathcal{V}', \chi' \rangle$, *such that* $\mathcal{M}' \models \alpha^\Sigma$.

*Proof.* In the proof of Lemma 18 we verified the pertinence of the formulas in maximally n-consistent sets and maximally w-consistent sets based on the structure of the given formula to establish the satisfiability relation. Each existential label required the existence of one neighborhood or world for the verification of a given subformula validity. The universal label for neighborhood required no neighborhood at all. It only added properties to the neighborhoods which exist in a given neighborhood system. The procedure is a demonstration that we only need to gather a finite set of neighborhoods and worlds, for any wff in $F_n$.

**Theorem 4.** *PUC-Logic is decidable.*

*Proof.* If $\nvdash \alpha^\Sigma$, then it must be possible to find a template which satisfies the negation of the formula. By the lemma above, there is a finite template which satisfies this negation.

**Definition 31.** *Every label occurrence $\phi$ inside a formula $\alpha^\Sigma$ is an index of a subformula $\beta^{\Omega,\phi}$. Every label occurrence $\phi$ has a relative label depth defined by $\flat(\phi) = \aleph(\alpha^\Sigma) - \aleph(\beta^{\Omega,\phi})$.*

**Lemma 23.** *Given $\alpha^\Sigma \in F_n$, there is a finite model $\mathcal{M} = \langle \mathcal{W}, \$, \mathcal{V}, \chi \rangle$, such that $\mathcal{M} \models \alpha^\Sigma$ with the following properties: (a) $\mathcal{W} = \widehat{\Delta_k^\$(\chi)}$, where $k = \aleph(\alpha^\Sigma)$; (b) For every world $w \in \Delta_n^\$(\chi)$, $\$(w)$ has at most the same number of neighborhoods as labels $\phi$, such that $\flat(\phi) = n$; (c) Every neighborhood $N \in \$(w)$ has at most the same number of worlds as the labels $\phi$, such that $\flat(\phi) = n + 1/2$, plus the number of labels $\varphi$, such that $\flat(\varphi) = n$.*

*Proof.* (a) From Lemmas 21 and 22; (b) Every neighborhood existential label $\phi$, such that $\flat(\phi) = 0$ contributes, by the procedure of Lemma 18, to one neighborhood to $\$(\chi)$ for the model $\mathcal{M} = \langle \mathcal{W}, \$, \mathcal{V}, \chi \rangle$. The neighborhood universal requires no additional neighborhood to $\$(\chi)$ according to Lemma 22 explanation. In the worst case, all neighborhood labels $\phi$, such that $\flat(\phi) = 0$, are existential. The labels $\phi$, such that $\flat(\phi) = n$, $n \geq 0$, $n \in \mathbb{N}$ contributes to the systems of neighborhoods of the worlds of $\Delta_n^\$(\chi)$. In the worst case, all of this labels contributes to a neighborhood system of a single world; (c) The same argument works for the number of worlds in a neighborhood except that the number of worlds in a neighborhood is bigger than the number worlds in every neighborhoods it contains. In the worst case, the smallest neighborhood contains the same number of worlds as the number of labels $\phi$, such that $\flat(\phi) = n + 1/2$. In this case, we must add at least one world to each neighborhood which contains the smallest neighborhood in the considered neighborhood system. But the number of neighborhoods is limited by the number of labels $\flat(\phi) = n$, $n \in \mathbb{N}$. So, the biggest neighborhood reaches the asserted limit and the number of worlds of the model is linear in the number of labels.

**Theorem 5.** *The satisfiability problem is $\mathbf{NP}$-complete for PUC-Logic.*

*Proof.* A wff without labels is a propositional formula. It means, by [19], the satisfiability problem complexity for PUC-Logic must be at least $\mathbf{NP}$-complete. Given a wff with labels, by Lemma 23, we know there is a directed graph, as in the proof of Lemma 3 [23]. In this case, the satisfiability problem complexity depends on the endpoints of the graph. Those endpoints are always propositional formulas. So, the complexity of the satisfiability problem is the sum of the complexities of the problems for each endpoint. It means the biggest subformula dictates the complexity because the model of Lemma 23 has at most a linear number of worlds and the satisfiability problem is $\mathbf{NP}$-complete. So, the worst case is the wff without labels.

## 6    Counterfactual Logics

Lewis presented in [1] several logics for counterfactual reasoning. These logics were defined and organized on the basis of conditions imposed on the nested neighborhood function \$. The most basic logic is $V$, which has no condition imposed on \$. The axioms and inference rules of $V$ were defined in terms of Lewis' comparative possibility operator ($\preccurlyeq$).

**Definition 32.** $\alpha^\Sigma \preccurlyeq \beta^\Omega$ iff $(\beta^{\Omega,\bullet} \to \alpha^{\Sigma,\bullet})^\circledast$

We now prove that the axioms of $V$-logic are theorems of PUC-Logic and that the inference rules of $V$-logics are derived rules in the system PUC-ND. This result shows that PUC-Logic is complete with respect to $V$-logic.

– **TRANS** axiom:
$$((\alpha \preccurlyeq \beta) \wedge (\beta \preccurlyeq \gamma)) \to (\alpha \preccurlyeq \gamma);$$

– **CONNEX** axiom:
$$(\alpha \preccurlyeq \beta) \vee (\beta \preccurlyeq \alpha);$$

– **CPR**:

If $\vdash \alpha \to (\beta_1 \vee \ldots \vee \beta_n)$, then $\vdash (\beta_1 \preccurlyeq \alpha) \vee \ldots \vee (\beta_n \preccurlyeq \alpha)$, for any $n \geq 1$.

We present a proof of the Comparative Possibility Rule (CPR) rule for $n = 2$. We omit the attribute representation of the wffs denoted by $\alpha$, $\beta$ and $\gamma$ to simplify the reading of the derivations. We use Lemma 24 below for the theorem $\alpha \to (\beta \vee \gamma)$ and a derivation $\Xi$ of it.

$$
\begin{array}{c}
\dfrac{
\dfrac{
\dfrac{
\dfrac{
\dfrac{{}^1[(\beta^\bullet \to \alpha^\bullet)^\circledast \wedge (\gamma^\bullet \to \beta^\bullet)^\circledast]}
{(\beta^\bullet \to \alpha^\bullet)^\circledast \wedge (\gamma^\bullet \to \beta^\bullet)^\circledast}
}{
\dfrac{(\gamma^\bullet \to \beta^\bullet)^\circledast}{\gamma^\bullet \to \beta^\bullet}\circledast
}
}{\beta^\bullet}\circledast
\quad {}^2[\gamma^\bullet]\circledast
}{}
\end{array}
$$

**TRANS**

$$
\dfrac{
\dfrac{
\dfrac{\alpha^\bullet}{\gamma^\bullet \to \alpha^\bullet}\,2 \ \circledast
}{(\gamma^\bullet \to \alpha^\bullet)^\circledast}\circledast
}{((\beta^\bullet \to \alpha^\bullet)^\circledast \wedge (\gamma^\bullet \to \beta^\bullet)^\circledast) \to (\gamma^\bullet \to \alpha^\bullet)^\circledast}\,1
$$

$$
\dfrac{
\dfrac{
\dfrac{
\dfrac{
\dfrac{{}^1[\neg((\beta^\bullet \to \alpha^\bullet)^\circledast \vee (\alpha^\bullet \to \beta^\bullet)^\circledast)]}{\neg((\beta^\bullet \to \alpha^\bullet)^\circledast \vee (\alpha^\bullet \to \beta^\bullet)^\circledast)}
\quad
\dfrac{
\dfrac{\dfrac{{}^2[\beta^\bullet]}{\beta^\bullet}\circledast}{\alpha^\bullet \to \beta^\bullet}\circledast
}{
\dfrac{(\alpha^\bullet \to \beta^\bullet)^\circledast}{(\beta^\bullet \to \alpha^\bullet)^\circledast \vee (\alpha^\bullet \to \beta^\bullet)^\circledast}
}
}{\bot_n}
}{
\dfrac{\alpha^{\bullet,\circledast}}{\dfrac{\alpha^\bullet}{\beta^\bullet \to \alpha^\bullet}\,2\ \circledast}\circledast
}
}{(\beta^\bullet \to \alpha^\bullet)^\circledast}
}{(\beta^\bullet \to \alpha^\bullet)^\circledast \vee (\alpha^\bullet \to \beta^\bullet)^\circledast}\ \Upsilon
$$

**CONNEX**

$$\frac{\dfrac{^1[\neg((\beta^\bullet \to \alpha^\bullet)^\circledast \vee (\alpha^\bullet \to \beta^\bullet)^\circledast)]}{\neg((\beta^\bullet \to \alpha^\bullet)^\circledast \vee (\alpha^\bullet \to \beta^\bullet)^\circledast)} \qquad \dfrac{\Upsilon}{(\beta^\bullet \to \alpha^\bullet)^\circledast \vee (\alpha^\bullet \to \beta^\bullet)^\circledast}}{\dfrac{\bot_n}{(\beta^\bullet \to \alpha^\bullet)^\circledast \vee (\alpha^\bullet \to \beta^\bullet)^\circledast}}\;{}_1$$

$$\Pi \qquad \frac{\dfrac{^4[\alpha]}{\alpha}\,N,u \quad \dfrac{\Xi}{\alpha \to (\beta \vee \gamma)}\,N,u}{{}_4\;\dfrac{\dfrac{\alpha^\bullet}{\dfrac{\alpha^\bullet}{\alpha}\,N,\bullet}\,N}{\dfrac{\dfrac{\beta \vee \gamma}{\dfrac{\beta \vee \gamma}{\beta \vee \gamma}\,{\circledast},\bullet}\,N,\bullet}{\dfrac{\beta \vee \gamma}{\beta \vee \gamma}\,{\circledast},\bullet} \quad \dfrac{\dfrac{[\beta]}{\beta}\,{\circledast},\bullet}{\dfrac{\beta^\bullet}{\beta^\bullet \vee \gamma^\bullet}\,{\circledast}}\quad \dfrac{\dfrac{[\gamma]}{\gamma}\,{\circledast},\bullet}{\dfrac{\gamma^\bullet}{\beta^\bullet \vee \gamma^\bullet}\,{\circledast}}}{\dfrac{\beta^\bullet \vee \gamma^\bullet}{\beta^\bullet \vee \gamma^\bullet}\,{\circledast}}}$$

$$\Sigma \qquad {}_3\;\frac{\dfrac{\alpha^\bullet}{\alpha^\bullet}\,N \quad \dfrac{\Xi}{\alpha \to (\beta \vee \gamma)}\,N,u}{\dfrac{\Pi}{\beta^\bullet \vee \gamma^\bullet}\,{\circledast}} \qquad \frac{\dfrac{\dfrac{^3[\beta^\bullet]}{\beta^\bullet}\,{\circledast}}{\dfrac{\alpha^\bullet \to \beta^\bullet}{(\alpha^\bullet \to \beta^\bullet)^\circledast}\,{\circledast}}}{(\alpha^\bullet \to \beta^\bullet)^\circledast \vee (\alpha^\bullet \to \gamma^\bullet)^\circledast} \quad \frac{\dfrac{\dfrac{^3[\gamma^\bullet]}{\gamma^\bullet}\,{\circledast}}{\dfrac{\alpha^\bullet \to \gamma^\bullet}{(\alpha^\bullet \to \gamma^\bullet)^\circledast}\,{\circledast}}}{(\alpha^\bullet \to \beta^\bullet)^\circledast \vee (\alpha^\bullet \to \gamma^\bullet)^\circledast}$$

$$\dfrac{(\alpha^\bullet \to \beta^\bullet)^\circledast \vee (\alpha^\bullet \to \gamma^\bullet)^\circledast}{}$$

$$\Omega \qquad \frac{\dfrac{^1[\neg((\alpha^\bullet \to \beta^\bullet)^\circledast \vee (\alpha^\bullet \to \gamma^\bullet)^\circledast)]}{\neg((\alpha^\bullet \to \beta^\bullet)^\circledast \vee (\alpha^\bullet \to \gamma^\bullet)^\circledast)} \qquad \dfrac{\dfrac{^2[\alpha^\bullet]}{\alpha^\bullet}\,N}{\dfrac{\Sigma}{(\alpha^\bullet \to \beta^\bullet)^\circledast \vee (\alpha^\bullet \to \gamma^\bullet)^\circledast}}}{{}_2\;\dfrac{\dfrac{\dfrac{\bot_n}{\beta^{\bullet,N}}}{\dfrac{\beta^\bullet}{\dfrac{\alpha^\bullet \to \beta^\bullet}{\dfrac{\alpha^\bullet \to \beta^\bullet}{(\alpha^\bullet \to \beta^\bullet)^\circledast}\,{\circledast}}\,N}\,N}}{(\alpha^\bullet \to \beta^\bullet)^\circledast \vee (\alpha^\bullet \to \gamma^\bullet)^\circledast}}$$

**CPR**

$$\frac{\dfrac{^1[\neg((\alpha^\bullet \to \beta^\bullet)^\circledast \vee (\alpha^\bullet \to \gamma^\bullet)^\circledast)]}{\neg((\alpha^\bullet \to \beta^\bullet)^\circledast \vee (\alpha^\bullet \to \gamma^\bullet)^\circledast)} \qquad \dfrac{\Omega}{(\alpha^\bullet \to \beta^\bullet)^\circledast \vee (\alpha^\bullet \to \gamma^\bullet)^\circledast}}{{}_1\;\dfrac{\bot_n}{(\alpha^\bullet \to \beta^\bullet)^\circledast \vee (\alpha^\bullet \to \gamma^\bullet)^\circledast}}$$

**Lemma 24.** *Given a theorem $\alpha^\Sigma$, there is a proof of $\alpha^\Sigma$ in the context $\{N, u\}$, in which the variables $N$ and $u$ do not occur in the proof.*

*Proof.* If $\alpha^\Sigma$ is a theorem, then, by definition, there is a proof $\Pi$ without open hypothesis which ends with the theorem in the empty context. During the proof $\Pi$, the smallest context is the empty context. So, if we can choose variables which do not occur in $\Pi$ and add the stack of labels $\{N, u\}$ at the rightmost position of each rule context. We end up with a proof of the theorem in the context $\{N, u\}$. This is possible because there is no restriction which could be applied over the new variables.

We now present some ideas related to the logics **VN**, **VT**, **VW** and **VC**. For each logic, PUC-ND may change its rule set to acquire the corresponding expressiveness provided by the conditions. These changes can be done as follows:

**VN** • Rule 9 looses restriction (a);
   • Rule 19 and 22 loose second premise;

   • Introduction of the rule:
$$\frac{\dfrac{}{\alpha^\Sigma}\,\Delta, \circledast}{\alpha^\Sigma}\,\Delta, N$$

**VT** • We repeat the system for VN.

   • Introduction of the rule:
$$\frac{\dfrac{}{\alpha^\Sigma}\,\Delta, \circledast, *}{\alpha^\Sigma}\,\Delta$$

**VW** • We repeat the system for VT;

   • Introduction of the rule:
$$\frac{\dfrac{}{\alpha^\Sigma}\,\Delta, \odot, *}{\alpha^\Sigma}\,\Delta$$

**VC** • We repeat the system for VW;

   • Introduction of the rule:
$$\frac{\dfrac{}{\alpha^\Sigma}\,\Delta, \circledast, \bullet}{\alpha^\Sigma}\,\Delta$$

For all cases, we must apply: Restriction (a) $\alpha^\Sigma$ must fit into the contexts.

## 7   Related Works

As far as we know, there is only one natural deduction system which deals with counterfactuals, the system defined by Bonevac [11]. But this system is designed for the **VW**-logic, since it contains the rule of counterfactual exploitation ($\square\!\!\rightarrow$E), which encapsulates the weak centering condition. Bonevac's approach in the definition of rules for counterfactual operators does provide a better intuition of counterfactual logic. His systems are expressive enough to deal with modalities and strict conditionals. The labeling of worlds using formulas makes it easier to capture the counterfactual mechanics. We also found the work of Sano [12], who pointed out the advantages of using a hybrid formalism for counterfactual logic. Sano presented some axioms and rules for the $V_{\mathcal{HC}(@)}$-logic, which is an extension of the **V**-logic. Another interesting reference is the article of Gent [10], which presents a new sequent- or tableaux-style proof system for **VC**-logic. His work depends on the operator $[\![\,]\!]$ and signed formulas definitions. We have

recently found a sequent calculus provided by Lellmann [20] which treats the
$V$-logic of Lewis and its extensions. The language used by Lellmann depends
on modal operators, specially on counterfactual operators $\Box\!\!\rightarrow$ and $\Box\!\!\Rightarrow$ and the
comparative possibility operator $\preccurlyeq$. Another sequent calculus which is equivalent
to the $VC$-logic has recently been defined by Negri and Sbardolini [24].

## 8   Conclusions

In this paper, we proposed a new logic for counterfactuals, PUC-Logic. Lewis'
counterfactual logics can be systematically treated in PUC-Logic. The use of
two types of labels (neighborhood and world labels) gives us the ability to man-
age different types of quantifications which are largely used in the definitions
of counterfactual operators according to Lewis. We also propose a new natural
deduction system, the system PUC-ND, which is proven to be sound and complete with respect to Lewis' $V$-logic. Our approach makes it possible to build
the rules for counterfactual operators as derived rules of the system. Another
advantage of our approach is to avoid the use of modalities or strict conditionals
in the formulation of the natural deduction system PUC-ND, making it easier
to reuse well-known proof-theoretical results for propositional logic, such as the
normalization theorem.

The main topic for our future work concerns PUC-Logic applications to hypothetical queries in deductive databases. We have presented a logic that can be
used to express well-known counterfactuals, and it is certainly worth investigating if, through the use of some of these counterfactual logics, it would be possible
to implement a solution to the problem of the derivation of the *answer set* of
hypothetical queries in deductive databases in an efficient and purely logical way.
The implementation and viability of our proposal have not been evaluated yet.

## References

1. Lewis, D.K.: Counterfactuals. Blackwell Publishing, Oxford (2008)
2. Goodman, N.: Fact, Fiction, and Forecast, 4th edn. Harvard University Press,
   Cambridge (1983)
3. Bell, J.L.: Toposes and Local Set Theories. Dover Publications, Mineola (2008)
4. Bonner, A.J.: Hypothetical datalog: complexity and expressibility. Theor. Comput.
   Sci. (TCS) **76**, 3–51 (1990)
5. Knuth, D.E.: Semantics of context-free languages. Math. Syst. Theory **2**, 127–146
   (1968)
6. Gabbay, D., Giordano, L., Martelli, A., Olivetti, N.: Hypothetical updates, priority
   and inconsistency in a logic programming language. In: Marek, V.W., Nerode, A.,
   Truszczyński, M. (eds.) LPNMR 1995. LNCS, vol. 928, pp. 203–216. Springer,
   Heidelberg (1995). doi:10.1007/3-540-59487-6_15
7. Prawitz, D., Deduction, N.: A Proof-Theoretical Study. Dover, Mineola (2006)
8. Ramsey, F.P.: Philosophical Papers. Cambridge University Press, Cambridge
   (1990)

9. Malhotra, A., Younesi, E., Bagewadi, S., Hofmann-Apitius, M.: Linking hypothetical knowledge patterns to disease molecular signatures for biomarker discovery in Alzheimer's disease. Genome Med. **6**, 97 (2014)

10. Gent, I.P.: A sequent- or tableau-style system for Lewis's counterfactual logic VC. Notre Dame J. Formal Logic **33**(3), 369–382 (1992)

11. Bonevac, D.: Deduction: Introductory Symbolic Logic. Blackwell, Oxford (2003)

12. Sano, K.: Hybrid counterfactual logics. J. Logic Lang. Inform. **18**(4), 515–539 (2009)

13. Kifer, M., Swift, T., Grosof, B.: Practical knowledge representation and reasoning in Ergo. In: Tutorial, RuleML2016 (2016)

14. Golfarelli, M., Rizzi, S.: What-if simulation modeling in business intelligence. Int. J. Data Warehouse Min. **5**(4), 24–43 (2009)

15. Fernandes, R.Q.A., Haeusler, E.H.: A Topos-theoretic approach to counterfactual logic. In: Pre-proceedings of Fourth Workshop on Logical and Semantic Frameworks, Brasília (2009)

16. Dummet, M.A.E.: What is a theory of meaning ? (II). In: Evans, G., McDowell, J. (eds.) Truth and Meaning, pp. 67–137. Clarendon press (1976)

17. Abiteboul, S., Hull, R., Vianu, V.: Foundations of Databases. Addison-Wesley, Boston (1995)

18. Lambert, K.: Free Logic: Selected Essays. Cambridge University Press, Cambridge (2004)

19. Cook, S.A.: The complexity of theorem proving procedures. In: 3rd Annual ACM Symposium on the Theory of Computation, pp. 151–158 (1971)

20. Lellmann, B., Pattinson, D.: Sequent systems for Lewis' conditional logics. In: del Cerro, L.F., Herzig, A., Mengin, J. (eds.) JELIA 2012. LNCS, vol. 7519, pp. 320–332. Springer, Heidelberg (2012). doi:10.1007/978-3-642-33353-8_25

21. Pereira, L.M., Aparício, J.N., Alfares, J.J.: Counterfactual reasoning based on revising assumptions. In: Proceedings of the 1991 Internal Symposium Logic Programming. MIT Press (1991)

22. Renteria, C.J., Haeusler, E.H., Veloso, P.A.S.: NUL: natural deduction for ultrafilter logic. Bull. Sect. Logic **32**(4), 191–199 (2003). Univ. of Lodz, Polland

23. Fernandes, R.Q.A., Haeusler, E.H., Pereira, L.C.P.D.: PUC-Logic, ArXiv CoRR (2014)

24. Negri, S., Sbardolini, G.: Proof analysis for lewis counterfactuals. Rev. Symbolic Logic **9**(01), 44–75 (2016)

25. Li, G.: Knowledge discovery from knowledge bases with higher-order logic. In: Wong, W.E. (ed.) Proceedings of the 4th International Conference on Computer Engineering and Networks, pp. 451–457. Springer, Cham (2015). doi:10.1007/978-3-319-11104-9_53

26. Winslett, M.: Updating Logical Databases, Cambridge Tracts in Theoretical Computer Science, vol. 9. Cambridge University Press, Cambridge (1990)

# Inconsistency-Tolerant Database Repairs and Simplified Repair Checking by Measure-Based Integrity Checking

Hendrik Decker[✉]

PROS, DSIC, Universidad Politécnica de Valencia, Valencia, Spain
hdecker@pms.ifi.lmu.de

**Abstract.** Database states may be inconsistent, i.e., their integrity may be violated. Database repairs are updates such that all integrity constraints become satisfied, while keeping the necessary changes to a minimum. Updates intending to repair inconsistency may go wrong. Repair checking is to find out if a given update is a repair, i.e., if the updated state is free of integrity violations and if the changes are minimal. However, integrity violations may be numerous, complex or opaque, so that attaining a complete absence of inconsistency is not realistic. We discuss inconsistency-tolerant concepts of repair and repair checking. Repairs are no longer asked to be total, i.e., only some but not all inconsistency is supposed to disappear by a repair. For checking if an update reduces the amount of inconsistency, integrity violations need to be comparable. For that, we use measure-based integrity checking. Both the inconsistency reduction and the minimality of inconsistency-tolerant repair candidates can be verified or falsified by measure-based integrity checkers that simplify the evaluation of constraints. As opposed to total repair checking, which evaluates integrity constraints brute-force, simplified repair checking exploits the incrementality of updates.

## 1 Introduction

This paper is about inconsistency-tolerant database repairs, which relax the notion of 'repair' [3], i.e., of amending database inconsistency, and about using measure-based integrity checking [23,24] for relaxing the process of repair checking as introduced in [13], i.e., for finding out if a given update is an inconsistency-tolerant repair.

In this introduction, we informally outline the main ideas of the paper and their background. In Subsect. 1.1, we distinguish between preventing and repairing inconsistency. We also characterize repairs and their relaxation to inconsistency-tolerant repairs. In Subsect. 1.2, we first address conventional repair checking, and then simplified repair checking, which uses incremental integrity checking based on inconsistency measures. In Subsect. 1.3, we summarize the salient points of this paper.

In Sect. 2, we revisit some key issues on which the remainder of this paper is based. In Sect. 3, we re-define repairs of database inconsistency and discuss that

© Springer-Verlag GmbH Germany 2017
A. Hameurlain et al. (Eds.): TLDKS XXXIV, LNCS 10620, pp. 153–183, 2017.
https://doi.org/10.1007/978-3-662-55947-5_7

definition. In Sect. 4, we define a generic concept of repair checking, and unfold the main results about repair checking by measure-based integrity checking. In Sect. 5, we first assess the brute-force computation of repair checking, and then outline two ways of computing inconsistency-tolerant repair checking, one of them naive, the other simplified. In Sect. 6, we address related work. In Sect. 7, we conclude.

## 1.1   Prevention and Reparation of Database Inconsistency

In any given database state, inconsistency may manifest itself as the violation of one or several integrity constraints that are part of the database schema. Merging mutually inconsistent databases, trading off consistency for performance or availability, weakening isolation requirements for concurrent transaction processing, imposing fresh constraints on legacy data, lack of system support for data integrity, imperfection of data cleansing, faulty application code, DBMS migration or system upgrades, data hacking, file corruption due to hardware failures or transmission errors – these, and more, are possible reasons for databases to be or become inconsistent with the integrity constraints imposed on them.

Even though, as pointed out in [36], there are, in general, fields of reasoning for which some forms of inconsistency are negligible (e.g., many applications of naive set theory), or for which inconsistency may have equal status to consistency (e.g., fake detection, or argumentation), database inconsistency typically is either unintentional or fraudulent. Hence, database inconsistency is potentially harmful and thus undesirable for most applications. Hence, methods to either prevent or repair database states that are inconsistent with their integrity constraints are called for.

The prevention of integrity violation can be supported by careful database design [41,57], possibly enhanced by a careful control of concurrency, distribution, parallelism and replication [5,42,50,56], and can be accomplished by integrity checkers, a.k.a. 'integrity checking methods' [28,33,47]. In this paper, we focus on repairs of integrity violations and repair checking. More precisely, we are going to relax the conventional notion of repair, and discuss an inconsistency-tolerant way of checking if a given update is a repair that reduces integrity violations or not.

According to their definition in [3], repairs are characterized as database states that are consistent with the integrity constraints imposed on them and that differ minimally from an inconsistent predecessor state. In principle, each database state (i.e., each instance of some database schema) can be mapped into each other database state by some update. Hence, repairs can as well be understood as updates that eliminate the inconsistency of a given database state: all constraints in the integrity theory associated to the database schema that had been violated before the update, are satisfied in the repaired state. Additionally, the modifications comprised by updates that qualify as repairs are required to be minimal, in some sense, so that no superfluous changes are effected by a repair, in compliance with the well-known Occam's razor principle. We speak of such repairs as 'total repairs', since they are supposed to yield database states that are totally consistent with their integrity constraints.

As opposed to total repairs, we content ourselves with updates that do not necessarily eliminate all violations, but only some, while not introducing new violations that would equal or exceed the previous violations. To distinguish such updates from total repairs, we call them 'inconsistency-tolerant repairs'.

## 1.2 Brute-Force and Simplified Repair Checking

Total repair checking has been studied in [2,4,12,13]. It can be characterized as the problem to find out if a given update minimally repairs all violations of database integrity. Analogously, our relaxed concept of repair checking means to detect if a given update reduces the inconsistency of a given state, without involving superfluous changes.

Both total and simplified repair checking can be implemented in two phases. Firstly, check if inconsistency is eliminated or at least reduced. We call that the *inconsistency reduction checking* phase. Secondly, check the minimality of inconsistency reductions. We call that the *minimality checking* phase.

For the inconsistency reduction phase of total repair checking, the integrity satisfaction of each constraint is in general checked brute-force. That is to say, in order to find out if a constraint is satisfied or violated, the brute-force approach evaluates the full-fledged constraint as a query in the updated database state.

In the field of integrity checking, the adjective 'brute-force' is used to distinguish one of two well-known modes of verifying or falsifying that an update would preserve the consistency of a state which is modified by some update. As opposed to brute-force integrity checking, simplified integrity checking exploits the incrementality of updates, by focusing on the actual changes effected by the update [14]. Thus, only some simplified forms of constraints that are actually affected by the update need to be evaluated, instead of an often prohibitively expensive evaluation of all unsimplified integrity constraints [15,52]. Examples of known methods for simplified integrity checking are referenced in Subsect. 2.4.

Unfortunately, simplified integrity checking as in [15,52] is not applicable for total repair checking, since the former requires that the database to be updated is totally consistent with all of its constraints. That, by definition, is not the case for repairs. However, as detailed in Subsect. 2.4, simplified integrity checking has been generalized to measure-based integrity checking. Measure-based integrity checking generalizes simplified integrity checking by defining criteria which guarantee their applicability to updates of databases that are inconsistent with their constraints. The measures used by measure-based integrity checking serve for comparing the inconsistencies of database states before and after an update. Database states resulting from updates that are accepted by measure-based integrity checks may remain inconsistent, but are not more inconsistent than the state before the update [23,24].

As we shall see in Sect. 4, measure-based integrity checkers can be used to check if an update is an inconsistency-tolerant repair. We speak of inconsistency-tolerant repair checking by measure-based integrity checking as 'simplified repair checking' since, as opposed to a brute-force evaluation of integrity constraints, it may take advantage of the incrementality of updates.

Note that measure-based integrity checking is not applicable to total repair checking. The latter requires that the updated state is totally consistent, while measure-based integrity checking is inconsistency-tolerant, i.e., it only requires that inconsistency is reduced but not necessarily eliminated completely.

## 1.3  Survey of Contributions

The essential differences between total repair checking and simplified repair checking are the following. The main conceptual difference: Simplified repair checking is measure-based and inconsistency-tolerant, i.e., it accepts measurable reductions of integrity violations that may not totally eliminate inconsistency. As opposed to that, total repair checking disqualifies each update that does not yield total consistency. The main technical difference: Simplified repair checking is implemented by simplified integrity checking, which exploits the incrementality of updates, while total repair checking evaluates all constraints brute-force. The main practical difference: Checking inconsistency-tolerant repairs is more realistic and more feasible than checking total repairs for total inconsistency elimination, particularly for large databases or for integrity constraints that are more application-specific than the usual constraints as exacted by database normalization theory.

The three main pillars of our approach are, firstly, inconsistency-tolerant repairs [21,31], secondly, simplified integrity checking [15] and its inconsistency-tolerant extension [26,30] and, thirdly, database inconsistency measures [22,27,29]. The latter two have been combined to measure-based integrity checking in [23,24], which we now propose to use for simplifying the checking of inconsistency-tolerant repairs.

The main contributions of this paper are the following.

- A refinement of the definition of 'partial integrity-preserving repair' in [21,30], which did not include any notion of minimality, to 'inconsistency-tolerant repair'.
- The use of database inconsistency measures for defining the minimality of inconsistency-tolerant repairs, which generalizes minimality as defined in [3].
- An inconsistency-tolerant relaxation of total repair checking.
- The cost-effective use of simplified measure-based integrity checking, which normally serves to prevent an increase of inconsistency, for checking its decrease, and also for checking the minimality of inconsistency reductions.

## 2  Key Issues

In this section, we recapitulate some key issues that underlie the remainder of the paper. In Subsect. 2.1, we turn to databases, updates and integrity constraints. In Subsect. 2.2, we define, for convenience, a generic class of database methods called 'update checkers'. In Subsect. 2.3, we revisit database inconsistency measures. In Subsect. 2.4, we recall integrity checking and in particular measure-based integrity checking.

As a notational convention, we use the symbols $\Rightarrow$ and $\Leftrightarrow$ for meta-level entailment and, resp., meta-level equivalence, in definitions and result statements.

## 2.1 Databases, Updates and Integrity Constraints

We assume a basic familiarity with relational and deductive databases. For details, the reader may consult, e.g., [1,34,53].

Throughout the paper, let symbols $D$, $IC$, $U$ and adornments thereof by superscripts or subscripts always stand for a database state, an integrity theory and, resp., an update.

Updates and database integrity are revisited in Subsect. 2.1.1 and, resp., Subsect. 2.1.2 Semantic and syntactic restrictions that may apply to triples $(D, IC, U)$ considered in this paper are addressed in Subsect. 2.1.3.

### 2.1.1 Updates

Formally, an update is a finite bipartite set of database clauses (i.e., facts or deductive rules) to be inserted to or, resp., deleted from a given database state. Thus, updates effect the dynamics of databases. In particular, updates are used for repairing database inconsistency (see also [61]).

Essentially, the idea behind repair checking by integrity checking is based on the evidence that it is easier to use integrity checkers for checking the increase of inconsistency than to use them for checking the decrease of inconsistency. Thus, we are interested in undos of updates, as defined below, since an update decreases inconsistency if and only if its undo increases it.

**Definition 1** (*undo*). Let $\overline{U}$ denote the *undo* of $U$: for each element of the form *insert X* or *delete Y* in $U$, $\overline{U}$ contains *delete X* or, resp., *insert Y*, and nothing else.

Let $D^U$ denote the updated database state obtained by applying $U$ to $D$. We denote consecutive updates $U$, $U'$ of $D$ and then $D^U$ by $D^{UU'}$. Hence, $D^{U\overline{U}} = D$. That equality will be used for proving results in Sect. 4.

### 2.1.2 Database Integrity

An *integrity theory* is a finite set of first-order predicate logic sentences, known as *integrity constraints* (or simply *constraints*). They capture database properties that are supposed to remain invariant across state changes. A complementary viewpoint is that constraints embody semantic conditions that are meant to rule out states which would be faulty or meaningless. For simplicity, we only consider integrity theories that are logically satisfiable. Unwarranted unsatisfiability of integrity theories is dealt with in [8] and subsection 5.5 of [30].

Integrity constraints can be interpreted and processed as queries about the consistency of stored data. If a constraint $I$ evaluates to *true* in a given database state $D$, then we say that $I$ is *satisfied* in $D$; if it evaluates to *false*, then we say that $I$ is *violated* in $D$. If all constraints in an integrity theory $IC$ are satisfied, then we also say that $IC$ is *satisfied* in $D$, or, synonymously, that $(D, IC)$ is *consistent*. If any constraint in $IC$ is violated in $D$, then we also say that $IC$ is *violated* in $D$, or, synonymously, that $(D, IC)$ is *inconsistent*.

Let us revisit now the definition 3.1 in [30] of 'cases', i.e. instances of constraints in $IC$ that are of interest for defining database inconsistency measures (to be addressed in Subsect. 2.3), as well as for simplified integrity checking (to be addressed in Subsect. 2.4).

**Definition 2** (*case*). Let $I$ be a constraint. A variable $x$ in $I$ is called a global variable in $I$ if $x$ is $\forall$-quantified and no quantifier of the form $\exists y$ such that $x$ would be in its scope occurs left of $\forall x$ in the prenex form of $I$, obtained by moving all quantifiers in $I$ leftmost by well-known equivalence-preserving rewrites. For a substitution $\sigma$ the domain of which is the set of global variables in $I$, $I\sigma$ is called a *case* of $I$. If $\sigma$ is a ground substitution, then $I\sigma$ is called a *basic case* of $I$. Let *basic(IC)* be the set of all basic cases $I'$ of constraints $I$ in $IC$.

### 2.1.3   Syntactic and Semantic Restrictions

In later sections of the paper, certain syntactic or semantic restrictions on tuples $(D, IC)$ or triples $(D, IC, U)$ may apply, without them being mentioned explicitly. In particular, the applicability of database inconsistency measures and of methods for integrity checking or repair checking usually is confined to certain classes of input tuples $(D, IC)$ or triples $(D, IC, U)$. For instance, common restrictions are properties such as the range-restrictedness [51] or the safety [60] of database clauses and constraints. However, since our approach to repair checking by integrity checking applies to generic forms of inconsistency measures and methods, we do not go into further details with regard to semantic or syntactic restrictions that may apply to individual measures or methods.

Nevertheless, for simplicity, let us agree on the following general restriction. It avoids that we'd need to bother with differences between the satisfiability and the theoremhood of integrity constraints, or with undefined or third truth values, or with subtle epistemic distinctions. Such issues are dealt with in [54].

Throughout the paper, we assume that the semantics of each triple $(D, IC, U)$ is *binary*, i.e., each $I \in IC$, when queried against $D$, has a unique *yes/no* answer, and also the answer of $I$ when queried against $D^U$ is always either *yes* or *no*.

The semantics of significantly large classes of databases and constraints comply with the binary assumption, for instance all pairs $(D, IC)$ such that $D$ is relational and $IC$ is range-restricted, and also all deductive databases and integrity theories that are acyclic [9] and range-restricted.

## 2.2   Update Checkers

We are going to investigate ways to implement repair checking by integrity checking. For that purpose, it is convenient to have the following generic definition of methods for checking updates, be it for the preservation or the reduction of inconsistency.

**Definition 3** (*update checker*). A mapping *uc* of triples $(D, IC, U)$ to $\{yes, no\}$ is called an *update checker*.

In the literature, various approaches to inconsistency measuring, integrity checking or repair checking are proposed, each of them for some particular class of databases, constraints or updates. The approach developed in this paper is independent of any particular inconsistency measure or update checker. Thus, whenever, for some mapping *mp* from tuples $(D, IC)$ or triples $(D, IC, U)$ to some range of values, we say, "for each tuple $(D, IC)$ ..." or "for each triple $(D, IC, U)$ ...", we actually mean to tacitly add, "... such that *mp* is defined for the input $(D, IC)$" or, resp., "... $(D, IC, U)$".

## 2.3   Database Inconsistency Measures

For deciding if an update effectively reduces the amount of database inconsistency, the latter needs to be measurable, so that the inconsistency before and after the update can be compared. That is the purpose of database inconsistency measures.

In Subsect. 2.3.1, we distinguish database inconsistency measures from classical inconsistecy measures. In Subsect. 2.3.2, we give examples of database inconsistency measures that are of interest in the remainder.

### 2.3.1   Background and Definition of Database Inconsistency Measures

Most inconsistency measures in the literature are for quantifying the inconsistency in what is frequently called 'knowledge bases', but what effectively corresponds, in most cases, to sets of formulas in the syntax and semantics of propositional or first-order predicate logic. For convenience, let us call them *classical inconsistency measures.*

Classical inconsistency measures have their origin in [37]. For the purpose of inconsistency-tolerant integrity checking, database inconsistency measures have been introduced in [27] and further developed in [22,24,29]. The main application of database inconsistency measures is not, in the first place, to quantify the amount of inconsistency in given databases, but to make the inconsistency of consecutive database states comparable. In fact, the values of inconsistency between database states before and after updates do not necessarily have to be computed in order to become comparable. Rather, only the increase, decrease or invariance of inconsistency between such states is of interest for integrity checking and repairing.

For pairs $(D, IC)$, database inconsistency measures seize or count the amount of violated integrity constraints or cases thereof, or causes of the violation of constraints, i.e., those parts of $D$ that are responsible for constraint violations in $IC$ [19,24,25]. Abstracting away from what exactly is sized for comparing the inconsistency of states, database inconsistency measures are defined as follows.

**Definition 4** (*database inconsistency measure*). A *database inconsistency measure* $\mu$ is a mapping from pairs $(D, IC)$ to a partially ordered range of degrees of inconsistency. We denote the ordering by the infix predicate $\leq$; $X{<}Y$ means that $X{\leq}Y$ and $X{\neq}Y$. The negation of $\leq$ is denoted by $\nleq$, and the negation of $<$ by $\nless$.

The literature about inconsistency measures is replete with discussions of properties and conditions that arguably should be required from inconsistency measures (cf., e.g., [7,24,39,59]). However, except the property exposed in Definition 5, below, we do not impose any further condition on database inconsistency measures, such that they would have 'nice' properties. Most of these properties are elusive and their desirability tends to be application-specific. Moreover, some of the most popular of such properties do not hold up against the non-monotonicity of database negation [24,25]. However, it can be argued that the following property is desirable in general, and indeed, it is widely adopted in the literature. We also adopt it for each inconsistency measure considered in this paper.

**Definition 5** (*positive-definite measure*). Let $\mu$ be a database inconsistency measure with a least element in its range, denoted by $o$. We say that $\mu$ is *positive-definite* if and only if, for each pair of databases $D$, $D'$ and each pair of integrity theories $IC$, $IC'$ such that $IC$ is satisfied in $D$ and $IC'$ is violated in $D'$, $\mu(D, IC)$ $= o$ and $o < \mu(D', IC')$.

Each database inconsistency measure paced in Subsect. 2.3.2 is positive-definite.

Instead of 'database inconsistency measure', we may simply speak of an 'inconsistency measure' or just 'measure', from now on. Moreover, let the symbol $\mu$ always stand for an inconsistency measure.

### 2.3.2 Examples of Database Inconsistency Measures

For example, let $\iota$ and $\zeta$ be mappings of tuples $(D, IC)$ which output the set of integrity constraints that are violated in $(D, IC)$ and, resp., the set of constraints in $basic(IC)$ that are violated in $(D, IC)$ [24,29]. It is easy to see that $\iota$ and $\zeta$ are database inconsistency measures, and so are the mappings denoted by $|\iota|$ and $|\zeta|$, which output the cardinality of $\iota(D, IC)$ and, resp., $\zeta(D, IC)$. Clearly, the range of $|\iota|$ and $|\zeta|$ is numerical, with least element 0, while the ranges of $\iota(D, IC)$ and, resp., $\zeta(D, IC)$, viz. the powersets of $IC$ and, resp., $basic(IC)$, are not; they are partially ordered by $\subseteq$, and their least element is $\emptyset$.

Other examples of a database inconsistency measures are collections or counts of the causes of integrity violations. For relational databases and range-restricted constraints in clausal form, causes are sets of ground literals that correspond to the database facts whose presence or absence violate a basic case of some constraint [19]. Thus, the measure denoted by $\kappa$ in [23,24] maps tuples $(D, IC)$ to the causes in $D$ that are responsible for violating constraints in $basic(IC)$, and $|\kappa|$ maps $(D, IC)$ to the cardinality of the union of all causes of constraint violations in $basic(IC)$. For example, in relational databases, the unique cause of the violation of some ground instance $\leftarrow B$ of a conjunctive denial constraint precisely consists of the literals in $B$ [19]. For deductive databases and more general forms of constraints, causes are more involved but can be defined and processed effectively, as described in [20,24].

A border case example of an inconsistency measure is one with a binary range, named $\beta$ in [24], viz. the mapping that outputs $\beta(D, IC) = true$ if $(D, IC)$ is totally consistent, else $\beta(D, IC) = false$. The range $\{true, false\}$ of $\beta$ is ordered by the relationship $true < false$.

Besides these measures, also some others have been studied in [23,24,29], including an adaptation of the inconsistency measure in [38] to pairs $(D, IC)$.

Measures $\iota$, $\zeta$ and $\kappa$ illustrate one of several differences between classical inconsistency measures and database inconsistency measures. As we have seen, the range of database inconsistency measures is not necessarily numerical, and the ordering of that range is not necessarily total. The range of classical inconsistency measures, however, always is numerical and hence totally ordered [59]. All other essential differences have to do with the classical logic syntax and semantics underlying classical inconsistency measures, on one hand, and the syntax and semantics of database logic underlying database inconsistency measures, on the other. Perhaps the most fundamental difference consists in the non-monotonicity of database negation, as opposed to the monotonicity of classical logic. These differences are looked at in more detail in [25].

## 2.4    Measure-Based Integrity Checking

An update checker, the purpose of which is to filter out updates that would violate some integrity constraint, is called an *integrity checker*. If $ic(D, IC, U) = yes$, we say that $U$ is *accepted* by $ic$. If $ic(D, IC, U) = no$, we say that $U$ is *rejected* by $ic$. (Btw, neither acceptance nor rejection of $U$ necessarily would determine or preclude any further action by the database system, its administrator, its user or its application, of what to do with the output of $ic$. By default, $U$ is rejected if $ic(D, IC, U) = no$. But also a modification of $D$ or $IC$ or $U$ such that the modified triple becomes acceptable is an option, as in active databases, belief revision or truth maintenance systems. Or, updates that cause tolerable violations of "soft" constraints may be waived through. However, any decisions or actions taken after or triggered by the output of $ic$ are out of the scope of integrity checking.)

For simplicity, we assume that, for each integrity checker $ic$, there is a well-defined domain of triples $(D, IC, U)$ for which $ic$ is defined as a total mapping.

Thus, we do not have to be concerned with subtle differences between satisfiability and theoremhood of constraints nor with undefined or non-binary truth values, nor with non-termination of processing constraints as queries.

Except brute-force integrity checking, conventional integrity checkers are consistency-based, i.e., they postulate that the database to be updated is totally consistent with its constraints. They accept updates only if they preserve total consistency. The idea behind measure-based integrity checking has been to realize an inconsistency-tolerant form of integrity checking, which allows that both the database state to be updated and the updated state are inconsistent [26,27,29,30]. That is captured by the following definition.

**Definition 6** (*measure-based integrity checker*). Let $ic$ be an update checker and $\mu$ an inconsistency measure. $ic$ is called a *sound*, resp., *complete $\mu$-based integrity checker* if (*), resp., (**) holds, for each triple $(D, IC, U)$:

(*)   $ic(D, IC, U) = yes \;\Rightarrow\; \mu(D^U, IC) \leq \mu(D, IC),$

(**)  $\mu(D^U, IC) \leq \mu(D, IC) \;\Rightarrow\; ic(D, IC, U) = yes.$

If $ic$ is applied only to triples $(D, IC, U)$ such that $(D, IC)$ is consistent, then $ic$ is called a *consistency-based integrity checker*.

In words, (*) means that $U$ is accepted by $ic$ only if $U$ either decreases or does not change the amount of inconsistency as measured by $\mu$. Thus, the contrapositive $\mu(D^U, IC) \not\leq \mu(D, IC) \;\Rightarrow\; ic(D, IC, U) = no$ of (*) means that $ic$ rejects $U$ if $U$ neither decreases inconsistency nor does it leave it invariant. In particular, if $\mu(D, IC) < \mu(D^U, IC)$, i.e., if $U$ increases inconsistency, then each sound $\mu$-based integrity checker $ic$ outputs $ic(D, IC, U) = no$.

Conversely, completeness of $ic$ as formalized in (**) means that, whenever $U$ decreases the amount of consistency or leaves it invariant, then $ic$ accepts $U$. If $ic$ is complete and $ic(D, IC, U) = no$, then, by the contrapositive of (**), $\mu(D^U, IC) \not\leq \mu(D, IC)$ follows. Thus, $U$ is rejected because $U$ would neither decrease the measured amount of inconsistency nor leave it unchanged. If, additionally, $\leq$ is a total order, then $\mu(D^U, IC) \not\leq \mu(D, IC)$ is equivalent to $\mu(D, IC) < \mu(D^U, IC)$. If $ic$ is not complete, then $ic$ might over-cautiously reject an update $U$ even if $U$ decreases or does not change the amount of integrity violation in $(D, IC)$.

Obviously, neither consistency-based integrity checking nor brute-force integrity checking depend on any particular $\mu$. However, by Definitions 5 and 6, it is easy to see that, for each $\mu$ whatsoever, each consistency-based integrity checker vacuously is a $\mu$-based integrity checker, since it only accepts input triples $(D, IC, U)$ such that $(D, IC)$ is consistent. Also brute-force integrity checking is $\mu$-based, since it only accepts totally consistent pairs $(D^U, IC)$. In short, Definition 6 properly generalizes conventional concepts of integrity checking.

By results in [26,27,30], it turns out that, for each $\mu \in \{\iota, |\iota|, \varsigma, |\varsigma|, \kappa, |\kappa|\}$, many (though not all) known consistency-based integrity checkers, when applied to triples $(D, IC, U)$ such that $(D, IC)$ is inconsistent, are sound $\mu$-based integrity checkers, e.g., the ones in [17,48,52,55].

The completeness of consistency-based integrity checkers is less frequently preserved when they are applied to triples $(D, IC, U)$ such that $(D, IC)$ is inconsistent. In fact, some consistency-based integrity checkers are incomplete already when applied only to triples $(D, IC, U)$ such that $(D, IC)$ is consistent, e.g., the one in [40]. However, for relational databases and range-restricted constraints in clausal form, the method in [52] has been shown in [27,30] to be a complete $\zeta$-based integrity checker.

Inconsistency in $(D, IC)$ may be complex or opaque or unknown. Hence, the computation of $\mu(D, IC)$ may be unfeasible, in particular if $D$ is big. Thus, we are interested in integrity checkers that do not have to compute the measure on which they are based. Fortunately, many such methods are known, such as those in [17,48,52,55], the domains of which can be soundly extended to triples $(D, IC, U)$ such that $(D, IC)$ is not necessarily consistent. They accept $U$ only if $U$ does not introduce any new constraint violation, but are ignorant of the actual amount of integrity violation in $(D, IC)$, as seen in [26,27,30].

# 3 Repairs

Inconsistency-tolerant repairs, as defined in Subsect. 3.1, generalize total repairs since they do not insist that all inconsistency is eliminated. Thus, an inconsistency-tolerant repair is an update $U$ of a database state that is inconsistent with its constraints, such that the updated state becomes less inconsistent, and there is no subset of $U$ that could achieve the same or a larger amount of inconsistency reduction. The amount of inconsistency before and after an update intended as a repair can be compared by using some database inconsistency measure.

In Subsect. 3.1, we characterize total and inconsistency-tolerant repairs by a definition that covers both. In Subsect. 3.2, some straightforward consequences of that definition are discussed and illustrated by examples.

## 3.1 Repairs – Definition

We are going to re-define total repairs as a special kind of updates, in two steps: in Definition 7a, below, we define total inconsistency reductions, and in Definition 7b, we characterize total repairs as minimal total inconsistency reductions. It is easy to see that this definition is equivalent to the original one in [3]. Analogously, we define inconsistency-tolerant repairs, based on some inconsistency measure $\mu$, in Definition 7c and d.

**Definition 7** (*total and inconsistency-tolerant repair*). Let $D$ be a database, $IC$ an integrity theory that is violated in $D$, $U$ an update and $\mu$ a database inconsistency measure.

(**a**) $U$ is a *total inconsistency reduction* of, $(D, IC)$ if each constraint in $IC$ is satisfied in $D^U$.
(**b**) $U$ is a *total repair* of $(D, IC)$ if $U$ is a total inconsistency reduction of $(D, IC)$ and there is no total inconsistency reduction $U' \subsetneq U$ of $(D, IC)$.

(c) $U$ is a $\mu$-based *inconsistency reduction* of $(D, IC)$ if $\mu(D^U, IC) < \mu(D, IC)$.

(d) $U$ is a $\mu$-based *inconsistency-tolerant repair* of $(D, IC)$ if $U$ is a $\mu$-based inconsistency reduction and there is no $U' \subsetneq U$ such that $\mu(D^{U'}, IC) \leq \mu(D^U, IC)$.

From now on, we may simply speak of an 'inconsistency-tolerant inconsistency reduction' or an 'inconsistency-tolerant repair' whenever $\mu$ is understood implicitly. We also may speak of a 'measure-based repair', or a '$\mu$-repair' when we want to emphasize the relevance of $\mu$. Moreover, we may generically speak of a 'repair' $U$ if $U$ is a total or an inconsistency-tolerant repair. In fact, the latter generalizes the former, as we are going to see in Subsect. 3.2.1.

## 3.2   Repairs – Discussion

As opposed to total repairs, measure-based repairs may tolerate remaining inconsistency. Otherwise, they are closely related, as will become more obvious below, where we discuss Definition 7 and illustrate it by several examples. In Subsect. 3.2.1, we show that inconsistency-tolerant repairs (Definition 7c, d) are a proper generalization of total repairs (Definition 7c, d), and that the latter are border cases of the former. In Subsect. 3.2.2, we have a closer look at the minimality condition imposed on repairs. In Subsect. 3.2.3, we expose some useful properties of inconsistency reductions. In Subsect. 3.2.4, we illustrate that repairs may depend significantly on the inconsistency measure on which they are based.

### 3.2.1   Measure-Based Repairs Generalize Total Repairs

Clearly, Definition 7 excludes that $U = \emptyset$, since the empty update does not repair anything. However, it includes the case $\mu(D^U, IC) = o$, i.e., total repairs are border cases of inconsistency-tolerant repairs. At first, that may seem to be an oxymoron, but in the end, it only means that Definition 7d properly generalizes total repairs, as stated in Corollary 1 below.

As opposed to inconsistency-tolerant repairs (Definition 7c, d), the definition of total repairs (Definition 7a, b) does not recur on any database inconsistency measure. However, for each inconsistency measure $\mu$ whatsoever, each total repair is a $\mu$-repair, as entailed by the following corollary of Definitions 4, 5 and 7.

**Corollary 1.** For each triple $(D, IC, U)$ such that $IC$ is violated in $D$, the following holds.

(a) For each inconsistency measure $\mu$, $U$ is a total repair of $(D, IC)$ if and only if $U$ is a $\mu$-repair of $(D, IC)$ such that $\mu(D^U, IC) = o$.

(b) $U$ is a total repair of $(D, IC)$ if and only if $U$ is a $\beta$-repair of $(D, IC)$.

**Proof.** (a) The 'if' part of Corollary 1a is entailed by Definitions 5 and 7a. For the 'only-if' part, let $U$ be a total repair of $(D, IC)$. Since $(D, IC)$ is inconsistent and, by Definition 7a, $(D^U, IC)$ is consistent, $o < \mu(D, IC)$ and

$\mu(D^U, IC) = o$ hold, for each $\mu$, by Definition 5. Hence, $\mu(D^U, IC) < \mu(D, IC)$ follows. It remains to verify the minimality of $U$, i.e., to show that there is no $U' \subsetneq U$ such that $\mu(D^{U'}, IC) \leq \mu(D^U, IC)$. Suppose there were such a $U'$. Since $\mu(D^U, IC) = o$, it would follow that $\mu(D^{U'}, IC) = o$. That, however, contradicts the premise that $U$ is a total repair and hence minimal, according to Definition 7b, i.e., there is no $U' \subsetneq U$ such that $\mu(D^{U'}, IC) = o$. Hence, $U$ is a $\mu$-repair of $(D, IC)$ such that $\mu(D^U, IC) = o$.     □

(**b**) For $\mu = \beta$, part (**b**) follows from part (**a**).     □

### 3.2.2   Minimality of Inconsistency-Tolerant Repairs

Clearly, each total and each $\mu$-repair is a total and, resp., $\mu$-based inconsistency reduction, but not vice-versa, due to the minimality conditions in Definition 7b and, resp., Definition 7d. The following example features an update $U$ that satisfies $\mu(D^U, IC) < \mu(D, IC)$ as in Definition 7c, but not the minimality condition of Definition 7d. Typically, updates of that kind contain elements that do not contribute to the reduction of inconsistency. Example 1 also features an update that is an inconsistency-tolerant repair of $(D, IC)$.

*Example 1.* Let $D = \{p, q, r\}$, $IC = \{\leftarrow q\}$, $U = \{delete\, q, insert\, s\}$. It is easy to verify that, for each $\mu \in \{\iota, |\iota|, \varsigma, |\varsigma|, \kappa, |\kappa|\}$, $\mu(D^U, IC) < \mu(D, IC)$ holds, i.e., $U$ is a $\mu$-based inconsistency reduction. However, $U$ is not a $\mu$-repair of $(D, IC)$, since its subset $U' = \{delete\, q\}$ is a $\mu$-repair of $(D, IC)$: it yields the same amount of inconsistency reduction, since $\mu(D^{U'}, IC) = \mu(D^U, IC)$ holds, but in a minimal way, since the only proper subset of $U'$ is $\emptyset$.

Note that the minimality condition of inconsistency-tolerant repairs in Definition 7d must not be weakened, so as to simply require that there is no proper subset $U'$ of $U$ such that $\mu(D^{U'}, IC) < \mu(D, IC)$, as illustrated by Example 2.

*Example 2.* Let $D = \{p, q, r, s\}$, $IC = \{\leftarrow q, \leftarrow r, \leftarrow s\}$, $U = \{delete\, r, delete\, s\}$, and $U' = \{delete\, r\}$. Thus, $D^U = \{p, q\}$ and $D^{U'} = \{p, q, s\}$. It is easy to verify that, for each $\mu \in \{\iota, |\iota|, \varsigma, |\varsigma|, \kappa, |\kappa|\}$, both $U$ and $U'$ are $\mu$-repairs of $(D, IC)$, i.e., inconsistency reductions that are minimal according to Definition 7d, although $U' \subsetneq U$. However, also $\mu(D^U, IC) < \mu(D^{U'}, IC)$ holds, i.e., $U$ reduces inconsistency more than $U'$, i.e., $U'$ is not preferable to $U$.

Instead of the conditions in Definition 7b and d, several other, non-equivalent definitions of minimality are conceivable. For total repairs, that has been pointed out, e.g., in [6]. For inconsistency-tolerant repairs, one could, for instance, replace $U' \subsetneq U$ by $|U'| < |U|$, or, more generally, require that there is no $U'$ that would be better than $U$ according to some preference criteria. Such criteria could, e.g., be determined by assigning some weights to the cases of constraints, or to the causes of their violation, in order to differentiate between different degrees of tolerability associated to the respective inconsistencies. In this paper, we do not study such alternative minimality conditions, except to note that $U' \subsetneq U$ entails $|U'| < |U|$, i.e., requiring minimality of the cardinality of $U$ is strictly more demanding than subset minimality, and that many preference criteria are application-dependent, as opposed to subset minimality.

### 3.2.3   Useful Properties of Inconsistency Reductions

The following corollary is useful for computing repairs, as addressed in Sect. 5.

**Corollary 2.** For each measure $\mu$ and each triple $(D, IC, U)$ such that $U$ is a $\mu$-based inconsistency reduction of $(D, IC)$, some subset of $U$ is a $\mu$-repair of $(D, IC)$.

**Proof.** If $U$ is a repair, then we are done. So, suppose that $U$ is not a repair. Then, by Definition 7, there is a proper subset $U'$ of $U$ such that $\mu(D^{U'}, IC) \leq \mu(D^U, IC)$. Since $U$ is an inconsistency reduction, i.e., $\mu(D^U, IC) < \mu(D, IC)$, it follows that $U'$ is a $\mu$-based inconsistency reduction of $(D, IC)$. If $U'$ is a $\mu$-repair of $(D, IC)$, then we are done. If not, we iterate the preceding argument inductively, until we arrive at a subset $U^*$ of $U'$ and hence of $U$ that, by Definition 7d and the transitivity of $\leq$, is a $\mu$-repair of $(D, IC)$.     $\square$

Ad-hoc intents to reduce inconsistency by singleton updates often occur in practice. The following corollary says that each insertion or deletion of a single database item which is confirmed to be an inconsistency reduction does not have to be checked for minimality for qualifying as a repair.

**Corollary 3.** For each measure $\mu$ and each triple $(D, IC, U)$, each singleton $\mu$-based inconsistency reduction $U$ of $(D, IC)$ is a $\mu$-repair of $(D, IC)$.

**Proof.** We only have to show that $U$ is minimal, according to Definition 7d. The only proper subset $U'$ of $U$ is $\emptyset$, for which $\mu(D^{U'}, IC) \leq \mu(D^U, IC)$ never may hold, since $D^{U'} = D$.     $\square$

Inconsistency can often be reduced iteratively, by sequences of singleton updates so that constraint violations are repaired one by one while the overall inconsistency does not increase. However, to compose such a sequence into one atomic transaction does not necessarily yield a repair, as shown by Example 3.

*Example 3.* Let $D_f = \{s, t, t'\}$ be the fact base of a deductive database $D$, the rule base of which consists of the following five clauses: $p \leftarrow s, t$; $q \leftarrow s, t'$; $r \leftarrow {\sim}s, t$; $r \leftarrow s, {\sim}t'$; $r \leftarrow t, t'$. Further, let $IC = \{\leftarrow p, \leftarrow q, \leftarrow r\}$. For the sequence of updates $U_1 = \{delete\, t'\}$, $U_2 = \{delete\, s\}$, $U_3 = \{delete\, t\}$, we have $\iota(D, IC) = IC$, $\iota(D^U, IC) = \{\leftarrow p, \leftarrow r\}$, $\iota(D^{U_1 U_2}, IC) = \{\leftarrow r\}$ and $\iota(D^{U_1 U_2 U_3}, IC) = \emptyset$. By Corollary 3, $U_1$ is a $\iota$-repair of $(D, IC)$, $U_2$ is a $\iota$-repair of $(D^{U_1}, IC)$ and $U_3$ is a $\iota$-repair of $(D^{U_1 U_2}, IC)$. However, neither the transactional update $U_1 \cup U_2$ nor $U^* = U_1 \cup U_2 \cup U_3$ is a $\iota$-repair of $D$, since $U_2$ is not only a $\iota$-repair of $(D^{U_1}, IC)$ but also a $\iota$-repair of $(D, IC)$ such that $U_2 \subsetneq U_1 \cup U_2$ and $\iota(D^{U_2}, IC) \subseteq \iota(D^{U_1 U_2}, IC)$, and $U = \{delete\, s,\, delete\, t\}$ is a total $\iota$-repair of $(D, IC)$ such that $U \subsetneq U^*$.

### 3.2.4    Repairs Depend on Inconsistency Measures

By Definition 7c, d, repairs are parametrized by the inconsistency measure on which they are based. The choice of that measure may have a significant influence on repairs and repair checking. Examples 4a and b illustrate that, for two measures $\mu$, $\mu'$, a $\mu$-repair $U$ is not necessarily a $\mu'$-repair, since $\mu$ and $\mu'$ may measure the effect of $U$ differently.

*Example 4.* Let $D = \{p, q, r\}$ and $IC = \{\leftarrow q, \leftarrow s\}$.

($a$) Let $U_a = \{delete\ q, insert\ s\}$. Clearly, $U_a$ is a $\mu$-repair of $(D, IC)$ for each $\mu$ that assigns a higher weight of inconsistency to the violation of $\leftarrow q$ than to the violation of $\leftarrow s$. However, $U_a$ is not a $|\iota|$-repair of $(D, IC)$ (recall: $|\iota|$ counts the violated constraints in $IC$), since $|\iota|(D^{U_a}, IC) = |\iota|(D, IC) = 1$.

($b$) Let $U_b = \{insert\ t\}$, and $\xi$ be the measure that counts the facts in $D$ that contribute to some integrity violation and then divides that count by the cardinality of $D$. (Similar inconsistency measures have been studied in [38,43].) Since $\xi(D^{U_b}, IC) = 1/4$ and $\xi(D, IC) = 1/3$, $U_b$ is a $\xi$-repair, by Corollary 3. However, for each $\mu \in \{|\iota|, |\zeta|, |\kappa|\}$, $U_b$ is clearly not a $\mu$-repair of $(D, IC)$, since $\mu(D, IC) = \mu(D^{U_b}, IC) = 1$.

## 4    Repair Checking

Difficulties and complications of automated repairing of database inconsistency by event-condition-action rules are well-documented [11]. Unpredictability of what may happen tends to increase whenever a database is updated ad-hoc and 'by hand' for restoring consistency or for getting rid of some constraint violation. Thus, repairing may go wrong. Hence, repair checkers, i.e., methods for checking if an update actually is a repair, are needed.

In Subsect. 4.1, we define repair checking in analogy to integrity checking. In Subsect. 4.2, we modularize repair checking according to the definition of repairs as minimal inconsistency reductions into inconsistency reduction checking and minimality checking. In Subsect. 4.3, we show that inconsistency reduction can be checked by integrity checking. In Subsect. 4.4, we show that also minimality can be checked by integrity checking. This leads to the main results of this paper in Subsect. 4.5, that repair checking can be computed by integrity checking. Repair checking is simplified by using a simplified measure-based integrity checker to compute it.

The basic idea is that an update $U$ reduces inconsistency if and only if its undo increases it. As we have seen in Subsect. 2.4, increase of inconsistency can be determined by measure-based integrity checking, while not necessarily a decrease.

### 4.1    Repair Checking – Definition

The repair checking problem is to find out if an update $U$ is a repair of $(D, IC)$. Hence, each automated total repair checker can be described as an update checker. The output *yes* accepts $U$ as a repair in compliance with Definition 7, and *no* means that $U$ is not recognized as a repair.

Soundness and completeness of repair checkers are defined below. Definition 8 abstracts away from the distinction of repair checking of updates that are either meant to be total or inconsistency-tolerant repairs, in accordance with Corollary 1.

**Definition 8** (*repair checker*). Let $rc$ be an update checker, and $\mu$ an inconsistency measure. $rc$ is called a *sound,* resp., *complete $\mu$-repair checker* if (*), resp., (**) holds, for each triple $(D, IC, U)$.

(*)    $rc(D, IC, U) = yes \;\Rightarrow\; U$ is a $\mu$-repair

(**)    $U$ is a $\mu$-repair $\;\Rightarrow\; rc(D, IC, U) = yes$

In words, $rc$ is sound if its output $rc(D, IC, U) = yes$ identifies $U$ as a repair of $(D, IC)$, and complete if each repair $U$ of $(D, IC)$ is identified by $rc$.

Below, Corollary 4 highlights close relationships between repair checking and integrity checking.

**Corollary 4.** For each inconsistency measure $\mu$, the following holds.

(*a*) Each sound $\mu$ -repair checker is a sound $\mu$-based integrity checker.
(*b*) Each complete $\mu$-based integrity checker is a complete $\mu$-repair checker.

**Proof.** By Definitions 6, 7 and 8.    □

Neither the converse of Corollary 4*a* nor the converse of Corollary 4*b* hold.

## 4.2    Repair Checking – Modularization

Corresponding to Definition 7, repair checking of an update $U$ proceeds in two modular phases. First, check if $U$ reduces inconsistency. We call this phase the *inconsistency reduction check*. If $U$ has passed the inconsistency reduction check, the second phase of repair checking is to check if $U$ is minimal. We call this phase the *minimality check*. For the first of the two phases of repair checking, the following definition characterizes sound and complete inconsistency reduction checking. according to Definition 7*c*.

**Definition 9** (*inconsistency reduction checker*).    Let $\mu$ be an inconsistency measure, and $ir$ an update checker. $ir$ is called a *sound,* resp., *complete, $\mu$-based inconsistency reduction checker* if (*), resp., (**) holds, for each triple $(D, IC, U)$.

(*)    $ir(D, IC, U) = yes \;\Rightarrow\; \mu(D^U, IC) < \mu(D, IC)$

(**)    $\mu(D^U, IC) < \mu(D, IC) \;\Rightarrow\; ir(D, IC, U) = yes$

In words, $ir$ is sound if $ir(D, IC, U) = yes$ correctly indicates that $U$ reduces the inconsistency of $(D, IC)$ measured by $\mu$, and complete if each $U$ that reduces inconsistency is checked correctly by $rc$.

Next, we define the soundness and completeness of the second phase, viz. measure-based minimality checking, according to Definition 7$d$.

**Definition 10** (*minimality checking*). Let $\mu$ be an inconsistency measure, and $mc$ an update checker. $mc$ is called a *sound*, resp., *complete*, $\mu$-based minimality checker if (*), resp., (**) holds, for each triple $(D, IC, U)$ such that $U$ is an $\mu$-based inconsistency reduction.

(*)   $mc(D, IC, U) = yes \Rightarrow$  for each $U' \subsetneq U$, $\mu(D^{U'}; IC) \not\leq \mu(D^U, IC)$

(**)  for each $U' \subsetneq U$, $\mu(D^{U'}, IC) \not\leq \mu(D^U, IC) \Rightarrow mc(D, IC, U) = yes$

In words, $mc$ is sound if $mc(D, IC, U) = yes$ correctly indicates that $U$ is a minimal inconsistency reduction, and $mc$ is complete if the minimality of each repair of $(D, IC)$ is acknowledged by $mc$.

The following result is a straightforward consequence of Definitions 7–10. It entails that repair checking can be realized modularly by inconsistency reduction checking and, if the latter was successful, subsequent minimality checking.

**Corollary 5** (*modularization of repair checking*). Let $\mu$ be an inconsistency measure, $ir$ a sound or, resp., complete $\mu$-based inconsistency reduction checker, $mc$ a sound or, resp., complete $\mu$-based minimality checker, and $rc$ an update checker. $rc$ is a sound or, resp., complete $\mu$-repair checker if and only if (*) or, resp., (**) holds, for each triple $(D, IC, U)$.

(*)   $rc(D, IC, U) = yes \Rightarrow ir(D, IC, U) = yes$ and $mc(D, IC, U) = yes$

(**)  $ir(D, IC, U) = yes$ and $mc(D, IC, U) = yes \Rightarrow rc(D, IC, U) = yes$

## 4.3 Inconsistency Reduction Checking by Integrity Checking

In this subsection, we show how inconsistency reduction can be implemented by measure-based integrity checking. Also, we specify conditions that guarantee the soundness and the completeness of inconsistency reduction checkers.

Part $a$ of Lemma 1, below, shows that $U$ is not a $\mu$-based inconsistency reduction of $(D, IC)$ if sound $\mu$-based integrity checking of $(D^U, IC, \overline{U})$ accepts $\overline{U}$. Part $b$ shows that complete inconsistency reduction checking is guaranteed by sound measure-based inconsistency checking.

**Lemma 1.** For each measure $\mu$ and each sound $\mu$-based integrity checker $ic$, ($a$) and ($b$) hold.

($a$) For each triple $(D, IC, U)$ such that $ic(D^U, IC, \overline{U}) = yes$, $U$ is not a $\mu$-based inconsistency reduction of $(D, IC)$.

($b$) An update checker $ir$ is a complete $\mu$-based inconsistency reduction checker if (*) holds, for each triple $(D, IC, U)$.
   (*)   $ir(D, IC, U) = no \Rightarrow ic(D^U, IC, \overline{U}) = yes$

**Proof:**

(a) We have to show that $\mu(D^U, IC) \not< \mu(D, IC)$ if $ic(D^U, IC, \overline{U}) = yes$. If $ic(D^U, IC, \overline{U}) = yes$, then the soundness of $ic$ entails $\mu(D^{U\overline{U}}, IC) \leq \mu(D^U, IC)$, i.e. $\mu(D, IC) \leq \mu(D^U, IC)$. Hence, $\mu(D^U, IC) \not< \mu(D, IC)$. $\qquad\square$

(b) We have to show that $\mu(D^U, IC) < \mu(D, IC) \Rightarrow ir(D, IC, U) = yes$ holds, according to Definition 9, under the premise of ($*$). We show the contrapositive, i.e., $ir(D, IC, U) = no \Rightarrow \mu(D^U, IC) \not< \mu(D, IC)$. Let $ir(D, IC, U) = no$. That, by the contrapositive of ($*$), entails $ic(D^U, IC, \overline{U}) = yes$. The soundness of $ic$ entails $\mu(D^{U\overline{U}}, IC) \leq \mu(D^U, IC)$, i.e., $\mu(D, IC) \leq \mu(D^U, IC)$, hence $\mu(D^U, IC) \not< \mu(D, IC)$. $\qquad\square$

Part $a$ of Lemma 2, below, shows that $U$ is a $\mu$-based inconsistency reduction of $(D, IC)$ if complete $\mu$-based integrity checking of $(D^U, IC, \overline{U})$ rejects $\overline{U}$ and the range of $\mu$ is totally ordered. Part $b$ shows that sound inconsistency reduction checking is guaranteed by complete measure-based inconsistency checking if the range of the measure is totally ordered.

**Lemma 2.** For each measure $\mu$ and complete $\mu$-based integrity checker $ic$ such that the range of $\mu$ is totally ordered, the following holds.

(a) For each triple $(D, IC, U)$ such that $ic(D^U, IC, \overline{U}) = no$, $U$ is a $\mu$-based inconsistency reduction of $(D, IC)$.

(b) An update checker $ir$ is a sound $\mu$-based inconsistency reduction checker if ($*$) holds, for each triple $(D, IC, U)$.
  ($*$)  $ir(D, IC, U) = yes \Rightarrow ic(D^U, IC, \overline{U}) = no$

**Proof:**

(a) Under the premise of Lemma 2, we have to show that $\mu(D^U, IC) < \mu(D, IC)$ if $ic(D^U, IC, \overline{U}) = no$. Since $ic$ is complete, $ic(D^U, IC, \overline{U}) = no$ entails, according to Definition 6, that $\mu(D^{U\overline{U}}, IC) \not\leq \mu(D^U, IC)$, which is equivalent to $\mu(D, IC) \not\leq \mu(D^U, IC)$, since $D^{U\overline{U}} = D$. Since $\leq$ is a total order, it follows that $\mu(D^U, IC) < \mu(D, IC)$. $\qquad\square$

(b) We have to show that $ir(D, IC, U) = yes \Rightarrow \mu(D^U, IC) < \mu(D, IC)$ holds, according to Definition 9, under the premise of ($*$). Let $ir(D, IC, U) = yes$. That, by ($*$), entails $ic(D^U, IC, \overline{U}) = no$. From the completeness of $ic$, it follows that $\mu(D^{U\overline{U}}, IC) \not\leq \mu(D^U, IC)$, i.e., $\mu(D, IC) \not\leq \mu(D^U, IC)$, i.e., $\mu(D^U, IC) < \mu(D, IC)$, since $\leq$ is a total order. $\qquad\square$

The condition in Lemma 2 that the range of $\mu$ is totally ordered cannot be waived, as shown by Example 5.

*Example 5.* Let $D = \{p, q\}$, $IC = \{\neg q, \neg r\}$, $U = \{insert\ r,\ delete\ q\}$ and $ic_N$ be the well-known integrity checker in [52], which, based on $\zeta$, is complete for relational databases and constraints in clausal form, as mentioned in Subsect. 2.4. Clearly, we have $D^U = \{p, r\}$, $\overline{U} = \{delete\ r,\ insert\ q\}$, $\zeta(D^U, IC) =$

$\{\neg r\}$ and $\zeta(D, IC) = \{\neg q\}$, thus $\zeta(D^U, IC) \nsubseteq \zeta(D, IC)$ and $ic_N(D^U, IC, \overline{U}) = no$. However, $U$ clearly is not a $\zeta$-based inconsistency reduction of $(D, IC)$.

Part $a$ of Lemma 3, below, shows that $U$ is a $\mu$-based inconsistency reduction of $(D, IC)$ if complete $\mu$-based integrity checking of $(D^U, IC, \overline{U})$ rejects $\overline{U}$ and sound $\mu$-based integrity checking of $(D, IC, U)$ accepts $U$. Part $b$ shows that sound and complete inconsistency reduction checking of $U$ can be realized by sound integrity checking of $U$ and complete integrity checking of $\overline{U}$.

**Lemma 3.** For each measure $\mu$ and each sound and complete $\mu$ -based integrity checker $ic$, the following holds.

*(a)* For each triple $(D, IC, U)$, $U$ is a $\mu$ -based inconsistency reduction of $(D, IC)$ if and only if $ic(D^U, IC, \overline{U}) = no$ *and* $ic(D, IC, U) = yes$.

*(b)* An update checker $ir$ is a sound, resp., complete $\mu$-based inconsistency reduction checker if and only if $(*)$, *resp.*, $(**)$ holds, for each triple $(D, IC, U)$.
$$ir(D, IC, U) = yes \Rightarrow (ic(D^U, IC, \overline{U}) = no \text{ and } ic(D, IC, U) = yes) \ (*)$$
$$(ic(D^U, IC, \overline{U}) = no \text{ and } ic(D, IC, U) = yes) \Rightarrow ir(D, IC, U) = yes \ (**)$$

## Proof:

*(a)* Under the premises of Lemma 3, we have to show that $\mu(D^U, IC) < \mu(D, IC)$ if and only if $ic(D^U, IC, \overline{U}) = no$ and $ic(D, IC, U) = yes$. We first show the if-half. As in the proof of Lemma 2, we have that the completeness of $ic$ entails $\mu(D, IC) \nleq \mu(D^U, IC)$. From $ic(D, IC) = yes$ and the soundness of $ic$, it follows that $\mu(D^U, IC) \leq \mu(D, IC)$. From $\mu(D, IC) \nleq \mu(D^U, IC)$, it follows that $\mu(D^U, IC) < \mu(D, IC)$.

For showing the only-if half, let $U$ be a $\mu$-based inconsistency reduction of $(D, IC)$, i.e., $\mu(D^U, IC) < \mu(D, IC)$. That entails $\mu(D^U, IC) \leq \mu(D, IC)$. From that and the completeness of $ic$, it follows that $ic(D, IC, U) = yes$. It remains to show that $ic(D^U, IC, \overline{U}) = no$, which follows from the soundness of $ic$. □

*(b)* To prove that $ir$ is sound under the premise of $(*)$, we have to show that $ir(D, IC, U) = yes \Rightarrow \mu(D^U, IC) < \mu(D, IC)$ holds, according to Definition 8. Suppose that $ir(D, IC, U) = yes$. By $(*)$, that entails $ic(D^U, IC, \overline{U}) = no$ and $ic(D, IC, U) = yes$. Completeness of $ic$ entails that $\mu(D^{U\overline{U}}, IC) \nleq \mu(D^U, IC)$, and soundness of $ic$ entails that $\mu(D^U, IC) \leq \mu(D, IC)$. That is equivalent to $\mu(D, IC) \nleq \mu(D^U, IC)$ and $\mu(D^U, IC) \leq \mu(D, IC)$. That entails $\mu(D, IC) \neq \mu(D^U, IC)$ and $\mu(D^U, IC) \leq \mu(D, IC)$, hence $\mu(D^U, IC) < \mu(D, IC)$.

To prove that the soundness of $ir$ entails $(*)$, let $ic(D, IC, U) = yes$. We have to show $ic(D^U, IC, \overline{U}) = no$ and $ic(D, IC, U) = yes$. The soundness of $ir$ entails $\mu(D^U, IC) < \mu(D, IC)$, hence $\mu(D, IC) \nleq \mu(D^U, IC)$ and $\mu(D^U, IC) \leq \mu(D, IC)$. Clearly, $\mu(D, IC) \nleq \mu(D^U, IC)$ is the same as $\mu(D^{U\overline{U}}, IC) \nleq \mu(D^U, IC)$, from which $ic(D^U, IC, \overline{U}) = no$ is entailed by the soundness of $ic$. From $\mu(D^U, IC) \leq \mu(D, IC)$, the completeness of $ic$ entails $ic(D, IC, U) = yes$.

To prove that ir is complete under the premise of $(**)$, we show the contrapositive $ir(D, IC, U) = no \Rightarrow \mu(D^U, IC) \nless \mu(D, IC)$ of the implication

$\mu(D^U, IC) < \mu(D, IC) \Rightarrow ir(D, IC, U) = yes$. Suppose $ir(D, IC, U) = no$. By $(**)$, $ic(D^U, IC, \overline{U}) = yes$ or $ic(D, IC, U) = no$ follows. If $ic(D^U, IC, \overline{U}) = yes$, then the same argument as in the proof of Lemma 1a applies. So, assume that $ic(D, IC, U) = no$. By the completeness of $ic$, that entails $\mu(D^U, IC) \not\leq \mu(D, IC)$, hence $\mu(D^U, IC) \not< \mu(D, IC)$.

To prove that the completeness of $ir$ entails $(**)$, let $ic(D^U, IC, \overline{U}) = no$ and $ic(D, IC, U) = yes$. Thus, we have to show that $ir(D, IC, U) = yes$. From $ic(D, IC, U) = yes$, the soundness of $ic$ entails $\mu(D^U, IC) \leq \mu(D, IC)$. From $ic(D^U, IC, \overline{U}) = no$, the completeness of $ic$ entails $\mu(D^{U\overline{U}}, IC) \not\leq \mu(D^U, IC)$, i.e., $\mu(D, IC) \not\leq \mu(D^U, IC)$. From $\mu(D^U, IC) \leq \mu(D, IC)$ and $\mu(D, IC) \not\leq \mu(D^U, IC)$, it follows that $\mu(D^U, IC) < \mu(D, IC)$. Hence, the completeness of $ir$ entails $ir(D, IC, U) = yes$. □

Note that, for $U$ to be recognized as a $\mu$-based inconsistency reduction, both Lemmata 2 and 3 require to run a complete $\mu$-based integrity checker $ic$ on $\overline{U}$. However, Lemma 2 additionally requires a totally ordered range of $\mu$, while Lemma 3 additionally requires also the soundness of $ic$ and to run it also on $U$.

## 4.4    Minimality Checking by Integrity Checking

In Subsect. 4.3, we have seen how the inconsistency reduction of updates can be checked by measure-based integrity checking. In Lemma 4 and Corollary 6, below, we are going to see that also the minimality check of inconsistency reductions can be accomplished by measure-based integrity checking.

**Lemma 4.** For each measure $\mu$, each sound or, resp., complete $\mu$-based integrity checker $ic$ and each triple $(D, IC, U)$ such that $U$ is a $\mu$-based inconsistency reduction $U$ of $(D, IC)$, $(*)$ or, resp., $(**)$ holds.

   $(*)$   $U$ is not minimal if there is a proper non-empty subset $U'$ of $U$
           such that $ic(D^U, IC, \overline{U}') = yes$

   $(**)$  $U$ is not minmal only if there is a proper non-empty subset $U'$ of $U$
           such that $ic(D^U, IC, \overline{U}') = yes$

**Proof:**

$(*)$ Assume $U'$ to be a proper subset of $U$ such that $ic(D^U, IC, \overline{U}') = yes$. Thus we have to show that $U$ is not minimal. Let $U'' = U \setminus U'$. Since $U' \neq U$ and $U' \neq \emptyset$, it follows that $U'' \subsetneq U$. Hence, it suffices to show that $\mu(D^{U''}, IC) \leq \mu(D^U, IC)$. From $ic(D^U, IC, \overline{U}') = yes$, it follows that $\mu(D^{U\overline{U}'}, IC) \leq \mu(D^U, IC)$, i.e., $\mu(D^{U''}, IC) \leq \mu(D^U, IC)$, since $U\overline{U}' = U''$. □

$(**)$ Assume that $U$ is not minimal. Thus, by Definition 7d, there is a proper non-empty subset $U''$ (say) of $U$ such that $\mu(D^{U''}, IC) \leq \mu(D^U, IC)$. For $U' = U \setminus U''$, this is equivalent to $\mu(D^{U\overline{U}'}, IC) \leq \mu(D^U, IC)$, since $U'' = U\overline{U}'$. Since $ic$ is complete, $ic(D^U, IC, \overline{U}') = yes$ follows, by Definition 6. □

The contrapositive of Lemma 4, together with Definition 7d, yields Corollary 6, below. We state it explicitly, for facilitating the evidence of theorems in Subsect. 4.5. Informally, it describes how to obtain sound and complete minimality checkers by complete and, resp., sound integrity checkers.

**Corollary 6.** For each measure $\mu$, each complete or, resp., sound $\mu$-based integrity checker $ic$, and each triple $(D, IC, U)$ such that $U$ is a $\mu$-based inconsistency reduction $U$ of $(D, IC)$, an update checker $mc$ is a sound or, resp., complete $\mu$-based minimality checker if (∗) or, resp., (∗∗) holds.

$$mc(D, IC, U) = yes \;\Rightarrow\; \text{for each non-empty } U' \subsetneq U,\; ic(D^U, IC, \overline{U}') = no \quad (∗)$$

$$\text{for each non-empty } U' \subsetneq U,\; ic(D^U, IC, \overline{U}') = no \;\Rightarrow\; mc(D, IC, U) = yes \quad (∗∗)$$

**Proof:** From the premise that $ic$ is complete and (∗) in Corollary 6, the soundness of $mc$ follows by (∗∗) in Lemma 4. From the premise that $ic$ is sound and (∗∗) in Corollary 6, the completeness of $mc$ follows by (∗) in Lemma 4. □

## 4.5 Repair Checking by Integrity Checking

Lemmata 1–4 and Corollary 6 provide handles for unfolding Corollary 5 into the main results of this paper, as presented in Theorems 1–3, below. They state how inconsistency-tolerant repairs can be verified or falsified by measure-based integrity checking.

Theorem 1 devises a way to see that a given update is not a repair. By requiring that the used integrity checker is not just sound but also complete, Theorem 3 devises a sound and complete way to check if $U$ is or is not a repair. While only catering for the soundness of repair checking, Theorem 2 additionally requires that the range of the used inconsistency measure is totally ordered, but in turn only needs the completeness of integrity checking, and one run of integrity checking less than repair checking according to Theorem 3.

**Theorem 1.** For each measure $\mu$ and each sound $\mu$-based integrity checker $ic$, a) and b) hold.

*(a)* For each triple $(D, IC, U)$ such that $ic(D^U, IC, \overline{U}') = yes$ for some $U' \subseteq U$, $U$ is not a $\mu$-repair of $(D, IC)$.

*(b)* An update checker $rc$ is a complete $\mu$-repair checker if (∗) holds, for each triple $(D, IC, U)$.

(∗)  $rc(D, IC, U) = no \;\Rightarrow\; ic(D^U, IC, \overline{U}') = yes$, for some $U' \subseteq U, U \neq \emptyset$.

**Proof:** By Lemma 1 and (∗) in Lemma 4, we have the following.

*(a)* For each triple $(D, IC, U)$ such that $ic(D^U, IC, \overline{U}) = yes$ or $ic(D^U, IC, \overline{U}') = yes$ for some non-empty $U' \subsetneq U$, $U$ is not a $\mu$-repair of $(D, IC)$.

(**b**) An update checker $rc$ is a complete $\mu$-repair checker if the following holds, for each triple $(D, IC, U)$.

$$rc(D, IC, U) = no \Rightarrow ic(D^U, IC, \overline{U}) = yes, \text{ or there is a } U' \subsetneq U, U \neq \emptyset$$
$$\text{such that } ic(D^U, IC, \overline{U}') = yes$$

From that, Theorem 1 follows.                                              □

**Theorem 2.** For each inconsistency measure $\mu$ with a totally ordered range, and each complete $\mu$-based integrity checker, the following holds.

(**a**) For each triple $(D, IC, U)$, $U$ is a $\mu$ -repair of $(D, IC)$ *if*, for each $U' \subseteq U$, $ic(D^U, IC, \overline{U}') = no$.

(**b**) An update checker $rc$ is a sound $\mu$-repair checker if, for each triple $(D, IC, U)$ and each $U' \subseteq U$, (∗) holds.

$$rc(D, IC, U) = yes \Rightarrow ic(D^U, IC, \overline{U'}) = no, ic(D^U, IC, \overline{U}') = no \quad (∗)$$

**Proof:** By Lemma 2 and (∗) in Corollary 6, we have the following.

(**a**) For each triple $(D, IC, U)$, $U$ is a $\mu$-repair of $(D, IC)$ if $ic(D^U, IC, \overline{U}) = no$ and, for each $U' \subsetneq U$, $ic(D^U, IC, \overline{U}') = no$.

(**b**) An update checker $rc$ is a sound $\mu$-repair checker if (∗) holds, for each triple $(D, IC, U)$.

$$rc(D, IC, U) = yes \Rightarrow ic(D^U, IC, \overline{U}) = no, \text{ and} \qquad\qquad (∗)$$
$$\text{for each } U' \subsetneq U, ic(D^U, IC, \overline{U}') = no.$$

From that, Theorem 2 follows                                              □

**Theorem 3.** For each measure $\mu$ and each sound and complete $\mu$-based integrity checker $ic$, the following holds.

(**a**) For each triple $(D, IC, U)$, $U$ is a $\mu$-repair of $(D, IC)$   if and only if, for each non-empty $U' \subseteq U$, $ic(D^U, IC, \overline{U}') = no$, and $ic(D, IC, U) = yes$.

(**b**) An update checker $rc$ is a sound, resp., complete $\mu$-repair checker if and only if, for each triple $(D, IC, U)$, (∗), resp., (∗∗) holds.

$$rc(D, IC, U) = yes \Rightarrow \text{ for each non-empty } U' \subseteq U, ic(D^U, IC, \overline{U}') = no$$
$$\text{and } ic(D, IC, U) = yes \qquad\qquad (∗)$$
$$\text{for each non-empty } U' \subseteq U, ic(D^U, IC, \overline{U}') = no$$
$$\text{and } ic(D, IC, U) = yes \qquad\qquad \Rightarrow rc(D, IC, U) = yes \ (∗∗)$$

**Proof:** By Lemma 3 and Corollary 6, we have the following.

($a$) For each triple $(D, IC, U)$, $U$ is a $\mu$-repair of $(D, IC)$ if and only if

$$ic(D^U, IC, \overline{U}) = no \quad \text{and} \quad ic(D, IC, U) = yes \quad \text{and,} \quad \text{for each } U' \subsetneq U,$$
$$ic(D^U, IC, \overline{U}') = no,$$

($b$) An update checker $rc$ is a sound, resp., complete $\mu$-repair checker if and only if, for each triple $(D, IC, U)$, $(*)$, resp., $(**)$ holds.

$$rc(D, IC, U) = yes \;\Rightarrow\; ic(D^U, IC, \overline{U})) = no \;\text{ and }\; ic(D, IC, U) = yes,$$
$$\text{and for each } U' \subsetneq U, \; ic(D^U, IC, \overline{U}') = no \qquad (*)$$
$$ic(D^U, IC, \overline{U}) = no \;\text{ and }\; ic(D, IC, U) = yes$$
$$\text{and for each } U' \subsetneq U, \, ic(D^U, IC, \overline{U}') = no \;\Rightarrow\; rc(D, IC, U) = yes \qquad (**)$$

From that, Theorem 3 follows. $\qquad\qquad\qquad\qquad\qquad\qquad\qquad\qquad\qquad\qquad$ □

# 5 Computing Repair Checking

We are going to outline how the inconsistency reduction and the minimality checking phases of total and measure-based repair checking can be computed. We are also going to assess the costs of these computations.

In Subsect. 5.1, we describe how total repair checking is computed by brute-force integrity checking. In Subsects. 5.2 and 5.3, we outline how inconsistency-tolerant repair checking can be computed. The approach in Subsect. 5.2 is 'naive', since it actually computes the values of inconsistency measures. It does not recur on integrity checking. The approach in Subsect. 5.3 does not need to compute inconsistency measures. It uses simplified integrity checking, so we call it 'simplified repair checking'.

Along the way, we compare the three approaches among each other. Since the objectives of total and measure-based repair checking are not precisely identical, it may be considered unfair to compare the cost of their computation. However, a common goal of both is to reduce inconsistency in a minimal way.

In general, we argue that both the naive and the simplified approach process inconsistency-tolerant repair candidate updates, and thus are more realistic than total repair checking, which needs to process updates that are supposed to repair the totality of all integrity violations, without tolerating any remaining inconsistency. Only for relatively simple cases of constraints and updates, and not-too-large databases, total repair checking and naive measure-based repair checking seem to be computationally affordable. Simplified repair checking is less costly than both naive and total repair checking, inasmuch as measures do not need to be computed, and both the number and the complexity of constraints to be evaluated are reduced.

## 5.1    Computing Total Repair Checking

First, we describe the computation of total repair checking by brute-force integrity checking. Then, we indicate how total repairs can be obtained from a given inconsistency reduction. Last, we assess the cost of total repair checking.

By Definitions 8a and b, total repair checking may verify or falsify, for given triples $(D, IC, U)$, that $(D^U, IC)$ is consistent, and that $U$ is minimal, in two phases, as described subsequently.

**Phase 1** *(inconsistency reduction check).* Check if $U$ is a total inconsistency reduction of $(D, IC)$ by querying each $I \in IC$ against $D^U$. If some $I$ is not satisfied in $D^U$, then $U$ is not a total inconsistency reduction and hence not a total repair of $(D, IC)$. If each $I \in IC$ is satisfied in $D^U$, then $U$ is a total inconsistency reduction, hence proceed to Phase 2.

**Phase 2** *(minimality check).* For each $U' \subsetneq U$, check if $U'$ is a total inconsistency reduction of $(D, IC)$ by querying each $I \in IC$ against $D^{U'}$. If each $I$ is satisfied in $D^{U'}$, then $U'$ is a total inconsistency reduction of $(D, IC)$. Hence, $U$ is not a total repair of $(D, IC)$, If some $I$ is not satisfied in $D^{U'}$, then $U'$ is not a total inconsistency reduction of $(D, IC)$. If no $U' \subsetneq U$ is an inconsistency reduction of $(D, IC)$, then $U$ is a total repair of $(D, IC)$.

If, in Phase 1, $U$ has turned out to be an inconsistency reduction of $(D, IC)$, then, by Corollaries 1b and 2, at least one total repair of $(D, IC)$ exists. From each inconsistency reduction of $(D, IC)$, a total repair of $(D, IC)$ can obviously be obtained by iterating Phase 2, as in the proof of Corollary 2.

For assessing the cost of computing Phases 1 and 2, let $n$ be the cardinality of $U$, and $m = 2^n$. Thus, there are $m$ subsets $U_1, \ldots, U_m$ of $U$; one, say $U_m$, is the empty set. Hence, if $U$ is a total repair, then $m - 1$ brute-force integrity checks of $(D^{U_i}, IC)$ $(i = 1, \ldots, m - 1)$ are needed for deciding if $U$ is a total repair of $(D, IC)$. If $k$ is the cardinality of $IC$, then that amounts to $k \times (m - 1)$ full-fledged evaluations of constraints in $IC$.

## 5.2    Computing Naive Inconsistency-Tolerant Repair Checking

First, we describe a naive way of computing inconsistency-tolerant repair checking, by computing the values of inconsistency measures before and after updating. Then, we indicate how inconsistency-tolerant repairs can be obtained from a given inconsistency reduction. Last, we assess the cost of the naive computation.

According to Definition 7c and d, $\mu$-based repair checking can be implemented naively in two phases, as follows.

**Phase 1** *(inconsistency reduction check).* Compute the values of $\mu(D, IC)$ and $\mu(D^U, IC)$ and then check if $\mu(D^U, IC) < \mu(D, IC)$ holds. If it does, then $U$ is an inconsistency reduction of $(D, IC)$, else it isn't.

**Phase 2** *(minimality check).* Compute the measure $\mu(D^{U'}, IC)$ of each proper non-empty subset $U'$ of $U$ and compare it to $\mu(D, IC)$, as already computed in Phase 1. If, for each such $U'$, $\mu(D^{U'}, IC) \leq \mu(D^U, IC)$ does not hold, then $U$ is a $\mu$-repair of $(D, IC)$. Else, if, for some such $U'$, $\mu(D^{U'}, IC) \leq \mu(D^U, IC)$ holds, then $U'$ is a $\mu$-based inconsistency reduction of $(D, IC)$, hence $U$ is not a $\mu$-repair of $(D, IC)$.

If, in Phase 1, $U$ has turned out to be an inconsistency reduction then, by Corollary 2, at least one total repair of $(D, IC)$ exists. From each $\mu$-based inconsistency reduction of $(D, IC)$, a $\mu$-repair of $(D, IC)$ can obviously be obtained by iterating Phase 2, as in the proof of Corollary 2.

Clearly, $\mu(D^{U'}, IC)$ has to be computed for each subset $U'$ of $U$: for subsets $\emptyset$ and $U$ in Phase 1, and for proper non-empty subsets in Phase 2. For $|U| = n$, that amounts to the computation of $2^n$ measurements, one for each subset $U'$ of $U$. The cost of the computation of measures obviously depends on the definition of $\mu$. To compute $\mu(D, IC)$ for any of the measures $\iota, |\iota|, \zeta, |\zeta|, \kappa, |\kappa|$ involves the evaluation of each $I$ in $IC$ against $D$, for $\zeta, |\zeta|, \kappa, |\kappa|$ also an analysis of the search space, for identifying all violated cases or, resp., all causes of integrity violation. Thus, the order of magnitude of evaluating constraints for naive measure-based repair checking is roughly the same as for total repair checking. However, depending on the specific measure to be computed, the total cost of computing naive repair checking may turn out to be higher than that of total repair checking, for comparable sizes of candidate updates.

## 5.3  Computing Simplified Repair Checking

A computation of simplified repair checking by measure-based integrity checking is suggested by Theorems 1–3. The output $ic(D^U, IC, \overline{U}) = yes$ means that $U$ is not a $\mu$-repair, by Theorem 1. For $U$ to be a $\mu$-repair, the output $ic(D, IC, U) = yes$ is only necessary, but not sufficient. Sufficient conditions to identify updates as $\mu$-repairs are given by Theorems 2 and 3, which both require the use of a complete $\mu$-based integrity checker.

In any case, however, for computing simplified repair checking, a measure-based integrity checker should be used that simplifies the evaluation of constraints, such as the method in [52], or one of the many methods that have been developed as modifications, refinements or extensions of that approach [47] [49].

We are going to assess simplified repair checking according to Theorem 3, again by the two phases of inconsistency reduction and minimality checking, as described below. Note, however, that, if the range of $\mu$ is totally ordered, then the cost of $\mu$-based repair checking according to Theorem 2 is lower than that of a computation according to Theorem 3, since the totally ordered range of $\mu$ enables a less costly inconsistency reduction check.

**Phase 1:** Check if $U$ is a $\mu$-based inconsistency reduction of $(D, IC)$ by computing $ic(D^U, IC, \overline{U})$ and $ic(D, IC, U)$, according to Lemma 3.

**Phase 2:** Check if $U$ is minimal in the sense of Definition 7d by checking whether $ic(D^U, IC, \overline{U}') = no$ holds, for each non-empty $U' \subsetneq U$, according to Corollary 6.

For Phase 1, at most two runs of $ic$ are needed. For Phase 2, at most $2^n - 2$ runs of $ic$ are needed, where $n$ is the cardinality of $U$. Hence, maximally $2^n$ runs of $ic$ are needed for deciding if $U$ is a $\mu$-repair of $(D, IC)$ or not. Thus, the actual cost of repair checking by integrity checking depends on $ic$. If a sound and complete simplified integrity checker is available, then running such a method tends to be much less costly than brute-force integrity checking, as employed for total repair checking and for naive measure-based repair checking.

Recall from Subsect. 5.1 that the cost of total repair checking was $k \times (m-1)$ unsimplified constraint evaluations, where $m = 2^n$ and $k$ is the cardinality of $IC$. For ease of comparison, suppose that all constraints in $IC$ are expressed by a single constraint formula $I$ (the conjunction of all constraints). Then, for total repair checking, we'd have in the order of $m$-1 evaluations of $I$ against $D^{U_i}$ ($1 \leq i \leq m - 1$), where the $U_i$ are the non-empty subsets of $U$. Compared to that, $m$ evaluations of a simplification of $I$ for simplified repair checking (one more against $D$ than as for total repair checking) obviously tends to be much less costly.

The significant cost savings obtainable by simplified integrity checking have been noted in many studies in the literature, among them, e.g., [10,14,16,52]. They essentially amount to the difference between having to evaluate universally quantified formulas, as for brute-force repair checking, and evaluating their simplified instances obtained from ground substitutions of their global variables, as for most methods of simplified integrity checking. Often, that corresponds to the difference of evaluating possibly huge joins of relations and simple lookups of ground instances of such joins.

The same way as described in Subsect. 5.2, inconsistency-tolerant repairs can be computed from an inconsistency reduction, which we therefore do not repeat here. Note, however, that the use of simplified integrity checking for inconsistency reduction checking and minimality checking as needed in Phase 3 is far less costly than to compute the values of inconsistency measures, as in Subsect. 5.2.

## 6   Related Work

Related work on integrity checking, inconsistency measuring, repairing and repair checking has been duly referred to already.

Conventional work on repairing and repair checking is focused on complexity issues in relation with consistent query answering (CQA) [3,12]. As opposed to that, neither our use of measure-based integrity checking for simplified repair checking nor our alternative to CQA in [20] is hung up in the complexity nexus between CQA, repairing and repair checking. Much of the discussion of complexity issues refers to certain classes of constraints and databases. However, that discussion tends to miss the point of where cost issues of integrity checking may hurt most: Many constraints are universally quantified formulas that may involve potentially huge joins of database relations, and brute-force evaluation of all of them may result to be prohibitively expensive. As opposed to that, the use of simplified integrity checking for inconsistency-tolerant repair checking only has to evaluate certain instances of those constraints that are affected by the given update.

Work that remains to be mentioned is concerned with the question how to obtain promising repair candidates, or how to compute repairs. In Subsects. 5.1, 5.2 and 5.3, we have outlined how to compute repairs from given inconsistency reductions. What we have not dealt with, however, is the related question of how to systematically obtain candidate inconsistency reductions. In Subsect. 3.2.3, we have mentioned attempts of repairing inconsistency by ad-hoc updates or iterated singleton updates. Repairing by tuple deletions as proposed in [13,62] only works if there is no non-monotonic database negation. For obtaining total repairs, the authors of [35,58] propose to identify and explicitly represent all constraint violations, which however can easily become a prohibitively difficult task. Instead, the use of abductive logic programming procedures that generate update hypotheses for satisfying integrity constraints [18,44–46] seems to be a more promising approach to obtain suitable inconsistency-tolerant repair candidates, or at least inconsistency reduction candidates, which can then be checked as described in Subsects. 4.3 and 4.4. The use of abduction for repairing remains to be investigated further.

# 7  Conclusion

We have simplified repair checking in two ways. Firstly, by relaxing total repairs, which do not tolerate the least bit of inconsistency, to inconsistency-tolerant repairs. Secondly, by deploying measure-based integrity checking (which normally is used for preventing an increase of inconsistency) for simplified checks of update attempts to decrease inconsistency. Simplified repair checking is based on inconsistency measures, but does not need to compute such measures. Nor does total repair checking. However, the latter does check each constraint brute-force. As opposed to that, simplified measure-based repair checking is inconsistency-tolerant and less costly than total repair checking.

In general, however, simplified repair checking by integrity checking requires a complete measure-based integrity checker. Although many known measure-based integrity checkers are in general incomplete, there are significant classes of databases, integrity theories, updates and inconsistency measures for which their completeness can be guaranteed, or relaxed, while preserving the soundness of measure-based repair checking.

Typically, such classes require a certain form of representing constraints. For example, the integrity checker $ic_N$ (say) in [52] is incomplete, e.g., for the non-clausal constraint representation of $IC = \{\neg q \land \neg r\}$ when asked to check the update $U = \{delete\ q,\ insert\ r\}$ in a database $D$ that contains $q$ but not $r$. Clearly, $\zeta(D^U, IC) = \zeta(D, IC) = IC$, hence $U$ leaves the amount of inconsistency invariant. But $ic_N$ is ignorant of the violation of $I$ in $D$ and considers $I$ violated in $D^U$ due to the insertion of $r$. Hence, $ic_N(D, IC, U) = no$. If $ic_N$ were complete for arbitrary representations of constraints, it would have to output $yes$ in this example. However, as soon as $IC$ is represented in clausal form, by

$IC' = \{\neg q, \neg r\}$ as in Example 5, i.e., by two separate constraints, then we have $\zeta(D, IC') = \{\neg q\}$ and $\zeta(D^U, IC') = \{\neg r\}$, i.e., $\zeta(D^U, IC') \nsubseteq \zeta(D, IC')$, hence the output $ic_N(D, IC, U) = no$ becomes correct, and indeed, $ic_N$ is a complete $\zeta$-based integrity checker for range-restricted constraints in clausal form, as already mentioned in Subsect. 2.4.

At this point, it is interesting to mention that, for each database inconsistency measure $\mu$, a complete $\mu$-based integrity checker obviously can be obtained by actually computing the values of $\mu(D, IC)$ and $\mu(D^U, IC)$ for input triples $(D, IC, U)$, as described in Subsect. 5.2.

However, for avoiding to have to recur on an expensive computation of measures, it is desirable to realize repair checking by an integrity checking method that simplifies constraint evaluation and is sound and complete with regard to some convenient measure. That is a feasible option for the measure $\zeta$ and some known integrity checkers of updates in relational databases with constraints in clausal form. Ongoing work is concerned with identifying suitable measures $\mu$ and expressive classes of triples $(D, IC, U)$ of theoretical and practical interest, such that some measure-based methods can be shown to be sound and complete $\mu$-based integrity checkers for input from such classes. According to the main results in this paper, such integrity checkers can then be used for sound and complete simplified repair checking.

**Acknowledgement.** Preliminary stages of the work presented in this paper have been published in [31] and [32]. John Grant had provided valuable comment on early drafts.

# References

1. Abiteboul, S., Hull, R., Vianu, V.: Foundations of Databases. Addison-Wesley, Massachusetts (1995)
2. Afrati, F., Kolaitis, P.: Repair checking in inconsistent databases: algorithms and complexity. In: Proceedings of 12th ICDT, pp. 31–41. ACM Press (2009)
3. Arenas, M., Bertossi, L., Chomicki, J.: Consistent query answers in inconsistent databases. In: Proceedings of PODS, pp. 68–79. ACM Press (1999)
4. Arming, S., Pichler, B., Sallinger, E.: Combined complexity of repair checking and consistent query answering. In: Proceedings 19th International Conference on Database Theory (ICDT), vol. 48, pp. 21:1–21:18. LIPIcs (2016)
5. Bayer, R.: Integrity, concurrency, and recovery in databases. In: Samelson, K. (ed.) ECI 1976. LNCS, vol. 44, pp. 79–106. Springer, Heidelberg (1976). doi:10.1007/3-540-07804-5_24
6. Bertossi, L.: Consistent query answering in databases. SIGMOD Rec. **35**(2), 68–76 (2006)
7. Besnard, P.: Basic postulates for inconsistency measures. In: Hameurlain, A. (ed.) TLDKS 2017. LNCS, vol. 10620, pp. 1–12. Springer, Cham (2017)
8. Bry, F., Decker, H., Manthey, R.: A uniform approach to constraint satisfaction and constraint satisfiability in deductive databases. In: Schmidt, J.W., Ceri, S., Missikoff, M. (eds.) EDBT 1988. LNCS, vol. 303, pp. 488–505. Springer, Heidelberg (1988). doi:10.1007/3-540-19074-0_69
9. Cavedon, L.: Acyclic logic programs and the completeness of sldnf-resolution. Theor. Comput. Sci. **86**(1), 81–92 (1991)

10. Celma, M., Garcia, C., Mota, L., Decker, H.: Comparing and synthesizing integrity checking methods for deductive databases. In: Proceedings of 10th ICDE, pp. 214–222. IEEE Computer Society (1994)
11. Ceri, S., Cochrane, R., Widom, J.: Practical applications of triggers and constraints: success and lingering issues (10-year award). In: Abbadi, A.E., Brodie, M., Chakravarthy, S., Dayal, U., Kamel, N., Schlageter, G., Whang, K.-Y. (eds.) Proceedings of 26th VLDB, pp. 254–262. Morgan Kaufmann (2000)
12. Chomicki, J.: Consistent query answering: five easy pieces. In: Schwentick, T., Suciu, D. (eds.) ICDT 2007. LNCS, vol. 4353, pp. 1–17. Springer, Heidelberg (2006). doi:10.1007/11965893_1
13. Chomicki, J., Marcinkowski, J.: Minimal-change integrity maintenance using tuple deletions. Inf. Comput. **197**(12), 90–121 (2005)
14. Christiansen, H., Martinenghi, D.: Incremental integrity checking: limitations and possibilities. In: Sutcliffe, G., Voronkov, A. (eds.) LPAR 2005. LNCS (LNAI), vol. 3835, pp. 712–727. Springer, Heidelberg (2005). doi:10.1007/11591191_49
15. Christiansen, H., Martinenghi, D.: On simplification of database integrity constraints. Fundamenta Informaticae **71**(4), 371–417 (2006)
16. Das, S.K., Williams, H.: Integrity checking methods in deductive databases:a comparative evaluation. In: Proceedings of 7th BNCOD, British National Conference on Databases, pp. 85–116. CUP (1989)
17. Decker, H.: Integrity enforcement on deductive databases. In: Kerschberg, L. (ed.) Expert Database Systems, pp. 381–395. Benjamin Cummings (1987)
18. Decker, H.: An extension of SLD by abduction and integrity maintenance for view updating in deductive databases. In: Maher, M.J. (ed.) Proceedings of the 1996 Joint International Conference and Symposium on Logic Programming, pp. 157–169. MIT Press (1996)
19. Decker, H.: Toward a Uniform Cause-Based Approach to Inconsistency-Tolerant Database Semantics. In: Meersman, R., Dillon, T., Herrero, P. (eds.) OTM 2010. LNCS, vol. 6427, pp. 983–998. Springer, Heidelberg (2010). doi:10.1007/978-3-642-16949-6_23
20. Decker, H.: Answers that have integrity. In: Schewe, K.-D., Thalheim, B. (eds.) SDKB 2010. LNCS, vol. 6834, pp. 54–72. Springer, Heidelberg (2011). doi:10.1007/978-3-642-23441-5_4
21. Decker, H.: Partial repairs that tolerate inconsistency. In: Eder, J., Bielikova, M., Tjoa, A.M. (eds.) ADBIS 2011. LNCS, vol. 6909, pp. 389–400. Springer, Heidelberg (2011). doi:10.1007/978-3-642-23737-9_28
22. Decker, H.: Axiomatizing inconsistency metrics for integrity maintenance. In: Proceedings of 16th KES, pp. 1243–1252. IOS Press (2012)
23. Decker, H.: New measures for maintaining the quality of databases. In: Murgante, B., Gervasi, O., Misra, S., Nedjah, N., Rocha, A.M.A.C., Taniar, D., Apduhan, B.O. (eds.) ICCSA 2012. LNCS, vol. 7336, pp. 170–185. Springer, Heidelberg (2012). doi:10.1007/978-3-642-31128-4_13
24. Decker, H.: Measure-based inconsistency-tolerant maintenance of database integrity. In: Schewe, K.-D., Thalheim, B. (eds.) SDKB 2011. LNCS, vol. 7693, pp. 149–173. Springer, Heidelberg (2013). doi:10.1007/978-3-642-36008-4_7
25. Decker, H.: Database inconsistency measuring (2017, submitted)
26. Decker, H., Martinenghi, D.: A relaxed approach to integrity and inconsistency in databases. In: Hermann, M., Voronkov, A. (eds.) LPAR 2006. LNCS (LNAI), vol. 4246, pp. 287–301. Springer, Heidelberg (2006). doi:10.1007/11916277_20

27. Decker, H., Martinenghi, D.: Classifying integrity checking methods with regard to inconsistency tolerance. In: Proceedings of the 10th International ACM SIGPLAN Conference on Principles and Practice of Declarative Programming, pp. 195–204. ACM Press (2008)

28. Decker, H., Martinenghi, D.: Database integrity checking. In: Erickson, J. (ed.) Database Technologies: Concepts, Methodologies, Tools, and Applications, vol. I, pp. 212–220. IGI Global (2009)

29. Decker, H., Martinenghi, D.: Modeling, measuring and monitoring the quality of information. In: Heuser, C.A., Pernul, G. (eds.) ER 2009. LNCS, vol. 5833, pp. 212–221. Springer, Heidelberg (2009). doi:10.1007/978-3-642-04947-7_26

30. Decker, H., Martinenghi, D.: Inconsistency-tolerant integrity checking. IEEE Trans. Knowl. Data Eng. **23**(2), 218–234 (2011)

31. Decker, H., Misra, S.: Measure-based repair checking by integrity checking. In: Gervasi, O., et al. (eds.) ICCSA 2016. LNCS, vol. 9790, pp. 530–543. Springer, Cham (2016). doi:10.1007/978-3-319-42092-9_40

32. Decker, H., Pascual-Miret, L., Misra, S.: Repair checking by integrity checking. In: 27th International Workshop on Database and Expert Systems Applications, DEXA 2016 Workshop COIN, pp. 134–138. IEEE Computer Society (2016)

33. Doorn, J.H., Rivero, L.C.: Database Integrity: Challenges and Solutions. Idea Group Publishing (2002)

34. Elmasri, R., Navathe, S.: Fundamentals of Database Systems, 7th edn. Pearson, London (2016)

35. Fan, W.: Constraint-driven database repair. In: Liu, L., Özsu, M.T. (eds.) Encyclopedia of Database Systems, pp. 458–463. Springer, USA (2009)

36. Gabbay, D., Hunter, A.: Making inconsistency respectable: A logical framework for inconsistency in reasoning, part I — A position paper. In: Jorrand, P., Kelemen, J. (eds.) FAIR 1991. LNCS, vol. 535, pp. 19–32. Springer, Heidelberg (1991). doi:10.1007/3-540-54507-7_3

37. Grant, J.: Classifications for inconsistent theories. Notre Dame J. Formal Logic **19**(3), 435–444 (1978)

38. Grant, J., Hunter, A.: Measuring inconsistency in knowledgebases. J. Intell. Inform. Syst. **27**(2), 159–184 (2006)

39. Grant, J., Hunter, A.: Measuring the good and the bad in inconsistent information. In: Proceedings of 22nd IJCAI, pp. 2632–2637. IJCAI-AAAI (2011)

40. Gupta, A., Sagiv, Y., Ullman, J.D., Widom, J.: Constraint checking with partial information. In: Proceedings of PODS 1994, pp. 45–55. ACM Press (1994)

41. Hernandez, M.J.: Database Design for Mere Mortals: A Hands-On Guide to Relational Database Design, 3rd edn. Addison-Wesley, Boston (2013)

42. Ibrahim, H.: Checking integrity constraints - how it differs in centralized, distributed and parallel databases. In: 17th International Workshop on Database and Expert Systems Applications (DEXA 2006), pp. 563–568. IEEE Computer Society (2006)

43. Konieczny, S., Lang, J., Marquis, P.: Quantifying information and contradiction in propositional logic through epistemic tests. In: Proceedings of 18th IJCAI, pp. 106–111. Morgan Kaufmann (2003)

44. Kowalski, R., Sadri, F.: Integrating logic programming and production systems in abductive logic programming agents. In: Polleres, A., Swift, T. (eds.) RR 2009. LNCS, vol. 5837, pp. 1–23. Springer, Heidelberg (2009). doi:10.1007/978-3-642-05082-4_1

45. Kowalski, R.A., Sadri, F.: Abductive logic programming agents with destructive databases. Ann. Math. Artif. Intell. **62**(1–2), 129–158 (2011)

46. Lin, F., You, J.: Abduction in logic programming: a new definition and an abductive procedure based on rewriting. Artif. Intell. **140**(1/2), 175–205 (2002)
47. Ling, T.W., Lee, S.Y.: A survey of integrity constraint checking methods in relational databases. In: Kim, I.P.W., Kambayashi, Y. (ed.) Database Systems for Next-Generation Applications. Advanced Database Research and Development Series, vol. 1, pp. 68–78. World Scientific (1993)
48. Lloyd, J.W., Sonenberg, L., Topor, R.W.: Integrity constraint checking in stratified databases. J. Logic Program. **4**(4), 331–343 (1987)
49. Martinenghi, D., Christiansen, H., Decker, H.: Integrity checking and maintenance in relational and deductive databases and beyond. In: Ma, Z. (ed.) Intelligent Databases: Technologies and Applications, pp. 238–285. IGI Global (2007)
50. Muñoz-Escoí, F.D., Ruiz-Fuertes, M.I., Decker, H., Armendáriz-Íñigo, J.E., Mendívil, J.R.G.: Extending middleware protocols for database replication with integrity support. In: Meersman, R., Tari, Z. (eds.) OTM 2008. LNCS, vol. 5331, pp. 607–624. Springer, Heidelberg (2008). doi:10.1007/978-3-540-88871-0_43
51. Nicolas, J.-M.: A property of logical formulas corresponding to integrity constraints on data base relations. In: Proceedings of the Workshop on Formal Bases for Data Bases 1979 (1979)
52. Nicolas, J.-M.: Logic for improving integrity checking in relational data bases. Acta Informatica **18**, 227–253 (1982)
53. Ramakrishnan, R., Gehrke, J.: Database Management Systems. McGraw-Hill, New York (2003)
54. Reiter, R.: What should a database know? J. Logic Program. **14**(1&2), 127–153 (1992)
55. Sadri, F., Kowalski, R.: A theorem-proving approach to database integrity. In: Foundations of Deductive Databases and Logic Programming, pp. 313–362. Morgan Kaufmann (1988)
56. Shave, M.: Problems of integrity and distributed databases. J. Softw. Pract. Experience **10**(2), 135–147 (1980)
57. Sörensen, O., Thalheim, B.: Semantics and pragmatics of integrity constraints. In: Schewe, K.-D., Thalheim, B. (eds.) SDKB 2011. LNCS, vol. 7693, pp. 1–17. Springer, Heidelberg (2013). doi:10.1007/978-3-642-36008-4_1
58. Staworko, S., Chomicki, J., Marcinkowski, J.: Prioritized repairing and consistent query answering in relational databases. CoRR, abs/0908.0464 (2009)
59. Thimm, M.: On the compliance of rationality postulates for inconsistency measures: a more or less complete picture. KI **31**(1), 31–39 (2017)
60. Topor, R.: Safety and domain independence. In: Liu, L., Özsu, T. (eds.) Encyclopedia of Database Systems, pp. 2463–2466. Springer, USA (2009)
61. Wijsen, J.: Database repairing using updates. Trans. Database Syst. **30**(3), 722–768 (2005)
62. Wijsen, J.: On condensing database repairs obtained by tuple deletions. In: 16th International Workshop on Database and Expert Systems Applications (DEXA 2005), pp. 849–853. IEEE Computer Society (2005)

# Author Index

Printed in the United States
By Bookmasters